Help for the Child with Asperger's Syndrome

of related interest

Asperger's Syndrome
A Guide for Parents and Professionals
Tony Attwood
Foreword by Lorna Wing
ISBN 1 85302 577 1

How to Live with Autism and Asperger Syndrome
Practical Strategies for Parents and Professionals
Christine Williams and Barry Wright
Illustrated by Olive Young
ISBN 1 84310 184 X

Parent to Parent
Information and Inspiration for Parents Dealing
with Autism or Asperger's Syndrome
Ann Boushéy
ISBN 1 84310 774 0

Understanding Autism Spectrum Disorders
Frequently Asked Questions
Diane Yapko
ISBN 1 84310 756 2

Parenting a Child with Asperger Syndrome
200 Tips and Strategies
Brenda Boyd
ISBN 1 84310 137 8

Getting Services for your Child on the Autism Spectrum
DeAnn Hyatt-Foley and Matthew G. Foley
ISBN 1 85302 991 2

Help for the Child with Asperger's Syndrome

A Parent's Guide to Negotiating the Social Service Maze

Gretchen Mertz

Foreword by Tony Attwood

Jessica Kingsley Publishers
London and Philadelphia

Excerpts on pp.37–39 from *Developmental Dyspraxia* by Madeleine Portwood (1999) reprinted with permission from David Fulton publishers.
Diagnostic criteria for Asperger's Syndrome (p.30), Autistic Disorder (p.177), Developmental Coordination Disorder (p.178), and Selective Mutism (pp.178–9) reprinted with permission from the *Diagnostic and Statistical Manual of Mental Disorders, Text revision* Copyright 2000. American Psychiatric Association.

First published in 2005
by Jessica Kingsley Publishers
116 Pentonville Road
London N1 9JB, UK
and
400 Market Street, Suite 400
Philadelphia, PA 19106, USA

www.jkp.com

Library of Congress Cataloging in Publication Data
Mertz, Gretchen, 1959-
   Help for the child with Asperger's Syndrome : a parent's guide to negotiating the social service maze / Gretchen Mertz ; foreword by Tony Attwood.-- 1st American ed.
   p. cm.
   Includes bibliographical references and index.
   ISBN 1-84310-780-5 (pbk.)
   1. Asperger's syndrome--Patients--Services for. 2. Asperger's syndrome--Patients--Education. 3. Parents of autistic children. 4. Parenting. I. Title.
   RJ506.A9M47 2004
   649'.152--dc22

                                        2004012438

British Library Cataloguing in Publication Data
A CIP catalogue record for this book is available from the British Library

ISBN-13: 978 1 84310 780 4
ISBN-10: 1 84310 780 5

Printed and Bound in Great Britain by
Athenaeum Press, Gateshead, Tyne and Wear

To Matthew, Andrew and Catherine

How do you avoid being chronically angry while getting services and still be an effective advocate for your child? Gretchen Mertz threads the needle on this vital issue guiding the reader with the lessons she learned parenting her own child who has Asperger's Syndrome. This is a thoughtful and intelligent guide to effectively negotiating rather than fighting the fragmented system of services.

Robert Naseef, author of Special Children, Challenged Parents: The Struggles and Rewards of Raising a Child with a Disability

Contents

Part IV Daily Life: Progressing in the Maze

Foreword

Tony Attwood

If you live in the United States and your son or daughter has just had a diagnosis of Asperger's Syndrome, then you need this book. Many parents are concerned, once the child has a diagnosis, how they are to access, negotiate and coordinate the relevant support services. Gretchen Mertz is the mother of Andy, a child with Asperger's Syndrome, and she has been through the American maze of services for children with Asperger's Syndrome. She understands what parents are going through and provides practical and emotional guidance. The American social service system has only recently acknowledged Asperger's Syndrome and there are relevant services, but parents have to know how to apply, and the application process is not user friendly. Gretchen also has considerable experience of the legal system, the relevant legislation and the process of litigation, to ensure the services the child is entitled to are made available.

The book is a metaphorical guide and map with Gretchen providing information on the range of government and professional services, what they do, their responsibilities and how they can help the child and family. Although the diagnosis may have been made by a paediatrician, child psychiatrist or psychologist, the child is most likely to receive intervention and treatment through special education.

In particular I applaud Gretchen's description of how to encourage good parent/teacher relationships. She describes the secondary disorders that can be associated with Asperger's Syndrome and how to obtain assistance for conditions such as an anxiety disorder or depression. I also value her section on the effects of the child and their behavior on the family and marriage. This parents' guide will be a well-used source of knowledge and guidance in the homes that have a child with Asperger's Syndrome.

Acknowledgements

As a first-time author on a subject touched by many disciplines, it would have been presumptuous and probably impossible for me to write this book entirely in isolation. Many personal acquaintances helped give me the confidence that writing the book itself was possible and a good idea, and several of them read sections of it for readability. But how could I, a working parent researching and writing in off-hours, network with the necessary professionals? Some I knew from going through the social service system with my son. Others I just wrote to and asked for help, requesting them with no previous introduction to review and comment on my draft work, for nothing. Almost no one turned me down.

I am indebted to the following professionals, who read and wrote out comments for my private use on sections of the book where they had expertise on the subject matter. Dr. Lorna Wing, psychiatrist and dean of autism research, provided valuable assistance by writing pages of comments on the draft section on diagnosis; so did pediatrician SheaAnn Cronley. Clinical psychologist Abigail Segal-Andrews and psychiatrist Eileen Bazelon also reviewed it. Speech therapists Carol Kaminsky and Ellen Schwartz, and occupational therapist Abigail Huntington, all of whose professional skills I admire, commented on the sections relevant to their chosen fields. Special education teachers Janice Maidman and Amy Andrews-Price reviewed the section on special education as did special education lawyer Leonard Rieser. Dr. Robert Naseef, psychologist and family therapist, did the same for the section on coordinating different parts of a child's program and home life, along with Abigail Huntington.

I also received valuable assistance from my classmates in a creative writing class, who were kind enough to look at some sections and discuss them thoroughly. The teacher of that class, Ken Bingham, a long-time friend, also advised me through the submission process.

I would also like to thank Christina Kurz, who helped me refine the maze diagram.

Of course, in addition to unacknowledged friends who have encouraged me, my family has been the motivation, inspiration, and chief source of support for this book. Thanks go above all to my husband, Matt. Besides acting as sounding board for the book, and shouldering more than his share of the domestic work in order to give me more time to write, his confidence in me has made him my most important support.

Something's wrong

OT evaluation

Psychiatric
evaluation

Neurological
workup

Wrong
agency –
go back!

M
D
T

m
e
e
t
i
n
g

Diagnosis

IFSP

R
e
p
o
r
t
s

S
u
p
p
o
r
t

g
r
o
u
p
s

Litigation

E
n
d
l
e
s
s

v
o
i
c
e
m
a
i
l

Due process
hearing

Your insurance
doesn't cover this
condition – try
another diagnosis

IEP
meeting

We don't
handle this –
go away

This provider
is not in your
network –
try again

IEP

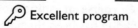 Excellent program

Preface

I write this book as a parent who has been through the process, coaching other parents through it. In Part I on diagnosis, I describe the diagnostic labels used by groups of professionals, and the meaning and criteria attached by them to those labels. However, as a parent, I regard these labels not as rigid definitions, but as guides for predicting behavior and getting help. The whole concept of diagnostic labels in the field of mental/developmental disorders is much more fluid than many people realize. Where there is fluidity there is a certain amount of malleability, and I discuss at length which diagnostic labels can trigger eligibility for which services. This is by no means to suggest that anyone should claim a false diagnosis in order to obtain desired services, only that out of two accurate descriptions or labels for a patient's symptoms, one may trigger eligibility for certain services while the other may not.

The correct language in discussing any form of disability (or difference, special need, challenge) changes frequently, and I have struggled to keep up. Asperger's Syndrome is one of several conditions included under the umbrella group Pervasive Developmental Disorders (PDD), the official name in the *Diagnostic and Statistical Manual of Mental Disorders* of the American Psychiatric Association. In the rest of the English-speaking world, the term autistic spectrum disorders is often used to denote the same class of conditions, especially informally. I have used both terms. At a couple points I have used the term "retarded" or "with mental retardation" to describe individuals with low cognitive abilities, fearing that the alternatives "with cognitive disabilities," or "lower functioning," which are sometimes preferred, were too imprecise, as some services are available only to individuals below a certain IQ. I most often used the term assistant or paraprofessional to denote those individuals who are employed to support individual students in the classroom or, less often, in other settings. In other literature these same workers are called wraparounds, shadows, aides, TSSs (therapeutic staff support), coaches, parapros, or paraeducators. With gender, I have usually used "he or she," and "his or her," but have occasionally slipped into he and his. Please read these references to include females as well. In educational circles, the term "mainstream" has been largely replaced by "include." However, I have continued to use mainstream, or "placed in a regular education class," as terms better known to the general public.

Introduction

When my son Andy was diagnosed with Asperger's Syndrome at age six, I read all about it and what treatments were supposed to help. I read books on sensory integration therapy, social skills training, and the best educational plans. I reviewed websites by people who had hired therapists from five different disciplines to work intensively with their children with autism or Nonverbal Learning Disability.

How could I get these services for my son? The school system where I lived was near bankruptcy. Our health insurance policy contained a clause saying it did not cover treatment of Pervasive Developmental Disorders. Everything I read seemed to be geared to families in affluent suburban school districts with mothers who did not have to work. When I turned to our school district I got voicemail.

It took weeks of toiling through networks of providers, insurers, and bureaucrats to set up anything, and the program had to be changed as my son developed. Eventually I developed more savvy in dealing with the so-called system. The word system is misleading because it implies a central management, but the social service system is a patchwork of agencies from healthcare and the educational establishment, most of which want to dump responsibility for any expense on some other segment of the system.

People advise you to stand up for your rights. While your child does have some legal rights, most of getting what you want involves negotiating the system rather than fighting it. Bureaucrats, whether from the healthcare system or the educational system, are less likely to say no than to direct you someplace else. It takes a lot of energy to move through the maze of service providers, insurance contractors and subcontractors, school district offices, and state agencies to find out what suitable assistance is available and how to obtain it for your child.

Diagnosis turns out to be not just a medical description, but also a legal tool requiring careful use. There are many overlapping diagnoses and some of them are entitled to more assistance than others. Finding out what diagnostic category triggers eligibility to what services requires as much energy as a knockdown fight, but is probably a lot more useful. You have to learn to keep all your child's evaluation reports, to ask some providers to word reports certain ways, and to know when to use which reports. You have to find people in the system who know its ins and outs, and who are willing to help you.

Each teacher or healthcare provider who deals with your child is a consultant: you are the manager. They work with your child for a few days or a few years, and may have valuable ideas on your child's needs and how to meet them, but they manage only one portion of your child's program. One parent whom I met in a therapist's waiting room told me she had thought that if a child needed a special program someone would be managing it. Instead, different entities provided parts of what the child needed but no professional was managing the whole program. That job always falls to the parent, which is just as well, because nobody else could do it as attentively. No one else could understand the child as thoroughly or be as committed to the colossal task of getting his or her needs met as the child's parent.

To all parents in this situation, I understand what you are going through. I understand the frustration of hitting a wall, either in understanding your child's behavior, in trying to modify behavior or effect development, in trying to get the right school setting, or in simply trying to find out what services are available. Because the network of social services is so uncoordinated, getting through it resembles getting through a maze. Because each child's needs are different, this process is different for everyone, and there is no clear road map.

Despite the attention in the last few years to special needs in general, and to autistic disorders in particular, getting through to the proper therapists and educators for a child with Asperger's Syndrome remains a daunting task, involving a maze of regulations, voicemail systems, insurance networks, and school bureaucrats. I salute the efforts of all parents to give their children what they need, but especially those who must struggle through that maze. This book is meant as a navigational tool through the maze. I hope it provides some emotional support as well.

PART I

Diagnosis

How to Make the Most of It

1

Finding a Diagnosis

Parents of children with psychiatric conditions or developmental disorders do not enter the social service maze upon receiving a diagnosis. They are drawn into the maze as they look for a diagnosis after noticing something is wrong. Often, with autistic spectrum disorders, the diagnosis does not come until years after the parents start looking for one. Experienced diagnostician Tony Attwood described six paths to an Asperger's diagnosis. Three of them involved having another diagnosis first, one involved diagnosis in adulthood (residual Asperger's Syndrome in an adult), and another involved diagnosis of relatives after one family member was diagnosed. In only one of the six paths was Asperger's the first diagnosis for a child without another family member already so labeled. Recent research indicates the average age of diagnosis is 11, years after symptoms have raised alarm (Howlin and Asgharian 1999).

Many parents of children with Asperger's have been visiting specialists for years before becoming aware that Asperger's Syndrome is the most suitable diagnosis for their child. Because symptoms of Asperger's Syndrome resemble those of other conditions, and because there is no definitive physical or psychological test for the syndrome, it is rare to simply walk into an Asperger's diagnosis. Also, Asperger's Syndrome, like other forms of autism, had been considered very rare until recently, so that diagnosis was not usually in the forefront of the first several diagnosticians' minds. Unfortunately, the process of visiting specialists, figuring out which specialist to visit, getting referrals, getting appointments, is itself a drawn-out chore at an emotionally difficult time for parents. It isn't cheap either. The process has earned the name "medical merry-go-round" not for any "merry" quality but for its "go-round" frustration. For working parents on a limited budget, the ongoing progression of finding a diagnosis with some suggestions on how to handle the condition, only to find that that particular diagnosis doesn't quite fit their child's situation, and to have to go through the process again, is a daunting task.

Are there any shortcuts through this process? There are probably no shortcuts, but there are some tips:

- Be aware that specialists tend to diagnose within their own specialty.

- Do not regard a given diagnosis as final.

- Find a diagnostician you trust.

- Get reports, but be careful what they say.

Diagnosticians find conditions within their own specialty

Ear/nose/throat doctors do not tend to find liver problems. Dermatologists do not find anemia. If they do happen to find some obvious clue that a patient is suffering from a condition outside their specialty, they refer them to the appropriate specialist, but they are not looking for conditions outside their own specialty. Occasionally patients with a physical problem wander around from specialist to specialist for a long time before they find the correct diagnosis. With psychological conditions, this situation is compounded by the number of overlapping diagnoses from different specialties, and sometimes the lack of time to do a full work-up, so that rather than being referred to the next specialist immediately, a child is more likely to get a diagnosis within the current diagnostician's specialty and only later referred to a diagnostician in another specialty.

Clinicians know it is easier to diagnose extreme forms of any condition, from heart attack to schizophrenia to autism. Dr. Peter Szatmari, writing on children at the milder end of the autistic spectrum, said:

> These children are in the borderland between the various developmental disorders and, to be sure, they share many clinical features. Identified by language pathologists, they became children with semantic-pragmatic disorder; identified by neuropsychologists, they became children with Nonverbal Learning Disabilities; identified by psychiatrists, they were labeled as having schizoid or schizotypal personality disorder; identified by psychoanalysts, they were those with atypical development. (Szatmari 2000, p.413)

This tendency among specialists is not something to bewail, but something to be aware of. Review your child's symptoms carefully with the pediatrician before going to a specialist, as primary care doctors are used to considering a wide variety of possibilities. If a child's school suggests an evaluation by a psychologist and is willing to pay for it, go through with it but do not rely solely on it. If the school authorities won't pay for an extensive, in-depth psychological evaluation, consider it along with the possibility of an evaluation by someone from another specialty, a psychiatrist or neurologist, or whatever you think would most likely yield helpful results, in consultation with your child's pediatrician. Regard each specialist as a consultant giving you the benefit of his or her special knowledge, rather than as the single final word.

Do not consider a given diagnosis as final

Sometimes the first diagnosis is just one part of the puzzle, the beginning of a learning process about your child. It is a label you go with while it seems suitable. Keep an open mind. Doctors often come up with what they call differential diagnoses, which is a list of possible diagnoses, and a working diagnosis, which is the diagnosis that seems to fit best based on what evidence they have at the time. Ask your child's doctors how certain they are of their diagnosis, and what other diagnoses they considered, and why they think this one is better.

Be aware also that criteria for diagnostic labels change over time, and that there are several sets of criteria for Asperger's Syndrome used by experts today. Also, many times criteria involve "significant impairment" in some area or other, and what constitutes significant impairment varies from one doctor to another.

I do not mean that you should shop endlessly for diagnoses, or deny that your child has serious problems if he does, but individuals may at one time seem to fit one set of diagnostic criteria and another set at another stage of development. Also, diagnoses in the area of developmental disorders/mental health are closer to descriptions of types than to diseases with inevitable courses.

Find a doctor you trust for the diagnosis

Although a diagnosis is not final, it is important. It helps you set up a plan to help your child. Find a doctor who inspires you with some confidence to do that. In many cases, the number of psychiatrists in an HMO (Health Maintenance Organization) network is far more limited than the numbers of other specialists, so there is much less choice in that area for patients than in other areas. If you are in an HMO and cannot find a doctor you trust to evaluate your child, consider paying a doctor outside the network. It may be expensive, but not as expensive as ongoing treatment which might follow the diagnosis. If your budget for your child's special needs is limited, this area of finding a diagnosis may be the one on which to spend your limited funds. The diagnosis may allow you to get ongoing treatment at someone else's expense.

Look for someone you trust, but whom should you trust? This may be someone you and your child feel comfortable with, someone to whom you and your child can open up. That might not be the evaluator who reviews your child's past history with you in the presence of your child the first time you meet. You want someone who appears able to consider different options, not someone who says, "Are you here for ADD?" when you first walk in.

If you are using someone from a medical profession, as opposed to a psychologist, check to see if he or she is board certified. Board-certified doctors have considerable training beyond the minimum needed for a medical license, and have passed "the boards," a big test in their specialty, usually lasting several days. Standards for board eligibility are also set by experts in the field, experts that the board-certified physicians agree are experts. Usually board eligibility involves a few years of practice after completion of an approved residency program. A physician can also be board certified in a subspecialty. Child psychiatry is a subspecialty within psychiatry, as neurosurgery is a subspecialty within surgery. There are boards in child psychiatry, and to be board eligible for them a doctor must be board certified in psychiatry and have some specified experience in child psychiatry beyond that. The *Official ABMS Directory of Board Certified Medical Specialists* is a multi-volume list of board-certified physicians in the US, set up by geographical area, and it may be available at your city library. It gives a brief biographical sketch of every board-certified doctor, including his or her medical school and previous experience. There are some excellent doctors who are not board certified, and some parts of the United States have more board-certified physicians than others (according to the 2003 ABMS directory, vast Montana has only seven board-certified child psychiatrists). You do not have to wait for a board-certified physician, but feel free to ask any doctor to whom you are considering taking your child if he or she is board certified or board eligible (qualified to sit for the boards).

Get reports but be careful how they are worded

Any doctor who did enough of an evaluation of your child to give a diagnosis should have enough information to write a report. They may charge extra for a report. Getting a written report has several uses. It helps you see the doctor's reasoning as he or she arrived at the diagnosis. It is useful to other doctors, therapists, or teachers involved with your child. It may make your child eligible for certain services. However, because no diagnosis is final, you have to be careful how the report is worded. It may lock your child out of certain services, or at least out of government or insurance company funding for certain services. If you have arrived at a stage where you know you want certain services for your child, you should make the doctor aware of your wishes beforehand. If you are just starting out in the process, you may want the doctor to use language which leaves the diagnosis a little more open. Keep any reports you get.

2

Be Aware of Similar and Overlapping Diagnoses

If you have your child evaluated because you feel he or she needs help in socializing with peers, expressing feelings, varying his or her activities, and with motor skills, your child might be given diagnostic labels other than Asperger's Syndrome, even labels outside the autistic spectrum of which Asperger's is a part. Despite the serious and unique nature of autism, it was not identified as a distinct disorder until 1943. Before then, autistic behavior was assumed to be the result of schizophrenia or mental retardation. Asperger's Syndrome was not known to the English-speaking world until 1981, and its sufferers are still sometimes confused with a variety of other disorders whose symptoms overlap with Asperger's to a degree.

Different diagnostic labels for the same individual are not simply a matter of misdiagnosis. Some individuals are on the edge of a diagnostic category. The business of labeling any kind of psychological differences from the norm is complicated not only because of the refusal of humanity to fit into neat categories, but also because different diagnoses have been constructed by different specialties. These specialties – psychiatry, psychology, occupational therapy, speech therapy – all have their lingo, but psychiatrists have the most influence over disorder classification. In order to avoid the chaos that would occur if every doctor used his or her own conception of various mental conditions to diagnose patients, the American Psychiatric Association publishes the multi-volume *Diagnostic and Statistical Manual of Mental Disorders*, usually called the DSM for short. This tome is the canon for the psychiatric community in the United States. Every recognized psychiatric malady is described and defined, and criteria required for diagnosis are set forth. The manual explains when two diagnoses can be overlapping and when they cannot be, and what criterion is ruling if two similar conditions cannot be overlapping. However, this manual is used by psychiatrists, not necessarily by psychologists, who have their own criteria and some of their own diagnostic categories. Also, the World Health Organization publishes its own respected, widely used list of diseases called the *International Classification of Diseases* (ICD), which includes autistic disorders. Its definitions of autism and Asperger's Syndrome, although very similar to the DSM's, are not identical. Also, definitions of autism and Asperger's Syndrome change over time. The DSM is now is its fourth edition, and its descriptions of autistic disorders have changed from one edition to another, and may change again.

Despite the fluidity of these definitions, parents have to have some understanding of them to get any benefit from a child's diagnosis. Let us start with diagnostic labels from the autistic spectrum, on which Asperger's Syndrome has an official place, and then go over labels with symptoms similar to Asperger's Syndrome outside that spectrum.

The elusive core of autism

When a doctor to whom my husband Matt and I had taken Andy for an evaluation told us she believed he was suffering from Asperger's Syndrome, which was considered a type of autism, I was shocked. Not because of the words Asperger's Syndrome, for I had never heard of it, but because of the word autism. I was familiar with autism as it was understood 25 years ago, and associated it with nonverbal or barely verbal children who were unable to express emotion. Andy did not fit that description at all. I also thought autism was called Pervasive Developmental Delay, which I had assumed entailed mental retardation. Andy was smart. How could someone be smart and pervasively developmentally delayed?

What exactly is autism? Today autism is considered a spectrum, also called Pervasive Developmental Disorder, with so-called classic autism or Kanner's autism, at the bottom. The DSM defines the spectrum of Pervasive Developmental Disorder as "characterized by severe and pervasive impairment in several areas of development: reciprocal social interaction skills, communication skills, or the presence of stereotyped behavior, interests, and activities." Classic autism[1] is defined as having gross and sustained impairment in

---

1   The DSM uses the term "Autistic Disorder".

reciprocal social interaction, marked and sustained impairment in communication affecting both verbal and nonverbal skills, and restricted, repetitive, and stereotyped patterns of behavior, interests, and activities. It includes children popularly thought of as autistic, that is those who don't talk, who hurt themselves, who are retarded along with these other difficulties. I had a vivid impression of autism from the words of Josh Greenfeld, a writer and father of an autistic child, describing his son at age four:

> At the age of four, Noah is neither toilet-trained nor does he feed himself. He seldom speaks expressively, rarely employs his less-than-a-dozen word vocabulary. His attention span in a new toy is a matter of split seconds, television engages him only for an odd moment occasionally, he is never interested in other children for very long. His main activities are lint-catching, thread pulling, blanket-sucking, spontaneous giggling, inexplicable crying, eye-squinting, wall-hugging, circle-walking, bed-bouncing, jumping, rocking, door-closing, and incoherent babbling, addressed to his finger-flexing right hand. But two years ago, Noah spoke in complete sentences, had a vocabulary of well over 150 words, sang the verses of his favorite songs, identified the objects and animals in his picture books, was all but toilet-trained, and practically ate by himself. (Greenfeld 1972, p.4)

My son Andy was nothing like that. He fed and dressed himself, though his fingers were clumsy. He talked, though his conversational style was stilted. He did not interact with his peers, but he did interact with his family. Although his interests were circumscribed, he could concentrate on subjects for a long, sustained time. In fact, most children with Asperger's Syndrome are in regular classrooms, whereas most of those with classic Autistic Disorder have some degree of mental retardation and many are nonverbal.

Another condition on the autistic spectrum is sometimes called simply Pervasive Developmental Disorder. The term Pervasive Developmental Disorder properly refers to the spectrum, not to a particular level, but there is a condition called term Pervasive Developmental Disorder – Not Otherwise Specified (PDD–NOS), which is sometimes referred to, technically incorrectly, as just PDD. It is supposed to be used for any condition on the autistic/PDD spectrum which does not meet the criteria for any more specific condition, but seems to be generally used to refer to those in the middle of the spectrum, or to those with some degree of mental retardation whose overall symptoms are not as severe as those associated with classic autism. Because classic autism has such a dire reputation and there is reluctance to label people in a negative way (unless they can get some benefit out of it), PDD–NOS is probably used for some cases of classic autism. It may also be used for some cases which are subsequently labeled Asperger's Syndrome, although that is less likely because Asperger's is distinguished from the other conditions on the spectrum by relatively normal verbal skills.

What then connects the spectrum? Why are people of such of such varied ability levels classified together? Josh Greenfeld, Noah's father, referred to autistic children as having "untouchable imperviousness to the usual course of human events." The root word autism, which existed before Leo Kanner presented his groundbreaking work in 1943, means something like "stuck in self." That term does describe the phenomenon throughout the autistic/PDD spectrum, of individuals lost in their own worlds and unable to come out, or able to come out only with difficulty of varying degrees.

Hans Asperger, who was not familiar with Kanner's work when he first identified his syndrome, wrote that the children he described had a "dash of autism."[2] When Kanner's autism and Asperger's Syndrome and other conditions were lumped together under the umbrella of Pervasive Developmental Disorder, there was concern that this would make it more difficult to discover the underlying etiologies which might be different in different individuals now being put in the same broad category. But supporters of the "lumping" argued that conditions were generally defined by symptoms, not etiology, and that there were many different causes for epilepsy and yet its sufferers were all placed together under its label.

Research has been done on whether the three "prongs" of an autistic spectrum disorder (social aloofness, communication impairment, and repetitive activities) are a true syndrome, as opposed to a random collection of symptoms which occur simultaneously in some individuals if you have a large enough sample. This research, based on large epidemiological studies carried out in England in the 1970s, shows that the three main symptoms are a true syndrome, raising the strong possibility that in autistic individuals these three symptoms all arise from the same underlying neurological damage (Wing and Gould 1979). This may be true even among varied autistic conditions, regardless of cognitive ability, vocabulary, and type of circumscribed interest.

---

2   Later in his career, Asperger became familiar with Kanner's work and commented on their respective syndromes.

One thing autism is not is the deliberate avoidance of people or withdrawal from them. It is not shyness. There is no disagreement on this point among professionals, but this common misunderstanding sometimes leads to delay in diagnosis because parents may be accustomed to thinking of autism as extreme shyness, and it never occurs to them as a possibility for a developmentally odd but not shy child.

It seemed odd that fine motor skills should be part of the same diagnosis, but that is what researchers are for. Large enough numbers of children presented with a similar set of symptoms to be considered statistically significant. It is just a syndrome, a collection of symptoms. No one knows why the symptoms go together. Perhaps the social skills area of the brain is near the fine motor part. From watching Andy, I have learned that fine motor skills deficits can contribute to hampered social development, and some occupational therapists seem to think that poor motor skills are the cause of all problems, but more likely the link points to an underlying neurological impairment.

The most prevalent name for the spectrum had been moving away from autism and toward Pervasive Developmental Disorder (although now autistic spectrum is becoming more popular). It is true that individuals along the spectrum all suffer from some major developmental delays: many of them from delays in cognitive development, the vast majority from delays in motor skills, and all from delays in social development. Yet I have noticed that every individual I come across in the autistic spectrum, whether personally or through reading, either living or fictional, seems to have uneven abilities. Classically autistic Noah learned to talk and then stopped talking when he made progress in other areas. A 5-year-old boy with whom I became acquainted through Andy's occupational therapy sessions, who was diagnosed as having Pervasive Developmental Disorder and mental retardation, tested in the 2-year-old range for expressive abilities but in the 4-year-old range for receptive abilities. Andy's subtest scores on an IQ test varied far more than is typical for most people, but that internal variation is typical for Asperger's Syndrome. In the movie *Rainman*, Dustin Hoffman's Rainman was very good at some things but not others. The DSM notes that: "The profile of cognitive skills is usually uneven, regardless of general level of intelligence." Perhaps Selective Developmental Delay would be a more accurate term.

Definitions of Asperger's Syndrome

Historical overview

Dr. Tony Attwood, a leading authority on Asperger's Syndrome, writes that a lack of social skills, limited ability to have reciprocal conversation, and an intense interest in a particular subject are its core features (Attwood 1998, p.13). The pattern of symptoms, and unusual profile of abilities, was first recognized as a condition worthy of being treated as a specific malady by Hans Asperger, a Viennese pediatrician. Unfortunately, he practiced and published in Austria during World War II. His paper on the syndrome, published in 1944, essentially sat on a shelf and did not make it into the consciousness of the English-speaking world until the 1980s. A treatment ward set up by him and a colleague, Sister Viktorine, was bombed during the war and Sister Viktorine was killed. Dr. Asperger continued practicing but in relative obscurity.

In contrast, Dr. Leo Kanner, also from Austria but working and publishing in the United States, published a description of a syndrome with more severe symptoms in 1943. His published writings were the ground-breaking work that led to the recognition of autism as a distinct category separate from mental retardation and emotional disturbance. To this day children who are generally thought of as autistic are referred to as having Kanner's autism or classic autism.

In 1981, psychiatrist Lorna Wing published an article on Asperger's Syndrome which brought Hans Asperger's work to the attention to the English-speaking medical world (Wing 1981). Since that time it has received increasing attention, and in 1994 the American Psychiatric Association included Asperger's Syndrome in the *Diagnostic and Statistical Manual of Mental Disorders, Fourth Edition* (DSM-IV). Much medical literature in the last 20 years has focused on the relationship of Asperger's Syndrome to classic autism, with some researchers concluding it is a subtype of autism and others concluding that autism and Asperger's are two separate syndromes. The DSM-IV considers them separate subtypes of Pervasive Developmental Disorder. The class of Pervasive Developmental Disorder is also known as autistic spectrum disorders. The DSM sets forth the following criteria for a diagnosis of Asperger's Syndrome:

DSM-IV Definition of Asperger's Syndrome: The Medical Standard in the United States

A. Qualitative impairment in social interaction, as manifested by at least two of the following:

(1) marked impairment in the use of multiple nonverbal behaviors such as eye-to-eye gaze, facial expression, body postures, and gestures to regulate social interaction

(2) failure to develop peer relationships appropriate to developmental level

(3) a lack of spontaneous seeking to share enjoyment, interests, or achievements with other people (e.g. by a lack of showing, bringing or pointing out objects of interest to other people)

(4) lack of social or emotional reciprocity

B. Restricted repetitive and stereotyped patterns of behavior, interests and activities, as manifested by at least one of the following:

(1) encompassing preoccupation with one or more stereotyped and restricted patterns of interest that is abnormal either in intensity or focus

(2) apparently inflexible adherence to specific, nonfunctional routines or rituals

(3) stereotyped and repetitive motor mannerisms (e.g. hand or finger flapping or twisting, or complex whole-body movements)

(4) persistent preoccupation with parts or objects

C. The disturbance causes clinically significant impairment in social, occupational, or other important areas of functioning

D. There is no clinically significant general delay in language (e.g. single words used by age 2 years, communicative phrases used by age 3 years)

E. There is no clinically significant delay in cognitive development or in the development of age-appropriate self-help skills, adaptive behavior (other than in social interaction), and curiosity about the environment in childhood

F. Criteria are not met for another Pervasive Developmental Disorder or Schizophrenia.

Other definitions of Asperger's Syndrome

Other respected organizations set forth slightly different criteria. The World Health Organization[3] and Gillberg and Gillberg (1989) (Swedish physicians) define the syndrome, and their definitions are widely used internationally. They are all very similar as far as the core features are concerned, although some of them include motor skills deficits and some do not. As funding for various forms of aid for the disabled becomes more available, diagnoses become more political. The DSM criteria are still more restrictive than some internationally used diagnostic criteria (that is, it is harder to fit the DSM definition of Asperger's than the Gillberg definition). Nonetheless, some people have noticed that each DSM edition covers more disorders than the last, such as Asperger's Syndrome, and think that the increase in defined maladies reflects a desire to turn any difference from the norm into a medical condition. Others think the increase reflects the growing attention to mental illness, especially to subtypes within existing labels. Whatever disagreements exist, in the United States the DSM remains the guiding standard for psychiatrists, and referral slips and receipts given by doctors to patients or their parents usually contain a numerical code which corresponds to a defined malady in the DSM. Rarely, if ever, will insurance companies cover treatment for any mental disorder not in the DSM. Government entities sometimes have their own definitions of certain disabilities, but they are usually heavily influenced by the DSM.

Individual cases

Whatever the criteria for an Asperger's diagnosis, individual cases are all unique. On the internet stories can be found posted by adults who think they have Asperger's Syndrome or by parents of children diagnosed with it. There are many books containing personal accounts, as well as a number of news accounts. Although the individuals described have the core symptoms of Asperger's Syndrome, their personalities and overall ability to function vary greatly.

Herbert, an adult in his forties who was not diagnosed until adulthood, is very articulate and seems to have a very good understanding of Asperger's. He

---

3   The World Health Organization publishes the *International Classification of Mental and Behavioral Disorders*, which gives criteria similar to the DSM.

seems so intelligent in his website and so aware of other people's feelings that it is hard to believe he has an autistic spectrum disorder. He suffered a lot in his youth, but it is difficult to tell how much of that was due to social awkwardness and how much due to the lack of kindness and understanding with which he was treated by members of his own family. Most of the Asperger's adults who maintain websites seem intelligent and articulate, and are at least competent enough to develop a website. However, Phil from Australia cannot hold a job and spends a lot of his energy fighting with the government over whether he should be classified as disabled. Ben in London, age 22 in 2001, sounds upbeat and perfectly normal in his website, not at all weird, yet he speaks of his social isolation and lack of employment. Some of the web Asperger's cases were misdiagnosed during some parts of their lives, and some spent time in psychiatric hospitals. Most of them felt their Asperger's diagnosis helped them to get a handle on what was going on with them.

The children described by their parents on websites and in other publications have varying degrees of general competence. Some are in regular education classes at school with a lot of support, such as a full-time aide or pull-outs for sensory integration training as needed, and some are in special education classes of various types. Some of them, mostly those described in mainstream newspaper articles, are quite bright with unusual interests, like trains (the classic Asperger's interest) or TV game shows. Echo Fling's son took much of his spoken language from *Thomas the Tank Engine* stories for a while (Fling 2000). Although the websites do not say so, I think some of the children described in them may have concurrent learning disabilities, not unusual in children with Asperger's Syndrome. I am also amazed at the degree of assistance which some of them get from their school districts. Most of the Asperger's Syndrome adults with websites got no special help as children, and suffered as a result. Most Asperger's Syndrome children are mainstreamed (Bauer 1996).

Some of the subjects of these stories show severe symptoms, while some seem so normal that you wonder if they actually have Asperger's. The best known story of an adult with Asperger's Syndrome is probably *Pretending To Be Normal* by Lianne Holliday Willey (1996). She certainly described tendencies toward Asperger's, features of it, but her symptoms as shown in the book did not measure up to the DSM criteria. She did not come across as impaired enough. Developmental pediatrician Stephen Bauer said that Asperger's Syndrome symptoms ranged from severe to shading into normal (Bauer 1996). I guess she is in the "shading into normal" section.[4] I hope Andy ends up in that category too. Many times relatives of Asperger's Syndrome individuals have some of the symptoms, but do not fit the strict diagnostic criteria set forth by the DSM.[5]

Similar diagnoses

High-functioning autism

High-functioning autism is not a separate diagnostic category: that is, it is not in the DSM but it is a frequently used term. It is generally used to describe autistic individuals of average or above average cognitive ability. Many physicians in England consider Asperger's Syndrome a type of high-functioning autism. In the United States, because of the influence of the DSM, autism and Asperger's are considered separate categories. The DSM-IV does not permit co-existing diagnoses of autism and Asperger's Syndrome, but considers them mutually exclusive. The key difference is that Asperger's individuals do not have the difficulties with language that high-functioning autistics do. Sometimes children are diagnosed with high-functioning autism at an early age (3 or 4 years), and then undergo intensive speech therapy. If it is successful to the point where the child can speak fluently, although stiffly, while retaining other aspects of autism, then the child now fits the criteria for Asperger's Syndrome. This diagnostic history is one of the "six paths" to an Asperger's diagnosis described by Dr. Tony Attwood.

If you are having trouble finding services for your child with Asperger's Syndrome and your community has no support group for parents of children with Asperger's, ask for advice from a local support group for parents of autistic children. The Autistic Society of America has chapters in every state. Both conditions are labeled as types of Pervasive Developmental Disorder, and some states provide assistance for individuals with Pervasive Develop-

---

4   In her book Lianne Holliday Willey said she had never been formally diagnosed, but more recently she reported that she had been pronounced by Dr. Tony Attwood, an Asperger specialist, as having Residual Asperger's Syndrome in an Adult.

5   Dr. Attwood calls this a "ghost syndrome" or "shadow syndrome."

mental Disorder. Support groups and advocates for autistic children are likely to know about any such assistance, as well as other programs for people across the autistic spectrum.

Nonverbal Learning Disability (NLD)

Other diagnoses/labels similar to or overlapping with Asperger's are Nonverbal Learning Disability (NLD), Attention Deficit Disorder (ADD), Obsessive/Compulsive Disorder (OCD), Sensory Integration Disorder (SID), and Developmental Coordination Disorder (DCD). Some of these are from fields outside psychiatry, and therefore not in the DSM. Of these, the most closely related to Asperger's Syndrome is Nonverbal Learning Disability (NLD), which comes from the field of neuropsychology, and is not listed in the DSM.

Definitions, or labels, in neuropsychology have a different basis than definitions in psychiatry. Psychiatry's DSM relies on observable criteria, that is, behaviors. Neuropsychology concerns itself with brain function. Neuropsychologists who study Nonverbal Learning Disability, notably Byron Rourke and Michael Roman, believe it results from some dysfunction in the subcortical white matter systems of the brain. Since medical science's knowledge of the neurologic basis of mental disorders is extremely limited at this time, most descriptions of Nonverbal Learning Disability are mainly lists of symptoms, like descriptions of Asperger's. The symptoms are very similar – trouble with social skills, fine motor skills, and academics. Children with Nonverbal Learning Disability are said to miss social cues, to be unable to interpret tones or facial expressions: "They often have a blank look, and humor is missing for them" (Stancliff 1997).

An evaluation for Nonverbal Learning Disability generally includes both behavioral criteria and psychometric tests, such as an IQ test and various types of memory tests. The different subgroups of an IQ test are grouped in categories, and the test yields separate scores for performance IQ and verbal IQ. If the verbal IQ is significantly higher than the performance IQ, and the individual manifests the symptoms described above, a psychologist will probably diagnose NLD.

Neuropsychologists have produced a body of literature on educational interventions for students with Nonverbal Learning Disability. In general, literature on NLD focuses on education, while literature on Asperger's Syndrome has a much broader range. Nonverbal Learning Disability literature portrays the malady as an academic disability accompanied by symptoms in social skills and fine motor skills. Asperger's, on the other hand, is usually portrayed as a disability in social interaction with accompanying symptoms in fine motor skills and academics. In academic circles there is some discussion on whether these two maladies (or conditions, if you prefer a more neutral term) are actually the same thing. Whether or not they are, you may find that educators not familiar with the term Asperger's Syndrome have been exposed to information on Nonverbal Learning Disability, which can be used for the benefit of your child.

However, there is no requirement in the special education laws for services or accommodations for students with Nonverbal Learning Disability, nor any significant funding for programs for them. If your child has received a diagnosis of Nonverbal Learning Disability and you are desperate for services or educational accommodations, you might try taking your child to a psychologist or psychiatrist to see if a diagnosis of Asperger's Syndrome is warranted. There is no guarantee of services with a diagnosis of Asperger's Syndrome either, but since it is a type of Pervasive Developmental Disorder schools have to make some provisions for students with it.

Attention Deficit Disorder (ADD)

Attention Deficit Disorder (ADD) has received far more attention than Asperger's Syndrome, and far more children are diagnosed with it.[6] Schools have a better idea of how to handle it. They are farther down the road with Attention Deficit Disorder than they are with Asperger's Syndrome, or with any of the milder autistic spectrum disorders. Superficially, some of the symptoms of ADD and Asperger's Syndrome are similar: difficulty paying attention in school, and academic and social difficulties. With Attention Deficit Disorder, short attention span is consistent, and seems to be the cause of accompanying academic and social difficulties. Children with Asperger's Syndrome, however, are capable of intense and lengthy concentration when a subject interests them. For them, difficulty concentrating in school seems to be due to withdrawal from the mainstream of life or the social scene.

---

6   According to the National Institutes of Health (NIH), Attention Deficit Disorder is the most commonly diagnosed behavioral disorder of childhood, estimated to affect 3 to 5 percent of school-age children ("Diagnosis and Treatment of Attention Deficit Hyperactivity Disorder" NIH Consensus Statement 1998 Nov. 16-18; 16(2):1-37).

Children with either condition tend to do best in a very structured class-room setting, but for different reasons. For children with Attention Deficit Disorder, structure is an outside force imposed on them to help train them to stay focused. For children with Asperger's Syndrome, structure helps because they feel more comfortable with it, and are less likely to withdraw or engage in self-stimulating behaviors such as hand flapping, nose picking, sticking their hands in their pants, etc. Sometimes children are correctly diagnosed with both disorders concurrently, but more often kids with Asperger's Syndrome are first incorrectly identified as having ADD. According to an OASIS survey, 65 percent of parents reported an incorrect diagnosis of Attention Deficit Disorder before getting a diagnosis of Asperger's Syndrome (Bashe and Kirby 2001, p.69). This is not a disaster since some of the accepted interventions overlap, such as structured classrooms and social skills clubs, but such a diag-nosis does not lead to a very full understanding of the child or a useful prog-nosis. Pharmaceutical treatments for Attention Deficit Disorder are always not appropriate for individuals with Asperger's Syndrome.

Obsessive-Compulsive Disorder (OCD)

Another condition whose criteria overlap with those for Asperger's Syndrome is Obsessive-Compulsive Disorder (OCD), an anxiety disorder whose suffer-ers engage in ritualistic, repetitive behavior. Asperger's sufferers also engage in ritualistic, repetitive behavior. A young child who is the subject of one website on Asperger's (Asperger's Syndrome in Our Family) was originally diagnosed with Obsessive-Compulsive Disorder after a hospitalization. She was treated with medication which her parents found to be helpful. As a general rule though, Asperger's sufferers seem to enjoy their ritualistic activities while Obsessive-Compulsive sufferers do not. Obsessive-Compulsive sufferers seem to feel something terrible will happen if they do not perform their rituals. They need help in changing their view of reality, whereas Asperger's sufferers need help learning social skills and conversational skills. Yet anxiety often plays a large role in the lives of both groups so therapy in that area might be similar. One drawback to a diagnosis of Obsessive-Compulsive Disorder is the prejudice against those labeled with a mental illness. Although Asperger's Syndrome can be considered a mental illness, the label itself has not attracted the scorn more traditional mental illness labels have (although its sufferers might have).

Developmental Coordination Disorder (DCD)

Developmental Coordination Disorder (DCD), also called dyspraxia or developmental dyspraxia, is a condition described in the DSM-IV, and therefore recognized by many insurance companies. It is largely the province of occupational therapists. Its essential element is deficiency in the development of motor coordination – clumsiness – and the DSM specifies that such a diagnosis can be made only if there is no discernible neural damage or abnormal finding on neurological examination. Also, this diagnosis can be made only if it is severe enough to interfere significantly with activities of daily living or school performance. It is well known that retarded children and children with any type of autistic disorder tend toward motor clumsiness. According to the DSM, Developmental Coordination Disorder should not be diagnosed if the criteria for a Pervasive Developmental Disorder (including Asperger's Syndrome) are present, or if mental retardation is present (although there is an exception for mental retardation cases where the lack of development of coordination exceeds what is expected for that level of mental retardation). Whatever the official diagnosis and whatever the root cause, in children the lack of normal motor skills presents developmental challenges, including difficulties in socializing with peers and functioning at school. Consider this schoolday in the life of Danny, a young boy with Developmental Coordination Disorder:

> The rest of the class is seated and ready to begin work, with pencils out and pages opened, before Danny sits down after spending ten minutes struggling with his coat. He is upset anyway because he wasn't allowed to join a game of tag. He has been publicly rebuked, "You can't run, you just push and spoil the game." Danny is questioned about his lateness; he can't find any reason, his eye contact is poor and he stares at the ceiling wondering what is for lunch.
>
> While trying to listen intently to the next set of instruction he swings too far backward on his chair. The class is disrupted again and Danny's behavior is becoming increasingly worrisome for his teacher. Unfortunately it's time for PE. Danny hates PE. Everyone laughs at him. The unintentionally sexist remarks given emphasize still further his failure to conform. "When the music starts I want the girls to walk around the hall and the boys to jump in place. When the music stops all change: Boys walk round and girls jump."
>
> The music starts and Danny begins to move with a quick marching step in a clockwise manner. He slowly realizes that he is the only boy doing so. He slows down, trying to merge with the group in the center

and starts to jump: he hasn't realized that by this time the music has stopped and only girls are jumping. The children are divided into pairs. It has to be done that way as no one would ever choose Danny as a partner. It is to be a simple catching game, throwing a large soft ball from one child to another. Danny can't judge the ball's position in space or speed. He stands with his legs in a wide, awkward stance and almost falls before the ball is thrown to him. His tongue is protruding and he licks his lips anxiously as he waits. The ball arrives and he flings his arms wildly into space. His arms cross somewhere in the region of his chest and the attempt has sent the ball to the opposite end of the hall.

Danny is pleased when PE is finally over. He puts his sneakers back on with Velcro fasteners (there was no way he could manage laces) and thinks it would be easier to tie the sleeves of his sweater round his waist than to try to put it on. Back in the classroom he picked up his pencil to complete the math, which is still unfinished. He knows how many "fish" to add to a line to make 14 but they look more like tennis balls than like sea creatures. His hand aches because he gripped the pencil so tightly – sometimes there was even a slight tremor. His work always looks messy. The pencil always seems to make smudge marks all over the page. Even when the teacher writes "good work" or places a sticker at the end of the page, he knows she doesn't really mean it because it always looks so untidy. Sometimes he was so angry with his work that he rips it up or scribbles over it before anyone could see it. His name was barely legible – a mixture of upper and lower case letters – he just can't master the shapes.

Thank goodness it is lunchtime. He supposes he would be at the back of the line. Danny finds it impossible to stand still and is always being accused of deliberately pushing into other children. Once he had fallen against the fire alarm and the whole school was evacuated. When Danny started kindergarten he enjoyed sitting down to eat with the other children but by first grade no one wanted to sit next to him. He could not manage a knife and fork and his food was usually scattered over the rest of the table. The problem was avoided when he changed to a packed lunch from home: sandwiches, chips, fruit and a juice box with a straw presented fewer problems.

Danny's verbal skills had improved a lot after having regular speech therapy. He was referred at age three because his vocabulary consisted of ten indistinct words. His articulation was now age appropriate but he could easily lose the thread of a conversation if more than two or three ideas were contained in a sentence. He confused words when speaking quickly like, "I am taking my school to bike," and sentences were taken literally. For example when asked to stand on his toes he placed one foot on top of another.

His teacher thought he was lazy. Written work was never completed in the allotted time and his concentration span at best was varied between five and ten minutes and he constantly wandered around the classroom. He did not enjoy the privilege of taking messages because he could never remember them. Although he gave good responses in class his ability was measured mostly by responses committed to paper. He could not set his work out appropriately. His writing was illegible to anyone but himself. The best part of the day was the afternoon session – a time for individual reading. Danny's ability was measured two years above his chronological age but despite this he was unable to excel. When reading his tone was flat and monotonous. His pitch varied from line to line and words were pronounced at different speeds.

At home Danny was always on the go and appeared restless even when watching his favorite television program. He was very excitable and when a funny character came on he jumped off his seat and clapped his hand vigorously. Temper tantrums were becoming more frequent and he was irritated by the labels in the back of his clothes. His parents were concerned that he had no friends, and spent most of his time at home alone in his bedroom reading or using the computer, refusing to join in games of "Snap" or play with Legos or Mega Blocks. He had always had erratic sleeping patterns and a bedtime routine had not been established. He frequently woke during the night complaining of nightmares. (Portwood 1999, pp.34–35)

Most parents of children with Asperger's will probably recognize parts of this description. The theory here seems to be that deficits in motor coordination are responsible for social, behavioral, and academic problems. In some children they probably are, but something more seems to be going on in children with Asperger's. Most Asperger's children have Danny's symptoms plus. The social skills deficits of individuals with Asperger's cannot be ascribed entirely to lack of motor skills. That is one reason the writers of the DSM separated the two conditions. Motor skills deficits are generally only an optional criterion for Asperger's Syndrome anyway. It is theoretically possible to have Asperger's Syndrome while having good motor skills, but in fact children with Asperger's usually have poor motor skills, well behind their peers. One of the reasons the whole class of autistic disorders is called Pervasive Developmental Disorder is because they include delays in several areas, in motor skills, as well as social skills and emotional maturity. If only social skills were affected, the condition would not be pervasive. Nonetheless, the programs occupational therapists have developed for children such as Danny can be very helpful to children with Asperger's also.

Few private insurance companies will pay for the treatment necessary for Pervasive Developmental Disorder, including autism and Asperger's Syndrome, but some will pay for treatment of Developmental Coordination Disorder, although individual plans vary greatly. If you feel your child, whatever his exact diagnosis, has similarities to Danny and would benefit from the treatment programs devised for his condition, discuss insurance coverage with your pediatrician or an occupational therapist before discussing it with your insurance company. Occupational therapists are very familiar with what diagnoses get coverage for occupational therapy, and they are usually familiar with all common insurance plans. Pediatricians write referrals and put the diagnoses on them. Consult with them. Don't make up any symptoms; just be careful about how you describe them.

Sensory Integration Disorder (SID)

Similar to Developmental Coordination Disorder, and probably overlapping nearly completely in a kid like Danny, is Sensory Integration Dysfunction (SID; also called DSI for Dysfunction in Sensory Integration to separate it from the abbreviation for Sudden Infant Death Syndrome). This disorder was first described by A. Jean Ayres, an occupational therapist, about 40 years ago. It has recently received more attention with the publication of *The Out-Of-Sync Child*, by Carol Stock Kranowitz (1998). Sensory Integration Dysfunction is a neurological disorder of the processing system. While a person may have acute vision, sharp hearing, and other working senses, there is some deficit in the brain's ability to process or integrate all the countless bits of information it gets from the senses. This deficit supposedly leads to difficulties interacting with other people, in athletics, and in school work. The theory here is remarkably like the theory of autism expressed by Uta Frith in *Autism: Explaining the Enigma*, that the key problem in autism is an inability to integrate pieces of information into coherent wholes. Carol Kranowitz says that many symptoms of Sensory Integration Dysfunction are common to symptoms of other disabilities. She also says that Sensory Integration Dysfunction "intensifies the bigger problems of children with autism, pervasive developmental delay, and serious language difficulty" (Kranowitz 1998).

Oversensitivity to stimuli is a common trait of autistic disorders. Many autistic children will wear only soft fabrics, and do not respond well to cuddling, even as infants. Many find loud noises painful:

> People everywhere, talking, wearing bright colors. The talking is like the pounding of horses' hooves. The bright colors are blinding, the talking hurts my ears, the bright colors hurt my eyes. Oh why can't people be quiet and wear dull colors?[7]

Temple Grandin said:

> My hearing is like having a hearing aid with the volume control stuck on "super loud." It is like an open microphone that picks up everything. I have two choices: turn the mike on and get deluged with sound, or shut it off. (Grandin 1992, p.107)

Occupational therapists have developed a treatment called sensory integration training, which is often used on children with autistic spectrum disorders, Attention Deficit Disorder, dyspraxia or Developmental Coordination Disorder, or children with no particular diagnosis whose parents bring them to occupational therapists for help. Many parents and therapists swear by it, but it has met with limited recognition from the medical profession.[8] Sensory Integration Dysfunction is not listed in the DSM, and therefore treatment for it is rarely funded by insurance companies or any entity other than parents.

Definitions and criteria for diseases are always in a state of flux. The definition of Asperger's Syndrome set out in DSM IV is the official definition in the United States until there is another edition. Meanwhile researchers are refining definitions, discovering subtleties previously undiscovered. Some of these refined definitions will appear in the next version of the DSM. In the meantime, the most imaginative diagnosticians will tell you that there are overlaps, that patients cannot be fit into neat categories. Dr. Lorna Wing, who introduced the term Asperger's Syndrome to the English-speaking world, had

---

7   Diane Mear, 1994, as cited by Tony Attwood (1996) in *Asperger's Syndrome: A Guide for Parents and Professionals*, p.42.

8   This treatment is discussed further in Chapter 7.

this to say about the diagnoses defined by various researchers, including Non-verbal Learning Disability and Kanner's autism:

> All of these workers were, so to speak, fishing in the same pool of social and communication disorders, but, because of their specific foci of interest, their catches were different in some ways but overlapping in others. (Wing 2000, p.421)

However, insurance companies, school districts, and other assistance programs, have to have clear definitions in order to dispense limited funds. Dealing with fluidity in diagnostic labels is beyond their ability. Therefore, parents must be very careful in obtaining, keeping, and submitting diagnostic reports on their child.

3

The Usefulness of Diagnosis

Considering that all these labels are just overlapping descriptions of symptoms with, at best, hints at the underlying causes, parents sometimes wonder of what real use they are. Once a diagnosis of Asperger's is obtained, the treatment path is not clear. There is no set course of treatment for Asperger's Syndrome because of the lack of any universally accepted technique for treating any autistic spectrum disorder, the uniqueness of the individuals who have it, and the disconnectedness of social services. Therefore, opinions on the usefulness of such a diagnosis vary.

More harm than good?

Generally, the identification of a specific condition spurs research into the conditions and support for those afflicted with it. Unfortunately, the 30 years following Kanner's identification of autism saw the development and refining of the theory that parental neglect, specifically maternal rejection, was the cause of autism. In 1961, Tony Vandegrift, the 4-year-old son of army sergeant Anthony Vandegrift and Berthajane Vandegrift, was diagnosed as autistic, but the parents were never told of the diagnosis. They were not told because the mother was blamed for the condition, and doctors felt she needed treatment and manipulated her into it. Her account of this ordeal, *Tiger By The Tail* (2001), slams the psychiatric profession for its manipulation of people and its assumption that "maternal rejection" was the cause of any emotional disturbance in a child. Although her son did not speak at age 8, no doctor suggested speech therapy. The only treatment at that time was psychotherapy. Since the cause of autism was assumed to be emotional abuse, it made sense that psychotherapy would be necessary to deal with it. Both Mrs. Vandegrift and her son underwent psychotherapy at the very strong recommendation of army doctors, which therapy she found punitive and stupid. Although the

Vandegrift family may have been a little more dependent on their doctors than civilians, their doctors were following the standard treatment of the time. Even though mental retardation and epilepsy, long known to be results of organic brain damage, occur in a staggering percentage of autistic individuals, autism was not thought of as a neurological condition.

Today the world of medical science is convinced that autism and every other label discussed in this chapter is the result of an underlying neurological impairment, not of poor parenting. In the popular world, autistic disorders have been getting great press, with numerous sufferers and parents writing memoirs. Parents today do not need to be afraid that having their troubled children evaluated and given a diagnostic label of Asperger's Syndrome or something similar will be a source of shame. Both child and parents are more likely to attract scorn without a diagnosis.

The "it's just a label" theory

Berthajane Vandegrift would have appreciated frank talk from her son's doctors, but there does not seem to be any indication in her book that Tony could have been significantly helped by a straightforward diagnosis; only that his parents would not have been so mistreated. "Physician, do no harm" seems to be the message.

In the late 1960s, novelist and screenwriter Josh Greenfeld and his wife Foumiko Kometani knew there was something seriously wrong with their son. Noah, who was ultimately diagnosed as autistic, did not walk until age 2, talked for a while and then gave up speaking permanently, and at age 4 spent most of his days banging on things. They tried to find out what was wrong:

> What's the matter with Noah? For the longest time it seemed to depend upon what diagnosis we were willing to shop around for. We'd been told he was mentally retarded; emotionally disturbed; autistic; schizophrenic; possibly brain-damaged; or that he was suffering from a Chinese-box combination of these conditions. But we finally discovered that the diagnosis didn't seem to matter; it was all so sadly academic. The medical profession was merely playing Aristotelian nomenclature and classification games at our expense. For though we live in one of the richest states in the nation, there was no single viable treatment immediately available for Noah, no matter what category he could eventually be assigned to. (Greenfeld 1972, pp.4–5)

Noah appeared to fit the criteria for classic autism, and was subsequently held up as an example of an autistic child by college psychology textbooks, yet Josh Greenfeld felt that the term autism was meaningless. It certainly did not seem to be of much use to either the child or his parents.

Doctors did not mistreat the Greenfelds, but although there are now more services, their journey down the diagnostic trail seems similar to many taken today. It often seems as if the scenario is as follows: A parent comes to a doctor and describes a child's symptoms. The doctor then gives a diagnosis based on the symptoms. The parents go home and research the diagnosis, and learn that it means only that the child presents with the symptoms the parent described.

A friend of mine and her husband had suspected for some time their son had some form of autism when they took him to a doctor who specialized in autism for an evaluation. After talking to the father and observing the boy at play (about two hours altogether), the doctor confirmed that autism was the most likely diagnosis and billed them $750. They felt that this was a lot to pay for what they had received; essentially an official label for what they already knew. The doctor did give them a report which they might be able to use later to get services for their son. Sometimes the diagnostic process is just one more ring of the social service maze. You have to pay for the report to get the services you know your child needs.

My son Andy's first occupational therapist, who was seeing him in a social skills group and for fine motors skills therapy, took me aside and told me she thought his Asperger's diagnosis was wrong, that he had too much empathy for someone with Asperger's, and that we should set up a neuropsychological evaluation. I was irritated because we had invested a lot already in getting a diagnosis that made sense. I knew no diagnosis could be proved definitively, and I did not think putting him through a neuropsychological evaluation would alter his treatment plan, whatever label it might provide. She stressed that it was important to have the right diagnosis, so I spoke with the psychiatrist who had diagnosed him with Asperger's and the school psychologist. Both of them felt the Asperger's diagnosis was correct, or correct enough, and agreed there was unlikely to be any change in the treatment plan. To quote the psychologist, "It's not like we're going to do brain surgery," just special education — social skills training, occupational therapy, and speech therapy. We did not pursue a neuropsychological evaluation. Of course, we already had a diagnosis which seemed to fit and from whose suggested interventions he seemed to benefit. If we had not had such a diagnosis, I would have wanted to get one.

Treatments overlap for high-functioning autism, Nonverbal Learning Disability, Sensory Integration Dysfunction, and Developmental Coordination Disorder. When I told our pediatrician that the diagnosing psychiatrist was not 100 percent sure of the Asperger's Syndrome diagnosis for Andy and had in fact given us Anxiety Disorder as another possibility, she said the treatments for Asperger's Syndrome would help anyone with his symptoms. Many boys in treatment groups with my son, that is social skills groups, have different diagnoses – often Attention Deficit Disorder, and sometimes no diagnosis – but they are getting much the same treatment. Of course the correct diagnosis is vital for a full understanding of the individual's special needs, but many people are on the edge of a diagnostic category, and some of the categories merge together.

Fans of Asperger's Syndrome diagnoses

In the last few years the BBC News in England has published articles on people misdiagnosed as mentally ill, usually with schizophrenia, treated with antipsychotic medication, and subsequently, presumably correctly, diagnosed with Asperger's Syndrome. The articles strongly implied that an earlier correct diagnosis would have made all the difference in the world and portrayed the missed diagnoses as an outrage. An article entitled "Autism Misdiagnosis 'Ruined A Life,'" published by the BBC News on June 27, 2000 told the story of Sean Honeysett, who was "wrongly diagnosed as being mentally ill." The article never said what mental illness he was diagnosed as having, but did say a variety of antipsychotic drugs did not help him. Eventually, when he was an adult, his mother came across literature on Asperger's Syndrome and thought he might have it. She read more about it and went to a psychologist who was supposed to be an expert in it and described her son's symptoms. The psychologist then pronounced that he had Asperger's Syndrome and expressed horror that it had never been picked up before, even though at the time Sean was diagnosed as "mentally ill" no doctors in England knew anything about Asperger's Syndrome. It also seems odd that a psychologist could be so sure about an Asperger's diagnosis in an initial evaluation of a patient with a long history of treatment for mental illness, especially without seeing the patient. I did not give as much credit as the article did to a psychologist who specializes in autism coming up with an autistic spectrum diagnosis when the mother came in with a list of symptoms after reading up on Asperger's Syndrome. The article reported Sean was still heavily dependent on psychiatric services four years after his Asperger's diagnosis but was being gradually weaned from the antipsychotic medication he had been taking. It did not say what, if anything, was being done to treat his Asperger's symptoms. The mother was relieved when Sean's diagnosis was changed to Asperger's Syndrome from whatever mental illness it had previously been: "Mrs. Honeysett's first reaction was one of relief: 'I thought my son's not a nutter.'" I am not sure why she considered a serious, lifelong developmental disorder such as Asperger's Syndrome (which is sometimes classified as a mental illness) such an improvement over a more traditional psychiatric diagnosis, probably because of prejudice against mental illness.

There are other stories of people eventually diagnosed with Asperger's whose symptoms were attributed to schizophrenia or obsessive-compulsive disorder and who were inappropriately treated.[1] To them, an Asperger's Syndrome diagnosis means at least fewer antipsychotic drugs, and usually clearer understanding from family members. Also, in my experience there is less prejudice against Asperger's Syndrome than there is against "mental illness," especially schizophrenia.

Other individuals or their parents have found a diagnosis of Asperger's Syndrome very helpful. Herbert, an intelligent, articulate adult with Asperger's Syndrome, has published a lengthy website of his early trials and tribulations, and his discovery that he was "mind-blind" and that scattered throughout the world was a whole flock of other people like him. A few books on autism and Asperger's made it possible for him to start teaching himself how to interpret other people. He said again and again that he had been clueless for 45 years ("like a Zombie") and that he suffered needlessly as a result; needlessly because he required only a little explanation. His diagnosis of Asperger's Syndrome (from what he says I think he may have been self-diagnosed) was the starting point for him to stop being clueless, to start making sense of other people, their behavior, and why they reacted to him the way they did.

---

1 See "Mother Claims Drugs Ruined Daughter's Life," in *Hillingdon & Uxbridge Times*, 1 June 2000, by Emily Rogers. The article tells the story of the adult daughter of Maureen Eldrod, who had Asperger's Syndrome but was committed to a psychiatric hospital in England and given medications; treatment Ms. Elrod thought inappropriate.

Liane Holliday Willey's first experience with the term Asperger's was when one of her children was diagnosed with it. As she learned more about the syndrome she suspected she had it also, and eventually was diagnosed as having "Residual Asperger's Syndrome in an Adult." She went on to write several books about living with Asperger's Syndrome. She embraced her diagnosis:

> Today, I am stronger than ever...Since receiving my official diagnosis...I see the world through fresh rose colored glasses...Now my differences have a name. Now I know there are others like me. Now I can really find a way to express myself clearly. Now I can turn my attention to building cohesion and coherence among the community that is Asperger's. And most importantly to me, I can now help my young daughter find her way, for she, like me, is an Aspie. (Holliday Willey 2001)

Other adults with Asperger's who have posted websites have found some satisfaction in communicating with others over the web, realizing that many others were out there. Some have joined or formed clubs for Asperger's adults.

The value of the diagnosis for an adult seems to be largely in self-esteem, in helping them understand themselves and that there are others like them. Potentially, the value of the diagnosis is much greater for a child because of the hope of effective intervention and treatment. Nonetheless, even for a young child the value is hard to determine at this point because Asperger's Syndrome has not been diagnosed on a large scale until recently, and those diagnosed as children have not had a chance to grow up. Even when they do, research on the issue may be difficult because a diagnosis is not a guarantee of treatment, if effective treatment even exists. Generally the diagnosis is made by a psychologist or psychiatrist who recommends certain not very specific treatments, usually social skills training and possibly sensory integration training or some other form of occupational therapy. The parents are left to search for an appropriate program in the area where they live, and for funding if an appropriate program does happen to be available. Nor are schools much help; most school systems have few or no programs tailored for Asperger's kids.

The main value of the diagnosis at this point seems to be an understanding of the child. Many parents have known that something was wrong with their child but didn't quite know what. Many have received other diagnoses for their child that were close but didn't quite fit, perhaps Attention Deficit

Disorder or some other form of learning disability. For them, if Asperger's Syndrome seems to explain their child where other diagnoses did not, there is at least a sense that now they know what is going on, and they no longer feel they are simply stumbling around; although that sense is often tempered with sadness since Asperger's Syndrome is such a serious condition. That is the feeling Echo Fling (2000) described in her book *Eating An Artichoke: A Mother's Perspective on Asperger's Syndrome*.

The medical merry-go-round, the process of going to doctor after doctor looking for a diagnosis, and receiving different ones, usually whatever that doctor specializes in, is exhausting, expensive, and probably harmful to the child. My family was lucky that we did not have to go through that. The psychiatrist we hired and paid out of pocket did a thorough evaluation, and she had the school psychologist to help her. There are many stories of searches for a diagnosis, and sometimes the lengthy absence of a correct one made for a hard road, even though Asperger's Syndrome is only a collection of symptoms with no miracle treatment.

I can state unequivocally that I found my son's diagnosis helpful. I had never heard of Asperger's Syndrome until the term was applied to him, but when I read descriptions of the syndrome after his diagnosis I thought to myself, "That's Andy." Sure I already knew he had the traits of the syndrome, but the diagnosis made me realize they were more serious and long term than I had thought (he was 6 years old at the time). Yes, I had already felt before the diagnosis that he would benefit from some kind of social coaching, but did not know where to find any. Getting the diagnosis was no guarantee of any social skills training, but it made me look harder for it, and though not easy to find, there is some available. The diagnosing doctor also recommended occupational therapy. I had known Andy was clumsy but had not considered occupational therapy as I had come from a family of klutzes, none of whom had any related diagnosis. Once I entered the world of occupational therapy with Andy I realized occupational therapy included far more than help with fine motor skills, and in fact offered help for almost every aspect of life affected by Asperger's Syndrome. Prior to getting the Asperger's diagnosis, my husband and I had rejected with scorn a suggestion of pharmaceutical intervention. After the diagnosis, which seemed accurate and serious, we explored the possibility further, consulting various medical professionals we knew about a trial of medication and reading about what medications might help.

What if the Asperger's Syndrome diagnosis is wrong? It must happen sometimes. Will your child be harmed? That depends largely on the attitude people take to him as a result of the diagnosis. If they assume he is a hopeless social misfit, it is bound to have a negative effect. Of course, such an attitude would have a negative effect even if the diagnosis were accurate. Would the child be given the wrong treatment? The treatment consists largely of training in social, conversational, and motor skills. If he needs help in these areas, such special training should help even if his underlying condition is something other than Asperger's Syndrome. The main harm from an inaccurate diagnosis is probably the lack of a more accurate one. If a child has early onset schizophrenia, or obsessive-compulsive disorder, an incorrect Asperger's Syndrome label may obscure or delay the more accurate diagnosis. As specialized medications play big roles in treating those conditions, the child may be deprived of effective treatment. In an article on diagnosis of childhood onset schizophrenia, Drs. Schaeffer and Ross reported on a study involving 17 children who were eventually diagnosed with and treated effectively for schizophrenia (Schaeffer and Ross 2002). All of them went through other labels first, one of which was Pervasive Developmental Disorder, and these did little to help. It was only after treatment with antipsychotic medication that their symptoms improved. This is not to suggest that you should be concerned about possible psychoses, but that you should get what help you can from each diagnosis, and not regard one as final and absolute.

Diagnostic labels and bureaucracy

Whatever use diagnostic labels might be in daily life, for self-esteem, general understanding, etc., their most tangible use is in getting services, that is, in getting funding for services. This is a very tricky area, and you will feel the need for a navigational chart. In *A Client Called Noah*, Josh Greenfield (1972) described his son Noah's annual classification meeting with his school district. The parents met with some bureaucrats to review his case, particularly his classification. At the end of the meeting he was retained in his current program with the classification of "retarded." Since Noah fitted the criteria for classic autism, he could have been classified as either autistic or retarded. Josh Greenfeld pointed out that funding per diem for an autistic student greatly exceeded that for a retarded student. Nonetheless, their son was classified as retarded because they thought the program he was in was the best available for him.

A diagnosis of a Pervasive Developmental Disorder can make a child eligible for Supplemental Security Income (SSI), if the family meets certain income requirements. In some states, the diagnosis makes a child eligible for a Medical Assistance card. Most private insurance companies will not pay for treatment of any autistic spectrum disorder. They are more likely to cover services, such as occupational therapy, for Developmental Coordination Disorder. Symptoms of Developmental Coordination Disorder are often seen in children with Asperger's, but the DSM prescribes that a diagnosis of Developmental Coordination Disorder should not be given to an individual with an autistic spectrum diagnosis. A child with Asperger's might have the same fine motor skills "challenges" (i.e. handicaps) as a child with Developmental Coordination Disorder, plus some additional ones. Those are just the definitions the DSM uses. It hardly seems fair that an insurance company would cover treatment for motor skills deficits in one individual but not in another solely because that other had additional handicaps.

Generally school districts have some kind of support programs for the communication impaired; this is a requirement of the federal Individuals with Disabilities Education Act. Sometimes, although these programs are not designed for Asperger's children, given the limited options available such a class may be the best placement for some students with Asperger's Syndrome. Echo Fling's son with Asperger's Syndrome was in such a class, largely because it was small, structured, and quiet. At one point we were considering such a class for our son, but were told by a representative of our school district that a student with a diagnosis of Asperger's was not eligible. This was particularly galling as our school district offered virtually nothing for students with Asperger's. Another mother I came across, from a suburban district, had a similar experience. Classes for the communication impaired are for students with difficulties solely in the area of communication, although it is hard to imagine any child in such a distinct category. School districts tend to be giant bureaucracies which attempt to categorize people into specific niches. Students with disabilities have to be squeezed into the existing official diagnostic labels. Yet these labels represent only medical science's best attempt at understanding various conditions. For individuals, the lines between the categories are anything but distinct. Because a child's school situation is so important, some parents choose the program they think best for their child and then shop for the required diagnosis. Other parents do the same based on what their health plan covers.

Because Asperger's is an autistic spectrum diagnosis, and the picture people generally have of autism is so grim, sometimes an Asperger's diagnosis closes more doors than it should. I once called a private school which specialized in educating students with "learning differences." The person there with whom I first spoke told me they did not handle children with Asperger's. Yet their program seemed to me suited to Andy's needs. I called again and spoke with someone else. This time I did not say that Andy had Asperger's, but described him. He learned facts easily but his reading level tested significantly below what his IQ predicted. His IQ was in the high average range, but the subtest scores varied widely. He had difficulties socializing with peers but got along well with grown-ups, and he had some nervous habits. This admissions officer assured me that this type of kid was right up their alley. Of course, it would be impossible to ever get a school district to pay for a private placement at such a school, no matter how suitable, if it did not explicitly claim to educate children with Asperger's Syndrome.

Besides opening or closing doors in bureaucracy, labels can set expectations. I once took a book out of the library, *Good Friends Are Hard To Find* (Frankel 1996), because I thought it might give me ideas for helping Andy. It is a primer on social skills for children, written for parents, to help them teach their children social skills in dealing with peers. I had to request it specially as it was not in our library branch. In the introduction, I was disappointed to see this disclaimer: "This book will not help the child with autism, who is in his own world, or the child with general delays in learning, motor and social behavior. These children need intensive programs offered by psychologists and recreational therapists." Dr. Frankel seemed to be saying that his suggestions were not for Asperger's children, as well as discounting the difficulty in finding appropriate programs offered by psychologists and recreational therapists. I have yet to come across any recreational therapists doing anything designed for kids with Asperger's. Then I looked at a couple of the hypothetical "problem" situations which he outlined steps to solve:

> Jason is seven years old and has never gone over to another child's house, nor has he invited another child over to his house. He has plenty of books. He likes to draw, has art materials and lots of videotapes. He doesn't know how to play any games which the other children his age play. At school, while the other children are playing handball, Jason is playing in the sandbox by himself. (Frankel 1996, p.25)

I don't know how many children with Asperger's like to draw, but substitute train sets, maps or anatomy sets for art supplies and it sounds pretty familiar. Here is another:

Nine-year-old Jeremy spends much of his free time watching TV or playing videogames. He doesn't know how to play any board games or the games the other boys are playing at recess. He shows little interest in sports. He has no toys at home that are interesting to other children his age. One time Michael, also age nine, came over to his house to play. They spent the whole time watching T.V., barely saying a word to each other. After the play date, Michael told his parents he was bored. Michael declines invitations to come back. (Frankel 1996, p.18)

If these scenarios sound familiar to you, Dr. Frankel's book has many practical suggestions for teaching children how to deal with social situations. It is true that the problems of children with Asperger's go deeper than those described by Dr. Frankel. His book's focus is on practical skills, not on innate problems with processing or other-worldliness. Yet his suggestions struck me as likely to be of great help to parents of children with Asperger's Syndrome. Children with Asperger's need to be taught social skills. They don't pick them up on their own. The suggestions in Dr. Frankel's book can be helpful, despite his disclaimer at the beginning.

One place where Andy's diagnosis has opened doors is at my workplace. My employer has been extremely generous in letting me work a flexible schedule to allow me to take him to various services. Generally the firm frowns on employees' constantly changing their hours. All I had to do was confidentially relay to the personnel director and my supervisor that I had a child with an autistic disorder (no one there had ever heard of Asperger's), and they were willing to do whatever they could to help.

Is autism on the rise?

There is a widespread impression that the prevalence of autism is rising. "One thing is clear: its incidence is growing," said the *Seattle Post-Intelligencer* in a report on autism. "There's one topic that virtually everyone agrees on: The number of children being diagnosed with this pervasive neurological disorder is booming," according to Deborah Weisberg in the *Pittsburgh Post-Gazette* (19 December 2000). "No one disputes it. Cases of autism…are rising sharply," reported the *New York Times* on its front page (26 January 2004). The Center for Disease Control concedes: "Studies published between 1985 and 1995 reported higher prevalence rates [for autism] than studies published prior to 1985."

The rising rates of autism diagnoses have led to a search for environmental causes of the disorder, but no link has been proven and most of the theories are speculative. One autistic boy's mother whom I met, a sales representative for a "clean" energy company, blamed fossil fuels for the increase. The best known environmental factors alleged as causes for the rise are probably the MMR vaccine and chemicals in wheat and milk. The possible vaccine connection has been studied and found to be without merit. The chemical allergies theory is harder to prove or disprove. Many parents have treated their autistic children with the megavitamins recommended by proponents of this theory as well as trying other treatments and have felt their children improved, but it is hard to tell what brought on the improvements. Given the overwhelming evidence of a very early etiology for autism, perhaps from conception, and the lack of any confirmed evidence supporting the megavitamin treatment, that theory does not seem very likely either.

From reviewing articles published in medical journals, I found no reason to think the actual prevalence of autistic disorders in the population has increased. Studies which found a higher prevalence used a broader criteria in defining autistic disorders. Lorna Wing, superstar British autism researcher, reviewed 16 studies on the epidemiology of autistic disorders and found no firm evidence of an increase in prevalence over time (Wing 1996). She concluded that the impression that there is an increase is due to broadening of the diagnostic criteria to include milder cases, increased awareness of autism, and a change in referral patterns. She conceded a shift toward later childbirth might have an effect on prevalence if there is a real link between autism and higher maternal age. Dr. Eric Fombonne, psychiatrist and noted autism epidemiologist, reviewed more recent studies and reached essentially the same conclusion, that the diagnosis rate has increased but not the actual case rate (Fombonne 2003).

Even if there is some increase in true prevalence (as opposed to number of diagnoses), broadening of the definition, increased awareness of the milder forms, and improved diagnostic techniques and screening must be responsible for the majority of increases in diagnoses. Since Asperger's has received considerable attention in the last 20 years and practically none before that, it is no wonder that Asperger's diagnoses have risen dramatically. Autistic disorders have received a lot of attention in the United States since the movie *Rainman*. The number of references to autism in the news media have skyrocketed. The demand for services has also skyrocketed. The California Department of Developmental Services reported a 273 percent increase in the number of individuals receiving services for autism from 1987 to 1998 (1999, p.8, Table 3), and the number has continued to increase. According to the *Pittsburgh Post-Gazette*, agencies in Allegheny County, "as well as those across the nation, are struggling to keep up with the demand" (Deborah Weisberg, 19 December 2000). That article goes on to report that because of the increased demand parents have had to wait for months to have their child evaluated and sometimes for another year to begin therapy. When the Seattle School District started a program for higher functioning autistic students with 42 spots, families moved from across the country to get an appropriate placement for a child.

One benefit to the increase in diagnoses of Asperger's Syndrome is advocacy. Schools do not have many programs now tailored to the needs of students with Asperger's syndrome but five years ago they had none. Generally, the increased interest in autism is a good thing. It is bound to result in more services. In 2001, 61 members of Congress joined the Coalition for Autism Research and Education, saying they would push to spend more federal money for research into autism. The Center for Disease Control and the National Institutes of Health are paying more attention to autistic disorders. Nonetheless, it takes some time before interest evolves into services, and even longer for access to services to reach all over our country.

PART II

Further Down the Maze

Starting Intervention

4

Finding a Program

Children with Asperger's Syndrome can learn to socialize with peers appropriately; it is just harder for them to learn these skills, as they do not pick them up naturally. Treatment is largely skill based. Just as children with poor fine motor skills can conquer the related difficulties through practice and compensatory strategies, so children with poor social skills can practice socializing and learn strategies that work for them.

With some disabilities – classic autism, cerebral palsy – intervention is most effective if done before age 5. Asperger's Syndrome is rarely diagnosed before age 6. According to Tony Attwood, the average age of diagnosis is 8 years (Attwood 1998, p.23). How much can be done at age 8? A lot. Social skills groups, disguised as clubs, give children and adolescents practice at socializing, and let them have some fun interacting with other kids. If nothing else, participation in such groups can help their self-esteem. They know that other kids, typical kids, belong to clubs and social groups. Now they can too, and enjoy it. Occupational therapists can consult in schools, to teach children tricks to stay organized and to compensate for poor motor skills, or to help with handwriting. Children with classic autism need speech therapy early to learn to talk. Children with Asperger's learn to talk on their own (more or less), but speech therapists can help them learn conversational skills, and sometimes run social skills groups for that purpose. Of paramount importance is organizing the right school program, with occupational therapy, speech therapy, and social skills involved.

The right program is not easy to find

After my son Andy's diagnosis, I read about Asperger's and learned all of the above, but I knew that getting the necessary services would be the biggest challenge. A year earlier, when Andy had been evaluated as having enunciation in the lowest 1 percent of his age group and in need of speech therapy, I had called our health insurance company to see what treatment they would cover. The answer was none. Unless Andy had a physical problem with his mouth or an identifiable neurological problem that affected his speech, insurance would not cover anything. The insurance company had referred me to our school district. When I called the school district, after several calls from one office to another, I was told that if he was not in school they could not do anything. In retrospect, they should have referred me to the early intervention system.

At that time I had no understanding of how the early intervention system is supposed to work, that the federal Education for Individuals with Disabilities Act requires states to have programs for preschoolers with disabilities from ages three to five, and that these programs are administered by school districts. Children with certain covered disabilities, including language impairment, are entitled by law to remedial services at no expense to their parents, but I did not know any of that until after Andy was school age. Neither the evaluator at a local pediatric rehabilitation facility, nor any school district office, nor Andy's private speech therapist had mentioned it. Our pediatrician gave me a number for an early intervention agency, but by that time Andy was five, and that agency told me that by the time they processed his application he would be almost school age, so I might as well wait. My husband and I paid for therapy privately. By the time Andy was evaluated by the school district's speech therapist halfway through his kindergarten year, his speech had improved to the point where he was not eligible (he was also very conscious of how to speak in front of a speech therapist). Our insurance company had paid for the initial evaluation, but it had taken months to get that and I regretted not having gone to a private therapist from the beginning and paid for the evaluation out of pocket. Had we done so our son might have started speech therapy several months earlier.[1]

If you have sought help for a child with any kind of delay, you have probably experienced similar difficulty getting information and similar waits for evaluation. If you have sought help for a child in the nebulous area of social skills, or for a child who needs multiple services, the frustrations

---

1   I had the same regret with psychiatrists when looking for a diagnosis. We waited months to get an evaluation through our insurance, were unsatisfied with it, and paid for a private psychiatric evaluation eventually anyway.

increase exponentially. Children with Asperger's Syndrome fall into both categories, so it is the rare parent who has not felt getting the right program together is a quandary.

Speech therapy had been within our means. At the time of Andy's Asperger's diagnosis however, it was clear that he needed help with fine motor skills (which cost about twice as much per session), learning supports, and social skills training. He needed to be taught play skills by a professional. How would we pay for this? Where would we even find play skills therapy, from recreational therapists? There are too few of them, and most of them work for institutions like rehabilitation hospitals, designing recreational programs for people with physical disabilities. Even before Andy had been diagnosed with Asperger's, I had been thinking he would benefit from a small playgroup led by someone who specialized in teaching play skills, and had wondered whether any such groups existed in our city, the fifth largest city in the country. Our pediatrician did not know of any such group.

Help is out there

Although lack of information, lack of sufficient services, and lack of funding are daunting problems, there are services and funding out there. Although it may seem that an appropriate program for a child with Asperger's Syndrome does not exist in your locality in a way you can afford, the component parts probably are available. You just have to find them and piece them together. The Individuals with Disabilities Act guarantees services necessary for their education to children with autism, language impairment, and learning disabilities. You can argue that your child with Asperger's Syndrome fits into one or all of these categories, and ultimately a school district should acknowledge that the ability to hold a conversation with peers, the ability to write quickly enough to keep up with the class, or the ability to predict what a fictional character is going to do next are necessary for a student's education. Private insurance companies generally do not like to pay for long-term therapy for any developmental disorder, but will sometimes pay for limited occupational therapy. They will usually pay at least for an evaluation in occupational therapy and speech therapy. The people who do those evaluations may have some idea of how you can get the therapy if they think your child needs it. Both the American Occupational Therapy Association and the American Speech–Language–Hearing Association can supply you with lists of therapists in your area. A local pediatric hospital can be a resource. Someone there must know something about where you can find the services you think your child needs (you should probably start with the speech therapy and occupational therapy departments). You just have to keep calling until you hook up with someone helpful.

Maybe the hardest service to find, because it is not a well-established field, is therapy to promote social skills. It is also the most important intervention for individuals with Asperger's Syndrome since deficiency in that area is their core symptom.

You want to find a small, structured playgroup run by a professional who specializes in teaching social skills. Where do you start? Social skills groups are not listed in the Yellow Pages. Fortunately, a variety of professionals offer social skills training, including occupational therapists, speech therapists, psychologists, and psychiatric social workers, and they are listed in the Yellow Pages. Better yet, your pediatrician or family doctor will know of some of these professionals.

Most of these therapists will not offer the service you want, but you have to persevere, calling all the therapists in those fields whose names you have collected, asking them if they know of any such group. This type of networking is exhausting for those of us who do not make cold calls lightly, but you can get used to it, especially if your child's development is at stake. You just have to budget time for it. Ask your pediatrician to ask around also, to take some of the burden off you, as well as anyone else, schoolteachers, relatives, clergy, you feel comfortable asking for the same favor.

You will probably find something suitable, or possibly inspire some professional to start such a group. In the meantime, other therapists can work on areas of social skills. Occupational and speech therapists cover an amazing number of areas. I had thought of speech therapists as working on enunciation, stuttering, and voice projection. I had thought of occupational therapists as concerned almost entirely with fine motor skills, and with getting injured people back to work. Both of them do a lot more.

5

Speech Therapy

Speech therapists, or speech-language pathologists, work on disorders from language-related learning disabilities to autism to difficulty swallowing. The closely related field of audiology is concerned with language processing as well as hearing. Conversational skills are within the purview of speech-language pathologists. These therapists are also concerned with nonverbal communication, including facial expressions, gestures, and posture. For decades, before Asperger's Syndrome was even known to the English-speaking world, speech therapists have been concerned with a condition called Semantic Pragmatic Language Disorder, the symptoms of which include poor conversational turn taking, unusual choice of words, and inappropriate tone of voice. They have developed a variety of techniques for treating this condition, techniques which can be useful to individuals with Asperger's Syndrome.

People with Asperger's can be taught not to talk for more than a minute without making sure someone else says something. They can be taught not to discuss the same subject for more than five minutes, or better yet to look for signs that whomever they are talking to is getting bored with the subject. They can study pictures of people's faces and learn to interpret emotions expressed nonverbally. A speech therapist can drill your child in interpreting body posture and in presenting appropriate body language. One suggestion offered for children with Nonverbal Learning Disability is to watch soap operas with the sound off, in order to pick up on body language. Believe it or not, such a program can be done under the direction of a speech-language pathologist. Speech therapists can help children practice proper eye contact, techniques for initiating a conversation, sustaining a conversation, and changing topics within a conversation. Sometimes, speech therapy focuses on prosody: appropriate inflection and melody to reflect the meaning of the words. Speech therapy can be used to work on proper communication of friendly, polite, sarcastic, or joking intent, a little bit like acting lessons might.

You may sometime hear the phrase "whole body listening" or "active listening," concepts based on the theory that listening involves the whole body, including eye contact, leaning forward slightly or orienting one's head, and mental concentration. A speech therapist can help your child practice these listening skills. These therapists also work on abstract language processing and use, that is idioms, jokes, and sarcasm. Speech therapists have experience in teaching clients to recognize different perspectives, to understand that different people can have different beliefs and ways of looking at things. Lack of such understanding is sometimes considered a key feature of autistic spectrum disorders. Speech therapists sometimes run conversational practice groups for children, a type of social skills training club. If your child is working with a speech therapist and you do not know of any social skills groups, try asking the speech therapist outright if he or she would consider working with your child in conjunction with a few other clients to practice conversational skills.

Speech pathologist Sally Bligh has developed a speech therapy curriculum for children who lack conversational skills. She recommends what she calls social language groups: small groups of children meeting with a speech therapist to practice conversational skills. Techniques used in these groups include modeling appropriate conversational responses, scripting (giving a child appropriate lines and having him deliver them), playing games which require some conversation, having a child give a talk on the subject of his special interest, and positive reinforcement for conversational success. To deal with monologues she recommends the rule, say two things and then ask a question. To deal with children who change the subject too abruptly, she recommends the therapist get the children to discuss a topic they like and then guide the discussion. She also has recommendations for children of different communication skill levels. She discusses five levels of communication skills, with a social language group plan for each level. Higher level groups play more complex board games like Clue, Monopoly, Trivial Pursuit. The children in some of these groups, the ones who can handle it, can make up list of things to do together, games to play together. These groups can also be used to practice body language interpretation.

The American Speech–Language–Hearing Association contains in its mission statement the goal of making high quality speech or language therapy available to all who need it. They have lists of therapists in practice in all areas of the country. There is a strong chance a speech therapist in your general area does this kind of work, if you are willing to pay for it. Expect to pay about $75 to $150 an hour depending on your community. Unfortunately, private insurance rarely covers this sort of therapy. Group therapy may be slightly cheaper, although probably harder to find, and just as beneficial to someone with Asperger's Syndrome.

Your best bet for getting funded speech therapy for a child with Asperger's is generally through your school district. Speech therapy is a related service under the federal Individuals with Disabilities Education Act (IDEA). Frequently, the school district speech therapists are booked up working with children with articulation disorders. Your child may be assessed and you may be told he or she does not qualify for speech therapy. Do not give up. Ask the classroom teacher to document the educational challenges your child faces as a result of poor expressive language skills. Present this documentation at the next Individualized Education Program (IEP) meeting, or request that an IEP meeting be convened to discuss this issue. Speech-language pathologists also study and treat language-related learning disorders. If your child is having problems with reading, either with phonics or with comprehension, they could be a result of some basic language-processing disorder, and therefore in the realm of speech therapy. If your child explains what he has read in a very odd or ineffective way, a speech therapist may be able to help. At least in theory speech therapists can teach children to draw inferences in order to improve reading comprehension and oral comprehension. Drag the school psychologist into the meeting to verify that reading problems could be the result of subtle language problems, and that a course of speech therapy aimed at helping your child comprehend what others are saying might push up the child's reading scores. The speech therapist can see your child on a consulting basis, working with the classroom teacher to put strategies in place to help your child engage in appropriate class discussion or work on comprehension skills, or can see him individually or in a small group.

6

Occupational Therapy

So what exactly is occupational therapy?

I had always assumed that occupational therapy had grown out of physical therapy, since from what I knew of occupational therapists' work in rehabilitation hospitals it seemed to be physical therapy for fine muscle control. I figured it had got its name from retraining injured workers to return to their occupations. In fact, occupational therapy grew out of treatment for the mentally ill.

Roots of occupational therapy

During most of the eighteenth century, the mentally ill, and possibly many retarded people as well, were locked up in asylums, sometimes in chains, with little light and fresh air. Toward the end of the eighteenth century, some reform-minded doctors starting treating these patients by taking them outside, and having them work with their hands. In the nineteenth century, this kind of treatment became more common. Mental patients were encouraged to work at gardening or farming, to be involved in recreational activities or classes, with an emphasis on manual labor. This therapy began to be called "activity therapy," and mental hospitals hired people to run these programs. However, these people, the predecessors of occupational therapists, had no training in anatomy or psychology. An American doctor, Herbert Hall, taught anatomy to arts and crafts instructors so that they could work with patients with motor skills deficits, so common in the neurologically impaired. Thus the profession was born that uses knowledge of anatomy to train people with disabilities to do the activities and occupations done by their nondisabled peers.

Use of this therapy spread to the assistance of the physically injured and handicapped, and received a big impetus during World War I when the army used occupational therapists to help injured soldiers. In 1917, the National Society for the Promotion of Occupational Therapy was founded, and this society later became the American Occupational Therapy Association. Training standards began to be developed for occupational therapists, and in 1935, the American Medical Association, along with the American Occupational Therapy Association, became involved in setting those standards. In 1946, a certification process was set up for occupational therapists based on an examination given nationwide. The first state licensure laws were enacted in 1976, and today almost all US states require occupational therapists to be licensed, and successful completion of an examination given by the American Occupational Therapy Certification Board is a requirement of licensure.

Occupational therapy is based on the use of everyday activities to help people with some kind of disability achieve a higher level of functioning. The disability can be physical, the result of an injury or birth defect, or the result of a psychological problem or developmental delay. Far from being restricted to helping injured workers return to their jobs or helping mental patients regain a sense of equilibrium, occupational therapy today is used with patient populations ranging from premature babies to the elderly. Nor are its concerns restricted to motor function. More and more, occupational therapy is concerned with sensory integration, coping skills, and social functioning.

Each state has its own laws governing licensing of occupational therapists, but they all rely heavily on standards set by the American Occupational Therapy Certification Board. In the United States, there are two levels of occupational therapy practitioners, Occupational Therapists Registered, who write OTR after their names, and Certified Occupational Therapy Assistants, who write COTA after theirs. To be certified as an OTR, the aspiring therapist must complete a bachelor's or master's program in occupational therapy (starting in 2007 all accredited programs will be master's programs) and then sit for the OTR examination given by the American Occupational Therapy Certification Board. To be certified as a COTA, the aspirant must complete a two-year, post-secondary program to be eligible for the test. COTAs work under the supervision of OTRs, but OTRs can set themselves up in private practice.

The number of occupational therapists in the USA has been rapidly rising. The perceived need for occupational therapy has generally been expanding since the mid-1960s, and the profession has grown phenomenally since then.

The prominent part occupational therapists played in the efforts of the last few decades to integrate people with disabilities into the rest of society fueled a large measure of this growth. The federal laws enacted in the same time period concerning special education have also contributed to the rise of the field, as public schools systems have hired more and more occupational therapists, becoming today their second largest employer (AOTA 1985; Abbott, Franciscus and Weeks 2001, p.101). According to the US Dept. of Labor, occupational therapy is one of the fastest growing health professions in the nation (Abbott *et al*. 2001, p.xii). In 1998, there were 73,000 occupational therapists working in the United States (US Dept. of Labor 2000, p.23). While that may sound like a lot, it really isn't. In a country with a population of 280 million people, that amounts to only about one occupational therapist per 3800 people, and one quarter of these therapists worked part-time. When you consider the number of children with some special need who could benefit from occupational therapy, on top of the numbers of mental patients and geriatric patients, and those rehabilitating after injuries, who compete for these therapists, then it really is not very many. It was in fact chronic shortages in the number of OTRs that led to the certification of COTAs. Demand for occupational therapy has skyrocketed in the last decade.

An amazing variety of skills come under the purview of occupational therapy. Besides the many activities which require use of one's hands, occupational therapy addresses sensory integration, social competence, and numerous skills and functions from bike riding to short-term memory.

Funding your child's occupational therapy

If you are looking for occupational therapy to help your child with Asperger's Syndrome or a similar disorder, you can try several routes to fund it. You can go through your private health insurance carrier, through Medicaid, for which your child may be eligible even if your income is high, through your school district or early intervention system, or you can pay for it yourself. There are a few private charities that fund therapy for sufferers of specific conditions, but usually those are more severe conditions than Asperger's Syndrome alone.

Private health insurance plans vary considerably, but most are reluctant to fund treatment of developmental disorders for any length of time. Our HMO would fund only 60 days of occupational therapy (60 calendar days starting on the date of the first treatment). When we switched (or rather were switched) to a company that was closer to a traditional fee for service plan, we found that it would not pay for any treatment of any form of Pervasive Developmental Disorder. It would, however, pay for treatment of Developmental Coordination Disorder. You have to be very careful of what diagnosis is on the request for authorization. Of course the parents do not write these requests, the treaters do, but you can discuss the issue with them. Generally, pediatricians and occupational therapists are savvy concerning negotiations with insurance companies.

Medical Assistance (Medicaid) is generally for low income people, but some states have an exemption to the income requirement for children with disabilities. Often this is not something middle-class parents check into. They are too busy fighting with their private insurance company or school district, and their pediatricians might not accept Medicaid or know as much about it as about private insurance. My home state, Pennsylvania, has such an exception (under fire now), but most Pennsylvania welfare workers are not aware of it. Apparently the laws are not being taken advantage of as much as they could be. Elected office holders such as your state legislator might be of use to you in determining for what benefits your child may be eligible from the state outside the educational system (or see Appendix VI for some state government numbers you can call). It might be hard to find professionals who accept Medicaid, but it does cover treatment of developmental disabilities.

The federal Individuals with Disabilities Education Act (IDEA) requires that school districts provide the necessary supports to educate children with disabilities. One of those supports for those with coordination problems is clearly occupational therapy. These supports must be made available to children ages three to five as well as to school aged children. The IDEA requires that these supports be provided at no charge to parents. However, although federal law requires that these supports be provided by school districts throughout the country to children from age three, in fact the standards for qualifying for services vary locally. Generally, in affluent school districts, it is much easier to qualify than in poor districts, where the child practically has to be missing fingers to get occupational therapy through the school district.

If you cannot get help from your insurance company or school district, or you feel your child needs more occupational therapy than the insurer or school district is willing to authorize, consult your budget and look for a therapist in private practice. They usually charge about $80 to $160 an hour. Be aware that a good, affordable occupational therapist in private practice is not easy to find. There is not an overabundance of occupational therapists, and most of them are employed by hospitals, rehabilitation centers, nursing homes, and school districts. Some rehabilitation hospitals see a lot of outpatients, but they usually charge private patients an arm and a leg (and then you need physical therapy too). Eventually we got our insurance company to authorize occupational therapy for Andy at a pediatric rehabilitation hospital, but had we paid for it privately it would have cost $168 an hour (the hospital and the insurance company had a contract price of $84 an hour; this was in 2000–01).

What to look for in an occupational therapist

When I was in high school, our health teacher took us to see a rehabilitation hospital for adults, which made an impression on me. Most of the patients were recovering from strokes or serious accidents. The physical and occupational therapists pushed the patients through stages of recovery and rehabilitation to make it possible for them to return to work or independent living. The director told us that some of the patients would prefer to sit around and watch television, while some pushed themselves through painful exercises. I had seen nursing homes before, and there the residents sat around and watched TV and no one pushed them to regain any deteriorating function. Later, the grandmother of some friends spent a month at the same rehab facility before moving in with them. She hadn't had a stroke or accident but had deteriorated to the point where she could no longer walk upstairs. At the rehab facility, they did a lot of work on stairs and other movements, and, according to my friends, increased overall mobility by about 50 percent. Therapists with the vision to set difficult but reachable goals, with the "tough love" necessary to push the patients or the ability to inspire them to push themselves, achieved tremendous results.

In my work at a law firm, I have reviewed hundreds of medical records. I continue to be impressed with the work of rehabilitation hospitals and the occupational therapists and physical therapists who practice there. I have also become familiar, in accident cases, with the work of another set of occupational therapists. Malingering plaintiffs are treated by these therapists forever, or until their insurance runs out. The treatment often seems to bring about no improvement; it just goes on and on. The reports these therapists write are boilerplate; the session notes say the same things over and over again. So besides finding funding, I knew we needed to find an occupational therapist we could trust, the same as with a psychiatrist.

First you have to find an occupational therapist who specializes in developmental problems, as opposed to recovering from broken bones. You need to find one who will make the most out of time he or she works with your child. Look for one who sets goals and pushes your child to reach them. The best therapists are probably the ones who push you to work with the child at home. It would be most cost effective to see the therapist only once a month to supervise a home program, although most therapists are not set up to work with such a schedule. The frequency of visits depends in part on your child's needs and learning style, and on the opportunity for the child to have supervised practice of skills at home.

How does occupational therapy help?

Motor skills

Even though their profession grew out of activities for mental patients, most of the work done by occupational therapists is on motor skills, especially fine motor skills. A very high percentage of children with Asperger's Syndrome need help with motor skills. This is an area that slows them down in school, particularly in handwriting, in life skills, such as in getting dressed, and maybe most important of all, in socializing. Socializing may not seem like an obvious category for which fine motor skills are important, but think of the social handicaps presented by having an unkempt appearance, sloppy eating habits, and for boys, the inability to perform worth a damn in any sport. The occupational therapists who ran Andy's social skills group reported that he had low muscle tone which affected his posture – he often slouched, and even lay on the floor when others were sitting on it. This lack of postural control also led to restlessness and fidgeting, also social handicaps. Earlier, Andy had trouble with enunciation and required a year of speech therapy. I had not realized it at the time, but the weakness of his oral muscles which led to poor enunciation requiring speech therapy was actually part of global muscle weakness. I do not believe motor skills are the cause of Asperger's sufferers' social problems (although if you talk with occupational therapists enough you might get that impression), but poor posture, poor enunciation, sloppy eating habits, fidgeting, and lack of ability at sports are all social handicaps, and when added together form a significant brake on social development.

Part of motor skills is motor planning, or praxis. Praxis is sometimes called the bridge between the idea of physical activity and execution of physical activity. People with poor motor planning look awkward and graceless in their movements. Developmental Coordination Disorder is sometimes called dyspraxia, or developmental dyspraxia, because its sufferers lack motor planning skills. Remember the Madeleine Portwood's description of Danny on page 37? His praxis ability was poor, and it affected him academically and socially. Writing on dyspraxia in young children, occupational therapists G. Gordon Williamson and Marie E. Anzalone discuss how important praxis is for toddlers exploring their environment. Toddlers with poor praxis may refrain from such exploration. Williamson and Anzalone state that "absence of flexibility and creativity are the strongest indicators of dyspraxia" (Williamson and Anzalone 2001, p.39). Absence of flexibility and creativity are also hallmarks of all autistic spectrum disorders. Early training in praxis might help, at least for some.

Besides their effect on social development, motor skills are important in their own right. They affect academic as well as social success, not to mention self-confidence. If you notice your child is clumsy, get him evaluated. Insurance companies will usually pay for an evaluation. You can also request an evaluation through your school district. If it is faster to get an evaluation outside the school district, do that and bring the report to the attention of the school district.

Social skills

Occupational therapists also work on social skills. Their historic mission has been to train people in activities essential to their role in life ("occupation"), and for children such an essential activity includes playing with other children. Most children learn to play with other children without any special training but children with Asperger's Syndrome do not. Occupational therapists teach children skills needed for playing. These skills include initiating a conversation, sustaining a conversation, joining or starting a group activity, knowing what other children like, playing games that other children like, and social problem-solving. (Speech therapists also work on these areas.)

The occupational therapists running Andy's social skills group noticed that if no one listened to him when he started to speak, he would continue to speak and his verbalizing became a monologue more and more distant from potential listeners. The ideas he expressed became more fragmented and removed from whatever the original conversation had been about. They taught him to tap a potential listener's shoulder or arm to get attention and then to speak to that person. Such a simple technique actually helped. I noticed Andy using it on the playground in the next few months.

Conversely, most people notice when other persons want to speak, and allow them to do so, but children with Asperger's must be taught this skill. Three-year-olds generally do not notice, and therefore interrupt others often, and two 3-year-olds will talk at each other in parallel rather than having a real conversation. Children with Asperger's Syndrome will still be doing so at age 10 unless trained otherwise; that is one reason why Asperger's Syndrome is classified as a developmental disorder. A child with Asperger's might be taught not to speak for more than 30 seconds without consciously re-evaluating his audience. This technique, like tapping someone on the shoulder to secure their attention before speaking, may be stiff at first, but they are tools that allow the child to get started in a social situation, and prevent him from becoming a complete bore (or boor) to those interacting with him. As he uses these strategies more often, they may become more natural.

Taking turns is generally a problem for children with Asperger's. As in conversations where they tend to either give a monologue or not participate at all, so in games they may want to dominate completely, using other children almost like props, or not play at all. Some sort of formal strategy to prevent such scenarios may have to be taught to the child, and drilled in a social skills group.

The best place for an occupational therapist, or anyone else, to teach a child these skills, strategies, and techniques is in a playgroup. Occupational therapists, speech therapists, and others (psychologists, social workers, school guidance counselors) run such groups for the socially challenged. These groups usually include children with a variety of social problems. Some may have Attention Deficit Disorder, some may be very short tempered, some may be emotionally disturbed, and some may have no particular diagnosis. Such diversity is okay, probably better than if they all had Asperger's. It would be best if some typical kids were mixed in, but that is hard to arrange. The kids should be approximately the same age and intellectual level.

These groups are hard to find but do exist. Call everyone you know who might know of one. Check with your child's pediatrician, psychiatrist or psychologist, speech therapist or occupational therapist. Call the occupational therapy department of a local pediatric hospital to see if they know anything. Try contacting specialized private schools. Even if these contacts do not know of a social skills group, they might know of someone who might know. Keep looking. These groups are out there although not in great numbers. If you cannot find one, ask your school guidance counselor or school speech therapist to start one. Insist your child needs such a group in order to learn to participate in class, to get the education to which he is entitled. Another alternative is to form one with parents of similar children. Come up with structured activities for the kids to do together and make it as fun as possible for them. Maybe a professional speech therapist, occupational therapist, psychologist, or pediatrician can give you some advice on such an enterprise. Part of what professional social skills therapists do is teach children popular games, and how to talk on the phone. You can do some of that yourself.

Organizational skills

Many individuals with Asperger's Syndrome and related disorders, both children and adults, have a hard time getting through aspects of daily life because of their minimal organizational skills. They often lose things, get lost themselves, or forget what they were doing. These difficulties are one reason why children with Asperger's Syndrome are sometimes first thought to have Attention Deficit Disorder. The large appendix to Liane Holliday Willey's (1996) book *Pretending To Be Normal: Living With Asperger's Syndrome* contains lists of practical suggestions for day-to-day problems for teenagers and adults with Asperger's Syndrome. These include picking out particular landmarks for navigation, and leaving early or late to avoid crowded situations.

Each person with Asperger's Syndrome is different, so what strategies work well for one may not work for another. Here is where you need an occupational therapist on a consultative basis. This consulting is probably best done within the school system, by a school staff occupational therapist, since at school the therapist can observe the child in action and consult with the classroom teacher. If a school therapist is not available, you can pay an occupational therapist in private practice to come into the school to observe and consult, preferably one who is already familiar with your child and his peculiarities. Make clear to the therapist what you want out of the consultation and describe whatever problems your child is having in as much detail as possible in advance, so your money is not wasted. The therapist may suggest strategies for your child or for the teacher to use in handling him, or both. Strategies for the child can be any trick to help him keep his supplies organized, to get to the correct place on time, or to remember his homework. Organizational goals can be written into the child's Individualized Education Program (IEP).

What you really want to do, ultimately, is get the child to figure out for himself what techniques work and what do not. Margaret Dewey (1991) comments on the need for problem-solving skills. Her son Jack has Asperger's Syndrome. One (relatively minor) problem her son had was that when he rode his bike he pulled his socks up over his pants legs to prevent their getting caught on the chain and he always forgot to pull them back down. Jack figured out a plan. He put a picture of an electric plug with a line through it on his bike lock (he always locked his bike). This symbol served as a reminder to him to "unplug" his socks. Liane Holliday Willey figured out coping strategies for herself. Socrates' counsel "Know yourself" remains true, and figuring out how to manage yourself leads to self-confidence.

Young children still need help, and figuring out coping strategies for an individual with a peculiar set of disabilities is part of the province of occupational therapists. What helps you get your books to class? What do you do when you forget your lunch money? What do you do when you miss the bus? These are skills you have to have to get through life, especially if you lose things a lot and lose track of time. Ideally, these strategies are part of an arsenal that instills self-confidence, and helps the child figure out other coping mechanisms on his own.

7

Related Therapies

Sensory integration therapy

In the last 20 years, occupational therapists have become increasingly concerned with something called sensory integration therapy. See Chapter 2, p.40 for a description of Sensory Integration Dysfunction (also called Sensory Integration Disorder, Dysfunction in Sensory Integration, SID, SDI, or DSI). This disorder was first described and treatment suggested by an occupational therapist, A. Jean Ayres (1979). In the last 40 years, especially in the last ten years, sensory integration training has won wide acceptance among occupational therapists, but narrow acceptance in the rest of the medical community. According to a 1999 survey of occupational therapists working with children with autistic spectrum disorders, 99 percent of them used sensory integration techniques in their work (Watling *et al.* 1999). Sensory Integration Dysfunction is not described in the DSM or covered under the Individuals With Disabilities Act. This disorder is not the same as autism, although it seems to overlap. It involves the processing of sensory stimuli, which often seems to be an issue with autistic children, including children with Asperger's Syndrome. Andy from infancy has been overly sensitive to loud sounds. His response to them has varied over the years, but it has been consistently atypical. He startled at them as a newborn, became almost catatonic as a toddler in the subway station when the train came (body rigid, hand clapped over mouth as in the image of Munch's painting The Scream), and was unable to handle noisy gatherings as a young child. Parents of children with autistic spectrum disorders often report that their children are very sensitive to touch, refusing to wear most clothes or to let a blanket touch their skin. As they get older, even the more able ones may refuse to wear a wristwatch. A big part of sensory integration training, or therapy, is de-sensitizing children to these stimuli and promoting more adaptive behavioral responses.

Another sensory system addressed through sensory integration is the "vestibular system," which coordinates body movements, balance, and equilibrium. Children with Sensory Integration Dysfunction can be either oversensitive or undersensitive to sensory cues in this area. Occupational therapists talk a lot about "arousal levels." According to an occupational therapist who tested him, Andy is said to be undersensitive to cues in this area. He spins around a lot, apparently in an attempt to gain enough stimulation. During an evaluation of Andy's sensory integration, an occupational therapist spun him around fast for a while and then stopped him suddenly, and attempted to measure how long his eyes moved back and forth. Apparently the longer the eyes move, the more sensitive an individual is to spinning stimuli. His eyes did not move at all, an indication that he barely registers vestibular stimuli.

Involved in the vestibular system is one's basic orientation in space, including a sense of where one's body is in relation to other objects or other people. According to theories of sensory integration, dysfunction in the vestibular system may be responsible for a person's not standing the appropriate distance from others. As dysfunction in the vestibular system is common among autistic people, and autistic people are commonly not aware of the appropriate distance to stand from another person, some therapists have theorized that vestibular system dysfunction is the source of autistic individuals' difficulty in this area; maybe partly true, but autistic people miss social cues altogether. Something more than Sensory Integration Dysfunction is going on with them. There are many people with sensory integration dysfunction who are not autistic.

Undersensitivity or oversensitivity to touch have also been blamed for various behavior problems. A child oversensitive to touch may react with a "fight or flight response" when accidentally bumped in a school hallway. Such jostling may be intolerable to the child. If undersensitive to touch, a child may jostle others and find himself in unpleasant social situations as a result, such as fights. Autistic children generally seem to be oversensitive to touch and sound. Oversensitivity to touch has been blamed for the failure of autistic infants and toddlers to cuddle, and for their absence of favorable responses to their parents' physical affection.

Sensory Integration Dysfunction is also blamed by proponents of sensory integration training for the self-stimulation ("stimming") exhibited by so many children with any autistic spectrum disorder: spinning around, finger-flexing, hand-flapping, for hours on end. According to the strictest proponents of sensory integration training, these behaviors are due to under-arousal and can be reduced through sensory integration training. Other therapists view "stimming" as a protective response to being overaroused (overly sensitive to stimuli): the child creates a sort of "white noise" with his own stimming to block out less predictable environmental stimuli. Some individuals are oversensitive to some types of stimuli and undersensitive to other types. Occupational therapists have developed a battery of tests called the Sensory Integration and Praxis Tests (SIPT), designed to measure an individual's abilities and arousal levels in different systems of sensory processing.

However, there are other ways in which to view self-stimulation behaviors. According to many psychologists, these behaviors are attempts to shut out the outside world. Psychiatrists would probably see such behavior as a response to anxiety and might suggest treatment with sedatives. Trouble with arousal levels can also be thought of as a form of developmental delay. Think of 2-year-olds you have known. They get very excited, "hyped up" easily, and go a little crazy during these times, which can be very annoying. Normal children eventually learn to control themselves. It is part of normal development. Children who do not learn to moderate their arousal levels, who still act like 2-year-olds in this regard at age 10, are suffering from a kind of developmental delay, even if not mentally retarded.

Although Sensory Integration Dysfunction may not fully explain self-stimulation behaviors, sensory integration therapy might help to some extent. You might try it before resorting to medication. Most occupational therapists are trained in sensory integration therapy to some extent, since it is a big part of occupational therapy today. While many occupational therapists use sensory integration as a framework for treatment, in order to administer the standardized battery of tests (SIPT), a therapist must go through further study and pass a certifying exam. There are many evaluation methods besides the SIPT that are appropriate for children with Asperger's Syndrome, and an occupational therapist can be a competent practitioner without specialty certification. However, the certification ensures that the therapist has pursued and been recognized for advanced training in this area.

What is sensory integration training? What do occupational therapists do with these kids that helps? To make children less sensitive to touch, they have them work with materials with a variety of tactile qualities such as flour paste, play-doh, hairy balls, rubber objects, prickly objects, bean bags. "Brushing" is also a big part of sensory integration training. That is literally massaging the kid with a brush, like you might groom a high-strung dog to keep it calm. In some well-funded school districts, occupational therapists take mainstreamed high-functioning autistic children, children with Asperger's Syndrome, and others with similar problems out of the classroom periodically to give them sensory integration treatments, including brushing, and then send them back to class. The idea is to keep them calm, functional, and alert in class. In a website entitled "Asperger's Syndrome in Our Family," Darin Jenzen describes services his 9-year-old daughter with Asperger's Syndrome receives in school: "There is no scheduled brushing…She is taken out and brushed as needed" (http://djenson.ourfamily.com/aspergers/index.html) (apparently she got scheduled brushing in prior years).

Besides brushing, another technique for calming is applying pressure, much like a deep pressure massage. Andy likes to be "squished." "Squish me," he says. He likes to have people (relatives) sit on him. Sometimes, when they are watching TV together, he will lie on the sofa while his sibling sits on top of him. A boy we met through occupational therapy with much more severe problems than Andy is calmed by pressure treatments in a sleeping bag. Temple Grandin (1996), the poster child for the able autistic individual, made for herself a pressure machine (modeled after a machine used for restraining cattle while they are vaccinated) to calm herself.

Another component of sensory integration training is swinging, to help with vestibular function. One therapist suggested getting Andy a Sit-N-Spin at home, to calm him down if he seemed to need it. Tony Attwood (1998) spoke of an adult with Asperger's Syndrome who used a trampoline to unwind every night; she passed it off to her neighbors as an exercise program recommended by her doctor. The effects of brushing, spinning, and swinging do not last very long, only a few hours. They are a management technique, not a cure.

Auditory integration training

A type of sensory integration training for which great claims have been made is auditory integration training. A very specific method of this therapy was developed by Dr. Guy Berard in France. According to Dr. Berard, processing problems may occur if one hears some sound frequencies better than others. He has designed a diagnostic audiogram, specific equipment used in training patients, and a specific training program lasting just ten days. To begin with, a patient is given an audiogram to determine to what sound frequencies he or she is particularly sensitive. Then, for ten days, the child spends several sessions a day wearing ear phones hooked up to a machine which modulates high and low frequency sounds to desensitize that individual's auditory system. Dr. Berard's program is based on an older method of auditory training developed by Dr. Alfred Tomatis (the "Tomatis Method"), which requires 50 to 100 hours of listening to specially prepared sounds. According to *The Sound of A Miracle* (1990) by Annabel Stehli, Dr. Berard's program cured her institutionalized, autistic 11-year-old daughter in just two weeks. Before the treatment Georgie Stehli had lived in an institution for years, but after the treatment she left the institution, went to college, got married, and now travels the world sharing her experience. This remarkable effect has not been replicated on any significant scale.

Proponents of auditory integration training make significant though generally less dramatic claims for it. They generally claim it improves attention span, memory and communication skills, and social behavior while reducing irritability and self-stimulatory behavior. Running a quick internet search on Auditory Integration Training will bring up a number of such claims, usually referring to them as "changes observed" or "improvements reported" following the treatment. They often refer to scientific studies, and while some studies have been done, they are not conclusive. Speaking of the more moderate claims, the American Academy of Pediatrics' Committee on Children with Disabilities had this to say: "AIT practitioners report that individuals who have received AIT demonstrate many benefits: improved attention, improved auditory processing, decreased irritability, reduced lethargy, improved expressive language and auditory comprehension. Unfortunately, little scientific documentation exists to support these assertions" (Committee on Children with Disabilities 1998). In the same statement, speaking on both the Berard method of Auditory Integration Training and the autism treatment "Many families incur substantial expense pusuing these treatments, and spend time and resources that could be used more productively on behavioral and educational interventions."

Insurance companies consider the treatment experimental. There are practitioners who travel around the United States offering this therapy, but it costs about $2000, is rarely covered by insurance, and has no guarantee of success or even reliable statistical evidence of efficacy, despite the great claims made for it. More recently, some occupational therapists have developed a therapy called therapeutic listening, which may be described as occupational therapy on insurance claims forms, but which is very similar to auditory integration therapy in technique and in claims.

Ordinarily, I would not give much consideration to such an unproven treatment – pay a large sum of money to hook autistic children up to a machine that plays special sounds to produce the effects claimed above. Yet I know Andy is very sensitive to sounds, and although he no longer starts at loud noises as much as he used to, I wonder if auditory sensitivity causes him to be distracted during conversations, or to block out sounds to which he should be listening. Sometimes I have thought of trying auditory integration training, but I have never done it, partly because it is hard to find.

Music therapy

Another type of treatment involving auditory processing is music therapy. Unlike auditory integration training, music therapy is not a specific course of treatment, but is broadly defined by the American Music Therapy Association as the prescribed use of music by a qualified individual to effect positive changes in the psychological, physical, cognitive, or social functioning of individuals with health or educational problems. As far as who is a qualified individual, there is not a licensing requirement as in occupational therapy, but there are bachelaurate programs and master's programs in music therapy offered by reputable universities. The curriculum usually overlaps heavily with music education curriculum, that is it includes a lot of education and psychology courses in addition to music. Music therapists work with mentally ill patients, patients in physical pain, and the elderly, as well as with children with learning problems. They are hired by school districts as well as medical facilities, but I have never run across any.

The claims made for music therapy by its proponents include lessening tension and anxiety, and strengthening communication skills and physical coordination. Well-known neurologist Oliver Sacks, author of *The Man Who Mistook His Wife for a Hat* (1985), in an interview published in the medical journal *The Lancet* answered a question on alternative therapies he had tried by saying: "Music therapy – which has amazing powers in many neurological conditions, allowing otherwise disabled Parkinsonian patients to walk and talk and demented patients to achieve a brief orientation and clarity" (The Lancet 2000). These claims, like those made for auditory integration training, do not have much statistical support.

Medical science, as embodied in peer-reviewed journals in medical libraries, does not view sensory integration training or auditory integration training favorably because there are no significant data to show benefits. The journal *Pediatrics* reported: "It is necessary to be aware that neurophysiologic retraining programs such as...sensory integration therapies, although reported by some to have beneficial results in selected cases, lack value" (Committee on Children with Disabilities 1985).

The same journal reported: "Despite anecdotal reports of beneficial results in selected cases, however, neurophysiologic retraining programs that purport to alter the underlying neurologic disorder have little effect on functional skills and are inappropriate for children with motor disabilities" (Committee on Children with Disabilities 1996). Music therapy, as discussed in medical journals, is viewed largely in terms of palliative care for the terminally ill.

Sensory integration training is probably helpful in teaching kids to control their arousal levels; that is, to calm themselves down when necessary, to get themselves pepped up when appropriate, and to keep themselves on an even keel during the many times when that is helpful. However, it has assumed such a prominent role in occupational therapy for children with developmental disorders that one gets the impression it is offered as a treatment of the core symptoms. It has not been proved to be such. The claims made for sensory integration therapy, auditory integration training, and music therapy are similar to those made for massage, exercise, and meditation, and may have a similar effect, although these last three are not particularly directed at individuals with medical or educational difficulties.

Physical therapy

Another type of therapy which can help ameliorate the symptoms of children with Asperger's Syndrome and related disorders is physical therapy. Like the therapies described above, it is closely related to occupational therapy. Physical therapy tends to concentrate more on gross motor skills. Children with Asperger's Syndrome, certainly those with Developmental Coordination Disorder, and often those with any autistic spectrum disorder, tend to have low muscle tone and poor gross motor skills. Even children with high-functioning autism, whose fine motor skills tend to be better than those of children with Asperger's Syndrome, sometimes grow up to have odd gait and posture as a result of poor overall coordination. Physical therapy can help.

Like occupational therapists, physical therapists have a bag of tricks for a variety of coordination and muscle problems. They can evaluate a child to see what exercises would help improve that child's gross motor skills, muscle strength, and overall coordination. Improvements in these areas can lead to improvements in posture and fine motor skills. The small muscles necessary for fine motor skills work from the large muscles, so the whole system is important. Low muscle tone is often a factor in the unusual posture of individuals with any autistic spectrum disorder (not the only factor as social perception also plays a role), and physical therapy can improve muscle tone or develop methods to compensate for low tone.

The main professional association for physical therapists in the United States is the American Physical Therapy Association, which pushes for stringent training and licensing standards. In all 50 states, physical therapists must be licensed in order to practice, and to get a license requires years of training and passing an exam. Also, unlike speech therapy and occupational therapy, a patient must have a prescription in order to get physical therapy. You cannot simply take your child to a physical therapist in private practice and pay the therapist to treat him. Your child's pediatrician can write the prescription; they are not too difficult to get.

Like occupational therapists, physical therapists work in a variety of settings, although a higher percentage of them are in healthcare settings. They usually work for hospitals or some sort of medical facility, nursing homes, or in private or group practices. A number of them (c. 7% of the 120,000 total, APTA 2001) work for school districts or for early intervention programs. School districts and early intervention programs have doctors who can evaluate your child and write the prescription at no expense to you (school districts often require a doctor's input for occupational therapy too). If you are looking for physical therapy outside the school district, your best bet may be a pediatric rehabilitation facility – they usually work with a lot of developmental disabilities – but they tend to be very expensive and private insurance usually will not pay for treatment of a developmental disability. Government medical insurance through the Children's Health Insurance Program (CHIP) or Medicaid does cover developmental disorders, but the household income must be fairly low to qualify. Some states have more generous programs, but the federal government will pay for children's health insurance only if the child lives in a household whose income is no more than 200 percent of the poverty level. If your school district will not help you and you don't qualify for CHIP or Medicaid, then perhaps you can get your private insurance company to pay for an evaluation (they are more likely to cover that than ongoing therapy) and ask the physical therapy evaluator to give you a set of exercises to work on at home. The insurance company may be willing to pay for another evaluation in another year, so you can get another set of exercises as your child develops. Possibly, your pediatrician can give you suggestions for a home program too. You can also try using the results of a private evaluation to help persuade your school district to supply physical therapy services for your child (more on this tactic in Part III).

Family therapy, training, or consultation

One other area in which a healthcare professional might be helpful is family therapy. This is not to suggest that your family needs group psychotherapy or that there is anything wrong with your parenting skills. But just as an occupational therapist can observe a classroom and suggest strategies that might help a child with Asperger's Syndrome, so an occupational therapist or some other professional can observe your home life, or simply discuss it with you, and suggest strategies for dealing with your child. Professionals from different fields can provide this service, occupational therapists, psychologists, psychiatric social workers, but it must be someone you trust and believe to be perceptive. In some states, a professional needs a special license to hold himself or herself out as a family therapist, but you do not necessarily need a licensed family therapist. An occupational therapist who provides such a service would not be able to call it family therapy, and therefore might use the term family consultation or training. It should be someone who is thoroughly familiar with autistic spectrum disorders. Generally, no outside source covers payment for this type of service, so you would have to pay for it, but it is a one-time expense, just for an evaluation and recommendations, not an ongoing therapy.

Summary

As Asperger's Syndrome is a developmental disorder, all treatment is really special education, broadly defined. Psychiatrists diagnose the disorder, help educate parents and teachers about it, and make recommendations for interventions, but, except for possibly managing pharmaceutical intervention to alleviate symptoms, they do not treat it. The healthcare professionals who intervene most intensively to help children with Asperger's Syndrome and similar disorders are from the fields of speech–language pathology and occupational therapy. Speech therapists work on the conversational skills which are such a challenge for Asperger's Syndrome sufferers. Occupational therapists also specialize in areas in which individuals with Asperger's Syndrome are likely to be delayed, motor skills, coping skills, controlling arousal levels, and play skills. Professionals from the related fields of audiology and physical therapy can help with some symptoms. Therapists from all these fields have been through years of training and need a license to practice. You can find many of them in private practice, though it can be difficult to get medical insurance to pay for treatment of a developmental condition. These therapists are also employed, although not in great enough numbers, by almost every school district and early intervention program.

PART III

The Education Machine

The Maze to End all Mazes

8

What's Needed for Students with Asperger's Syndrome

When the psychiatrist who diagnosed Andy gave us her diagnosis of Asperger's Syndrome in June of 1999, she spent a substantial amount of the session gearing us up to struggle with our health insurance company. She did not say anything about the school system. Perhaps that is because she is a doctor, and is therefore more used to dealing with insurance companies. Perhaps it is because Andy was in a private school at that time. Whatever the reason, she missed where the big struggle lay. We see her once or twice a year. Andy goes to school 180 days a year. Although we have struggled with our insurance company over payment for occupational therapy and social skills groups, for everyday life nothing except perhaps family life is more important than finding the right educational setting.

Diagnoses of Asperger's Syndrome, and related disorders, are usually made or confirmed by a psychiatrist or clinical psychologist, with suggestions for interventions and management. Special education is the most important of these, yet the diagnosticians usually know little about special education, which is governed by numerous laws and regulations. As Hans Asperger stated:

> Only pedagogical methods in the broadest sense of the word can really change people to the better, or put more precisely, can pinpoint the best of the developmental alternatives that are at a child's disposal and

make it possible for him or her to develop along these lines. (Hans Asperger 1950)[1]

There is information available on the appropriate school setting for Asperger's children: Tony Attwood, Lorna Wing, Sue Thompson and many others have written on that subject. The University of Kansas has started a Master's Program in Special Education focusing on Asperger's Syndrome (and another one focusing on autism). All the literature, from Hans Asperger on, stresses small, structured classes with a lot of predictability and routine. Also crucial is the understanding of the teacher, that he or she exercise patience and flexibility toward the student, and have appropriate supports from specialists.

According to Tony Attwood, the most important attributes of a good school for a child with Asperger's Syndrome are "the personality and ability of the class teacher, and their access to support and resources" (Attwood 1998, p.173). Because Asperger's Syndrome is unusual, and subtle but serious, the teacher will need to know something about the syndrome, although not necessarily to have worked with such students before. The teacher should take the time to learn about Asperger's and its implications. Ideally, a professional knowledgeable about Asperger's Syndrome can visit the classroom and observe the child, and then consult with the teacher on how to treat that student in various situations which may arise. Most school districts have autistic support classes, and while the teachers of those classes are used to working with lower functioning students on the autistic spectrum, they have an understanding of autism that most regular classroom teachers do not. They can be a resource.

Most students with Asperger's Syndrome can be managed in a regular classroom. However, the classroom should be quiet and orderly, with a regular routine. Temple Grandin, poster child for the successful autistic individual, described her primary school education thus:

> At age six I was enrolled in a typical first grade. The school was small and the class had only 12 kids. It was an old-fashioned, very structured classroom. Looking back, I know that a chaotic, unstructured classroom full of 30 kids doing lots of different things would not have

---

1   Hans Asperger 1950, cited by Maria Asperger Felder, MD, in Foreword to A. Klin, F.R. Volkmar, and S.S. Sparrow (eds) (2000) *Asperger Syndrome*. New York: Guilford Press, pp.xii-xiii.

worked for me. ...Most of the structure I had in my education was just part of the structure of the 1950s, but the orderliness and clear rules were very important to me. (Grandin 2000, p.xii)

Before working in my current job as a paralegal, I worked for six years as a junior high and high school English teacher, and before that was trained as a teacher, so I am familiar with some of the issues that can arise in a classroom with a variety of students. Special education expert Sue Thompson has come up with lists of compensations, accommodations, modifications, and strategies (CAMS) that students with Nonverbal Learning Disability should have, and Asperger's students need the same ones. These CAMS do not really address the deficits of students with Asperger's Syndrome, but they make it easier for them to get through the school day.

For students who have trouble finding their way around, teachers could write out directions on getting from place to place in school, complete with "landmarks." They could also eliminate negative consequences for tardiness. Educator Susan Thompson Moore suggests giving these students a map of the building at the beginning of the school year (Moore 2002). Students who have trouble with transitions can be helped by the teacher giving several verbal announcements about the next activity in advance, posting a simple written schedule on the board at the beginning of each day or section of the day (many students without Asperger's Syndrome can be helped by this), or writing out a high school student's daily schedule on a card which the student can carry from class to class.

Some students with Asperger's Syndrome have trouble following multi-step directions. Tasks should be broken down into sections for these students, or written out in steps. They may also need to be monitored closely to make sure they are following through.

Regarding curriculum issues, students with Asperger's Syndrome cannot be counted on to draw conclusions or put facts or concepts together in the way most students do. Therefore, it is important for the teacher to review past information before presenting new, related information, to explicitly point out similarities, differences, and connections, and methodically discuss cause-and-effect relationships of events with students. Students with Asperger's Syndrome also tend to interpret statements literally. Most young children do so, but children with Asperger's do it for a lot longer than most. Their ability to pick up implications is poor. Teachers must understand this and help the child interpret abstract connotations.

The teacher must be able to manage the child's participation in class discussion. Some people with Asperger's will pursue topics which interest them relentlessly. This is not appropriate in a class discussion, just as it is not appropriate in casual conversation. The student should not be shut off altogether, but the teacher may have to talk to that student about limiting his questions or comments to three, or setting up a participation schedule for that student in which he is not allowed to make comments or ask questions consecutively, but only after several (a specific number) of classmates have had turns in between. The speech therapist may be able to help here. It may seem odd, forced, and a lot of trouble to set up such a rigid schedule for class discussion, but this area focuses on more than getting a student with Asperger's Syndrome through the school day. Learning appropriate group discussion techniques is a difficult and important challenge for students with Asperger's Syndrome, and should be given great weight in their educational plans.

According to Lorna Wing: "The teacher has to find a compromise between, on the one hand, letting the child follow his own bent completely, and, on the other insisting that he conform" (Wing 1981, p.129). Ideally, teachers do this with every child; it is just more important for a child with Asperger's Syndrome. Children with Asperger's Syndrome are prone to depression from all the confusion and rejection they experience, so playing to the strengths is crucial. Therefore teachers should let them hold forth occasionally on the human digestive system or the history of booster rockets, whatever their special interest is, or do a special report or give a special presentation. Letting them follow their own bent might also mean letting them do something apart from the rest of the class for a while, perhaps reading while everyone else is making gingerbread houses or off at recess. Such segregation is not desirable but is sometimes necessary. Students with Asperger's Syndrome must also be explicitly taught to conform at times, since they are unlikely to pick it up on their own.

Finally, to get students with Asperger's Syndrome through their school days in a mainstream environment, the school staff must make provisions for their tendency to become overwhelmed. The noise, movements, and jostling of a school, combined with the demands of social interactions and academics which do not necessarily suit their thought patterns, can be insupportable stress for them. When overwhelmed by these stresses, they may shut down completely, become near catatonic, "zone out" and daydream in their own little world, react with anger or aggression, or start to cry. Teachers must understand this and make some provision for it. If possible, the teacher and student could have some prearranged signal the student could use to commu-nicate he or she is near meltdown (it is fortunate that individuals with Asperger's Syndrome are not very manipulative). For many young students though, this will not be possible. The teacher should monitor them for signs of overload. A special place should be prepared for the student for these times, possibly the school library or a secluded corner of the classroom, where he or she can take a breather until ready to rejoin the regular activity.

Besides the attitude of the teacher and the structure of the classroom, appropriate supports should be available at the school, such as occupational therapy, sensory integration therapy, and social skills training, and possibly a one-to-one paraprofessional assistant.

Occupational therapy is a crucial support for most students with Asperger's Syndrome. Although deficits in fine motor skills are not a required criterion for Asperger's Syndrome according to the DSM, most students with Asperger's Syndrome have such deficits to some degree. Like so much else about Asperger's Syndrome, these deficits are subtle but significant. These children are not missing fingers, they don't have palsy, and superficially they do not appear physically different from their peers. But over a couple of years of primary school, the slower ability to form letters can add up to slower development of the ability to write paragraphs, and later essays, and can ulti-mately hamper the ability to form complicated arguments. Eye tracking ability, or rather the lack of it, can slow down reading. Occupational therapy should be a support offered to students with symptoms of Developmental Coordination Disorder, or developmental dyspraxia. See the description of dyspraxic Danny on page 37. As discussed in Chapter 7, sensory integration issues also come under the province of occupational therapists. Sensory inte-gration issues are crucial in schools, which are often noisy and bustling. Many students desperately need help with organizational skills in order to get through school, and occupational therapists can help in this area.

Some students may require assistive technology – special devices. Although every effort should be made to teach students with poor fine motor skills to write, keyboarding may become necessary as more speed is required to take notes in class and to write papers. Students with Asperger's Syndrome may need keyboards available to them in class and to take home. Another piece of special equipment that might prove helpful to students with sensory integration issues is a "wiggle cushion." These small, low-tech cushions, something like seat-cushion-shaped beanbags, are designed to lessen the need to fidget while sitting in a chair. Along the same lines are footrests designed to help children keep their feet to themselves, or to minimize irritating nervous foot-tapping.

Another support which students with Asperger's Syndrome need is speech therapy. Often Asperger's students need conventional speech therapy for enunciation, as the muscles controlling the lips and tongue are subject to the global lack of muscle control so common in these students. At least as important though are the conversational skills that speech therapists teach. They can pull Asperger's Syndrome students out of their classrooms to work with them in small groups, they can observe them in their classrooms, at lunch or at recess, and then offer them or their teachers some strategies for handling communication issues which arise in those settings. They can practice oral reports with them before they are given in the regular classroom; they can rehearse show and tell.

If reading goals are part of your child's Individualized Education Program (IEP), make sure use of expressive language is somehow included in that part of the IEP. It should say something about the student being able to summarize or describe a story, not simply read it, and should set forth how this goal is to be met. The teachers may be used to students having less trouble with this area than simply learning to read all the words, but for children with Asperger's or related conditions such as Nonverbal Learning Disability, the opposite may be true. Writing instruction should be accompanied by a structured approach to writing paragraphs and compositions. There are many such strategies marketed heavily in the educational establishment, so the teachers should have heard of some. Your job is to make sure they are considering such an approach for your child rather than assigning your child open-ended writing exercises.

Another important support for students with Asperger's Syndrome is formal social skills training. Such training can be done by speech therapists as described above, but some schools now have little "clubs" run by the guidance counselor, for students whose social skills need some work. Such clubs could be run by a speech therapist, occupational therapist, guidance counselor, psychologist, special education teacher, or regular education teacher. I mean a group of four to six students, who might meet at lunchtime or after the regular school day for activities. It is disguised as a club, but is really social skills therapy. These could be just clubs, where the kids play checkers or board games, or maybe games which require interaction, the same type of play therapy described in Chapter 4. They could be less disguised and involve role playing for school situations. They should include activities which can be incorporated into recess. Many children with Asperger's Syndrome stay by themselves during recess, run in circles, or stare at a fan. Such social skills clubs could help these children learn to participate in other children's games at recess, and this could be part of their IEP. Ideally, these clubs could be the basis for friendships at school. Students from the same class could be in them, not necessarily all handicapped but with some similar interests. They could meet in their supervised club at recess one day, and then be expected to do the same activities with minimal supervision the next day at recess on the playground. This sort of club can also be preparation for joining a regular club in high school.

Dr. Tony Attwood (2000) has suggested that high school students with Asperger's Syndrome be excused from homework if it is a heavy burden for them. This may be a difficult decision since homework becomes important academically in high school. But he points out that school is very difficult and energy consuming for students with Asperger's Syndrome, and that adolescence is a particularly stressful time for them. He also stresses that social skills are the most important skills for adolescents with Asperger's to work on. Therefore, they do not need the added stress of homework.

Writing about elementary school students, Susan Thompson Moore recommended modifications in homework assignments depending on how much the student could handle (Moore 2002, p.84). She said her own son with Asperger's was so busy with his after school social skills group and martial arts classes, needed to help address deficits of Asperger's, that he couldn't do a full load of homework on top of them and school. His teachers agreed on the following homework schedule: Grade 1, 5 to 10 minutes, two or three days a week; Grade 2, 10 minutes, three or four days a week, Grade 3, 10 to 15 minutes, three or four days a week; Grade 4, 15 to 20 minutes, three or four days a week. She pointed out that a lot depended on the individual child, but strongly recommended that homework modifications be considered.

Of course a lot depends on the individual class too, some teachers assign much more homework than others, even in the same school and for the same age and type of students, and some students with Asperger's may learn more from doing homework at home in solitude than they do in class. Nonetheless, because school does put much more stress on students with Asperger's than it does for most students, and because they have so many other areas to work on, homework modifications should be considered for students with Asperger's.

As Asperger's Syndrome encompasses varying degrees of overall severity, some students cannot be served best in a regular classroom. If they are placed in a self-contained special education classroom, the class should be small and structured, with the same supports described above. Social skills and peer interaction should be a central part of the curriculum. Other students with Asperger's Syndrome might do best if placed in a regular classroom with one-on-one wraparound support, that is a full-time or part-time coach assigned to work with them in the regular classroom.

The question of whether children with special educational needs are better off in a self-contained classroom or mainstreamed with a full-time assistant depends on each case, and is beyond the scope of this book. I believe in the case of students with Asperger's Syndrome, there are few appropriate self-contained classes, thereby increasing the need for such assistants. Most existing special education classes simply do not have the necessary academic challenge for these students. Even so, the small size and structure of special education classes for autistic or language-impaired students can be very helpful to students with similar disabilities. Most students with Asperger's Syndrome are probably mainstreamed without assistants.

Understandably, parents and teachers tend to pay a lot of attention to keeping a child with Asperger's Syndrome functioning at school, and keeping up with academics. But make sure social skills goals and strategies for reaching them are part of your child's IEP. One goal may be that the child is participating in class discussion or holding at least two conversations with a classmate everyday. The teacher could set up a program in which the child starts the day with five chips in a bowl on his desk. Each time he talks appropriately, a chip is taken away. Or the child could be given chips, and use them to earn something. Depending on the child's needs, the program could start with getting chips for simply raising his hand. The next step could be getting chips for answering questions, or for asking appropriate questions, whichever is the weaker area. The next step, next because for children with Asperger's this step is usually harder than participating in structured, academic class discussion, would be to talk to peers, first just asking them something, then having some sort of practical exchange with them, and finally working up to small talk. Along with social goals, make sure the IEP specifies methods of measuring progress toward those goals. That way, you can support a request for more social skills coaching if progress isn't made.

Social skills goals can be outlined in a Behavioral Intervention Plan (BIP), but some parents and educators are reluctant to prepare a BIP for a child who is not a disruptive. Although my husband and I were very concerned about Andy's autistic behaviors at school, he never received a BIP. Discussion of a behavioral program was removed from the draft Comprehensive Evaluation Report prepared by the school psychologist when other IEP team members objected. They felt it would stigmatize Andy and create unnecessary paperwork. They read the term BIP to mean the child was disruptive, and thought others reading the report would get the same impression. Andy is not disruptive. He would have received no additional services if he had a BIP. It would be only a label and more paperwork for the school staff. Behavioral goals, including communication goals for a child with a disorder like Asperger's can be handled in a regular IEP. Although we were happy to accommodate the school staff in lessening their paperwork, it is crucial that such goals, and methods of measuring progress toward them, be included in writing somewhere in the IEP, whether in a BIP or not.

Whatever your child's placement, and type of paperwork he has, do not forget that the main deficit of Asperger's is social, not academic, and don't let the teachers, or the educational establishment as purveyor of IEPs, forget it either.

9

Just What You're Entitled To

Legal rights

Chapter 8 describes an appropriate placement. You may already have strong ideas about your child's education. But how do you get these desired elements? You need to spend as much time studying your legal rights as you do studying the literature on recommended programs. Science always seems to be ahead of the rest of society. Doctors such as Hans Asperger, Lorna Wing, and Tony Attwood are at the helm of the ship of progress, figuring out the needs of children with Asperger's Syndrome. Most schools are in the turbulence of the wake of that ship, with a few so far removed as to be unaffected by the ruffles. School districts are just starting to be aware of the prevalence and severity of Asperger's Syndrome. One of the Philadelphia school district's supervisors of autistic support programs told me he had learned at a conference that Asperger's Syndrome was a new learning disability first described in 1991. As Asperger's Syndrome was first described in 1944, it seems that it took about 50 years for the educational community to get the word (although perhaps that isn't so bad when you consider it took about 40 years for the medical community to catch on).

What are your child's legal rights? Nationally, two laws govern educational entitlements for students with special needs in the United States, the Individuals With Disabilities Education Act (IDEA) and Section 504 of the Rehabilitation Act. By far the most important of these is the IDEA.

The IDEA

The IDEA was passed by Congress in 1975, as the Education for All Handicapped Children Act. It required that states implement policies to identify disabled children and develop programs to meet their needs. Prior to the Act, not every place in the United States had special education programs. Some physically and mentally handicapped children never got an education at all, many were unnecessarily segregated, and most of the rest were in regular classrooms with no special supports. Some of you may have read the story of Karen Killilea, who had cerebral palsy and was school age in the 1940s, whose mother told her story in the best selling book *Karen* (1952). Public schools then had no programs for a child in a wheelchair, and would not accept her as a student. She attended kindergarten at a private Catholic school, but by age 6 she was too heavy for the little old nun to carry around while managing teaching responsibilities so Karen could not return to school. In *Tiger By the Tail* (2001) in the 1960s autistic Tony sat out of school for a year because his school district had no appropriate program for him.

For hundreds of thousands of children like Karen and Tony, the IDEA had an impact analogous to that which the great civil rights laws of the 1960s had on disenfranchised African Americans. Children who had previously been deprived of an education were now entitled to one. When Congress passed the Act in 1975 after years of study, it gave as its rationale for the law that there were 8,000,000 handicapped children in the United States, that 1,000,000 of these children were completely excluded from the public schools, and over half of the rest were not getting the necessary supports. Today every child with a disability is entitled to a free appropriate public education, and the supports necessary to such an education are to be provided free of charge. The IDEA has effected huge strides in special education. No longer are the Karen Killileas and Tony Vandegrits of this country excluded from schools and left at their parents' homes with no services. Yet, how many of the millions of students with disabilities described by the 1975 Act as attending school without the proper supports are getting them now is not clear.

The law requires each state to implement the policies set forth in the IDEA, so each state has enacted legislation on the subject, often using much of the same language as the federal Act. States may do more for students with disabilities than the IDEA requires, but not less. Each state and the federal government also have regulations giving specific directions for the implementation of the more general principles set out in the statutes. Over the last 30 years, there have been many court decisions interpreting portions of the state and federal laws. Therefore, there is a large body of law on the subject of special education, but the basic tenets of the IDEA govern this body of law.

The basic requirements of the IDEA are as follows. Children with disabilities are entitled to a free appropriate public education (FAPE). Previously states provided some special education programs, but they were not an entitle-ment. Students who needed them were not entitled by law to special educa-tion services; they got them if they were available. Now special education services are a statutory right for students who need them, and the child's program is supposed to be appropriate for that student, not just whatever program happens to be available. The necessary supports are to be provided free of charge. What constitutes an appropriate education has been the subject of many court decisions. It does not mean whatever the parents want, or the best supports available under the current state of scientific knowledge, but neither does it mean throwing children with Asperger's Syndrome into a regular education class with no special supports, or enrolling a child with high-functioning autism in a class for retarded children. The necessary supports required by the law can be interpreted, and often have been inter-preted, to include occupational therapy and speech therapy. Most importantly, the child is entitled to an appropriate education, even if the school district has no existing appropriate program.

The IDEA requires that a child's program be tailored to his individual needs, and the program is written out in an Individualized Education Plan (IEP). This document lists the child's needs, goals for him, methods of mea-suring progress toward those goals, and his placement and supports (see Appendix II). Once signed, it is a contract between the school district and the parents, and the parents can file a complaint if it is not carried out.

Equally revolutionary, the IDEA required that handicapped children be educated in the least restrictive environment. This is generally interpreted as meaning the child stays in a regular education class, with appropriate supports, in the neighborhood school if possible. If that is not possible then the child is placed in a special education class in the neighborhood school. If that is not possible, then the child is placed in a special education class at another school reasonably close to the child's home. If no appropriate program exists in the child's school district, then the district must create one or arrange for the child to attend an appropriate program at a neighboring district. If neither of those alternatives is possible then the district must pay for private education. This last option is generally reserved for children with serious, long-term medical conditions such as spina bifida, severe cerebral palsy, or children requiring very specialized education such as blind or deaf students. Instruction in the home is considered least desirable as most segre-gated. The school district is required to have this "continuum of placements" available to meet various student needs. (See Appendix IV for key sections of IDEA regulations.)

Section 504 of the Rehabilitation Act

Section 504 of the Rehabilitation Act,[1] enacted in 1973, does not aim to give remediation to students with disabilities, but to lower barriers to existing services. That is, where school buildings and classrooms may have been inaccessible to students with disabilities such as cerebral palsy and numerous other physical disabilities, school districts now had to make them accessible, or to provide some accessible buildings, or arrange for students with disabilities to be carried up steps. Previous to this law and the predecessor to the IDEA (the Education for All Handicapped Children Act), some children did not have a right to education at all. My state, Pennsylvania, requires a "thorough and efficient public school system" in every locality. This state law is different from saying every child has the right to an education. Section 504 outlawed practices such as requiring all entering kindergartners to pass certain tests as a condition of admission, such as tying their shoes; tests that were designed largely with the purpose of keeping retarded children out of the public schools. Section 504 provisions are similar to those of the Americans with Disabilities Act (ADA), passed in 1990. It promotes access, and outlaws discrimination, giving students with disabilities the means to help them benefit from existing programs, if they can benefit from them. It also did not provide any funding for states or local school districts to comply with its provisions; it simply required any entity receiving federal funding to comply.

You can use Section 504, as well as the IDEA, to get a school district to provide special assistive technology for your child. For a child with Asperger's Syndrome or a related disorder, such special equipment might be a keyboard, a word processor, special pens or pencils, wiggle cushions, footrests, or even earplugs.

Section 504 has also been interpreted as requiring educational systems to offer occupational or physical therapy where those therapies were necessary to enable the student to benefit or participate in existing educational programs. This line of reasoning with regard to occupational, speech, and physical therapy is similar to that of the IDEA. For those services to be

---

1   Despite its name, this statute is found at 29 U.S. Code section 794.

required, they must be necessary for the student's education; they are not provided for their own sake. If the parents simply think their child would benefit from such services beyond their educational needs, the school district is not required to provide them. However, it is usually easy to find an educational justification for such services. Also, the law makes it illegal to automatically exclude children with disabilities from extracurricular activities. They are entitled to reasonable accommodations there too. Some schools offer free music lessons. These could be helpful to a child with Asperger's Syndrome, and such a child cannot be excluded simply because he or she has Asperger's.

Section 504 covers a broader range of students than the IDEA does, since its definition of disabilities is broader than the IDEA's. All students who are covered by the IDEA are also covered by Section 504, but there are a number of other students not covered by the IDEA who are covered by Section 504. If a student is dropped from or denied an Individualized Education Plan, labeled as not needing or no longer needing one, he or she may still be covered by Section 504. Also, Section 504 applies to any entity receiving federal money, so it applies to some institutions of higher learning as well as to school districts. The paperwork entailed by Section 504 for a covered student is a 504 plan, rather than an IEP. (See Appendix III for a blank 504 plan and Appendix V for key sections of Section 504 regulations.)

10

How to Get It

Problems between the law and real life

Funding

The IDEA is a good law, and all 50 states have accepted it and the attached federal funding. However, the law is not always followed by cash-strapped school districts. The reasons for that are inherent in the discrepancy between the funding levels envisioned by the IDEA and those passed in federal budgets. The Act required enormous and expensive changes in the way states and local schools districts handled special education, and anticipated that the necessary increase in funding would be split 40/60 between the federal government and the states, with the federal government paying 40 percent of the cost and states and local entities the rest. Unfortunately, the federal government has never allocated enough money to pay 40 percent of the expenses of the IDEA. Federal funding levels have ranged from c. 9 percent to c. 20 percent of the required funding. States have been left with the rest. In states with decentralized education systems local school districts have been left to bear the brunt of the cost. Also, for reasons beyond the scope of this book, poverty-stricken areas have a much higher percentage of students with special needs, and therefore a much greater need for special education, than affluent districts, so the requirements of the IDEA hit them very hard financially.

Because the IDEA establishes entitlements, students with disabilities are entitled by federal law to special education supports and can sue to get them; local districts cannot ignore them. If they require a small class to learn, they are entitled to a small class by law. There is no federal law mandating small or even reasonable class size for regular education students. Sometimes special education takes a big share of a district's limited resources. Therefore, there is some resentment of special education students on the part of everybody else.

In urban districts with many special education students, while there may be more special education programs, the criteria for getting into those programs may be stringent. Speech therapists may be so taken up with students who can barely speak that they have little capacity for teaching conversational skills. Learning support may be limited to those with mental retardation or severe, obvious learning disabilities. Therefore, parents of students with unusual conditions such as Asperger's Syndrome have to fight for everything they get.

Lack of special classes for Asperger's

If no appropriate program exists to meet a students needs, then the school district is supposed to create one. Autism was added as a covered condition to the revised version of the law, the Individuals with Disabilities Act, in 1997. Therefore school districts are required to provide special education services for students with autism, the US Department of Education tracks the number of students identified as having autism, and most school districts now have programs for designed for autistic students.

My home school district in Philadelphia has autistic support classes, but they are geared toward lower functioning, nonverbal or barely verbal students. Many of these classes are very good. They usually have two teachers for eight students and a lot of wraparound paraprofessionals. The teacher of the autistic support class at Andy's school is very experienced and committed. Her assistant also seems very committed. The students in this class are entitled to year-round instruction (not by virtue of being in the class, but by virtue of their severe needs). As an additional perk, because table manners are part of their curriculum, they receive a free breakfast and lunch each school day. However, the students in this class are lower functioning and their curriculum is not appropriate for anyone who needs much intellectual challenge.

For higher functioning students with autism or Asperger's Syndrome, there are not many special programs. Many students with Asperger's either receive no supports or are placed in autistic support classes where the academic and conversation standards are too low for them. Most school administrators know very little about Asperger's Syndrome. Very few school districts have programs tailored for it.

In the fall of the year 2000 (the 2000–2001 school year), the Seattle School District started seven classes for mildly autistic children (those diagnosed with high functioning autism or Asperger's), with spots for 42 children. Each class was set up to have six students, one teacher, and two assistants. This was apparently the first time in this country that a school district has had such an extensive program for mildly autistic students. Three of the seven Seattle classes were slated for students with Asperger's Syndrome, and they were said to be unique because students could go back and forth between the Asperger's class and a regular classroom. One family moved from New York to Seattle to get its child into one of the 42 spots, and an August 7, 2000 *Seattle Times* article reported that parents of Asperger's children from around the country had said they were willing to pack up and move to Seattle for a shot at this program. The Seattle Times article quoted Michelle Garcia-Winner, a California speech therapist who works with a range of autistic children, as saying two similar classrooms were about to start in the San Francisco Bay area, and one already existed in New York. There must be more, since Philadelphia had one then and it was not mentioned in the article, but there are not many.

DeAnn Hyatt-Foley and Matthew G. Foley (2000), parents of a boy with Asperger's Syndrome, describe their difficulty in obtaining appropriate placement for their son. Early in his school career their son was placed in a class for emotionally disturbed children. According to some professionals, such a placement is one of the worst possible for a child with an autistic spectrum disorder (Klin and Volkmar). When the parents complained that the class was not appropriate and described his needs, the school administrator said she did not think the district had an appropriate program for him. This statement was not made with the expectation that the district would therefore find an appropriate program for him elsewhere or establish one themselves, but with a "Too bad" attitude.

Echo Fling (2000) in *Eating An Artichoke*, the story of raising her son with Asperger's, got him into a class for speech-impaired students. She managed to visit a lot of classes and felt this most suited to his needs. Fortunately her school district allowed him to be placed there. When we considered a class like that for Andy, we were told it was impossible, against the rules, for a student with a diagnosis of Asperger's Syndrome to be placed there. This was particularly galling since at the time it seemed that the district had nothing else to offer, and the officials saying he could not go into the speech-impaired class were not making any suggestions for where he could be placed. At that time our school district did have one class geared toward students with Asperger's Syndrome, but it had only eight spots and we were told it had a waiting list of 300 students. It was also an hour's drive away from us in a far corner of the city.

The mother of a boy with Pervasive Developmental Disorder whom I met through Andy's private occupational therapist felt her son had received adequate preschool supports, but she had a difficult time finding the right placement for him when he became school age and entered the regular school district. The school district wanted to put him in a class with a life skills curriculum (self-care, grooming, etc.), but she felt he was at a higher level than that. All the other existing classes were directed above his ability level, so he ended up in the life skills class. School districts do have programs for severely autistic students, because they have to, but very little for the milder cases.

Most students with Asperger's Syndrome can be managed in a regular classroom with supports. Personally, I would prefer to keep Andy mainstreamed if possible, but there is still plenty of reason for lament over the lack of special programs for Asperger's Syndrome students. Some students really need them. If they cannot be mainstreamed, Asperger's students today are stuck in programs designed for other types of disabilities in autistic support classes which are generally aimed below their ability level, learning support classes which focus on remedial academics, classes for the emotionally disturbed where they are particularly unlikely to learn appropriate social skills, or classes for the communication impaired. These last may be appropriate in some cases, but in other cases students with Asperger's Syndrome are directed away from them even if they are the most appropriate placement. There should be many more classes specially designed for students with Asperger's Syndrome to meet the needs of these now inappropriately placed students.

There are great potential benefits to classes specially designed for Asperger's students beyond the needs of the students in them. They cause a school district to be aware of these children and others like them. They necessitate a school district employing specialists in Asperger's Syndrome. They provide a place, if there are enough of them, where a student with Asperger's Syndrome can go for a year or two if regular education becomes too stressful. Ideally, these classes would prepare students for mainstream placement. As students are mainstreamed from the special class they will require supports, which may provide a model for supports for other students with Asperger's Syndrome who have always been mainstreamed.

Lack of support for mainstreamed students

The IDEA emphasizes that students with special educational needs should be mainstreamed as much as possible. "Least restrictive environment" is a phrase which shows up repeatedly in the IDEA and its implementing regulations. The historical roots of today's special education laws are in the civil rights movement and integration policies. In *Brown v. The Board of Education*, the US Supreme Court ruled that segregated education was inherently unequal, and advocates of children with disabilities relied successfully on that reasoning bringing court cases and pressing for special education legislation. According to current federal regulations: "Placement in special classes is to occur only if the nature and severity of the disability is such that education in regular classes with the use of supplementary aids and services cannot be achieved satisfactorily" (34 CFR 300.550). Supports necessary to keep students in a regular classroom, if they could possibly stay in a regular classroom with supports, are to be made available. Every IEP is supposed to say why the student is getting as extreme intervention as he or she is, rather than less, to justify any separation from the mainstream.

Traditionally, autism has been viewed as a severe disability warranting self-contained special education classes, and in fact, nonverbal, or barely verbal children with autism accompanied by mental retardation need a lot of intervention, probably warranting a self-contained classroom. But students with Asperger's Syndrome and high-functioning autism are often in a regular classroom. However, there is generally not enough itinerant or resource room support directed toward their special needs, so they are usually classified as needing learning support; not quite the right classification, and not quite the right kind of support. As the IDEA requires school districts to provide support for children with mental retardation, specific learning disabilities, autism, emotional disturbance (as well as several other specified disabilities), school districts usually have learning support classes and teachers, autistic support classes and teachers, and emotionally disturbed support classes and teachers. True Asperger's cases probably come closest to needing autistic support, but they are labeled as needing learning support because the autistic support programs are below their intellectual level, and they often do have learning problems. There is a fair amount of itinerant and resource room support for students classified as needing learning support but little for students classified as needing autistic support. In learning support resource rooms, students with Asperger's Syndrome are likely to get some individual attention and help for whatever academic problems they have, but little help for their problems with social and communication skills and peer interactions.

The least restrictive environment clause has been interpreted to mean providing enough supports to a child mainstreamed into a regular classroom for him to succeed there. This can mean a full-time paraprofessional, a coach in the classroom for a few hours a week, pull-outs for extra tutoring, special equipment, or making the regular education classroom wheelchair accessible. For students from the autistic spectrum, such supports are most likely some kind of paraprofessional coaching the child in the classroom part or full time. For students with Asperger's Syndrome they include the accommodations designed for student with Nonverbal Learning Disability, frequently extra help with handwriting, occupational therapy, expert consultation on sensory integration issues, possibly a keyboard to use instead of writing, and special consideration in assigning the child to the most orderly regular education class available. The law requires that the necessary supports be provided at no charge to the child's family.

Since Asperger's Syndrome was not even known in this country as a diagnosis at the time the IDEA was first passed (as the Education for All Handicapped Children Act) in 1975,[1] of course it has taken some time for appropriate supports for students with Asperger's Syndrome to be developed in schools. School systems are not exactly like the computer industry in responsiveness to consumer needs.

What kind of supports do students with Asperger's in regular education classrooms get now? It depends on the district. The World Wide Web is full of stories by adults who got no supports at all and suffered for the lack. Herbert Cross, an adult with Asperger's who publishes a website, went from school to school as a child, including a military academy which he said was the only place his father could find that would take him. They must have been a family inclined toward private schools. He was not very happy at the military academy, where he was completely isolated by the other students and received no support from the staff. Another boy, this one British, was forced to sit at the back of his class. These individuals were in school without a diagnosis. On the other hand, a child whom I know personally who does have an "official" diagnosis of Asperger's Syndrome received no special supports when he attended public school in Philadelphia in the 1990s. The staff at the school knew about the diagnosis and he may have received a little extra understanding from his teacher and principal as a result of that knowledge. His handwriting was poor and his mother sought occupational therapy for him, but was told he did not

---

1   Autism was added as a covered condition to the revised version of the law, the Individuals with Disabilities Act, in 1997.

qualify. He did not even have an IEP. His family moved to a suburban school district where an IEP was developed for him. He is in an "inclusion" class which has some special education and some regular education students, mostly regular, and two teachers for 16 kids. It is a very structured classroom. He also receives occupational therapy once a week, and is in a special class for gifted math students. Another boy in the same school with a similar needs profile, also labeled with Asperger's Syndrome, has a full-time paraprofessional assigned to him.

Problems in providing one-to-one paraprofessional assistants

Some parents see a one-to-one paraprofessional for their child as a means of keeping him mainstreamed, and of coaching him in social, coping, and other skills. Sometimes dedicated paraprofessionals are a means to reaching these goals. In my experience, though, there are several problems. The demand for trained paraprofessionals outstrips the supply. Many of the paraprofessionals employed are not very good; they end up being used as crutches by the students they serve, and their presence stigmatizes the student.

The demand for paraprofessional assistants or "shadows" has risen dramatically as parents and school districts strive to keep severely impaired children in regular education classrooms. As they are a considerable expense to a school district, school districts are often reluctant to agree to a personal assistant in an IEP for children who are not physically handicapped, unless some other source pays the bill. These assistants can be paid for by the school district, Medicaid, or by mental health services. If the child's IEP calls for a paraprofessional to coach the student through the school day, the school district is ultimately responsible, but can work with Medicaid or other sources to fund the service. Sometimes assistants paid for through Medicaid or a state's mental health department are better trained than employed directly by the school district, who often do not have more than a high school education. However, there is often a waiting list for therapeutic staff support from Medicaid contractors, with children on waiting lists for years for evaluations or for assistants after evaluations have determined the need for an assistant.

Unfortunately, even the better trained assistants I have seen in classrooms are sometimes reading the newspaper. Most of them do not know anything about Asperger's Syndrome. They act as a back-up if the child they are assigned to has some sort of fit, sparing the teacher the trouble. Often, the better trained assistants are supplied by some agency outside the school district, such as a Medical Assistance contractor or mental health agency, and they are not supposed to assist the child, or to assist the teacher with the rest of the class (which can sometimes make the situation less stigmatizing for the assisted child). They are supposed to keep the child on task, but often act as just behavior controllers.

Teachers of all age groups have told me that not only do the one-on-one assistants generally not actively bring the child to a higher level of functioning, but the children often come to rely on the assistants to do things for them, to help them get through lunchtime or around the school. If a student is mainstreamed with an assistant, the presence of the assistant marks the child as being unable to function on his own, excluding him further from his peers.

Problems with speech therapy support

As students with Asperger's Syndrome by definition are communication impaired, with poor conversational skills, you would think they would be entitled to speech therapy at school. School districts throughout the country have many speech therapists on staff or under contract, and many students receive help from them. Students with Asperger's Syndrome should be getting help from speech therapists with conversational skills, but many are not. School speech therapists' time is largely taken up with working with students with articulation problems, and difficulty learning to speak. Schools might not see the development of conversational skills as necessary to a child's education, and therefore not covered under the special education laws. However, development of class discussion skills, and the ability to explain what one has learned, are necessary to a child's education.

Andy has been lucky in his school speech therapist. Because his regular education school has an autistic support class and a communication-impaired support class, the school has a couple very fine speech therapists. One of these is taken up with teaching the communication-impaired support class, but the other worked with Andy once a week along with another boy from his class. She has also observed him in his class, at lunch and at recess, although her attempts to help him in these last two areas have been thwarted by the overwhelming noise in the school lunchroom and Andy's need to decompress in the playground after lunch. She has nonetheless been a valuable part of his IEP team. However, our earlier attempts to secure speech therapy for Andy through the school district for enunciation work failed. He was tested and found not to meet their criteria, even though an independent test had placed him in the lowest 1 percent of his group in enunciation skills, and his kindergarten teachers, as well as admission officers at another school where he had merely applied for admission, had commented on his speech deficit and its potential effects on his education.

The speech therapist at Andy's public school in Philadelphia covers four schools and is involved with 90 IEPs, so she works with 90 students. The national average number of students with whom school speech therapists work is 50 (Westat 2002). That is an awful lot, when you consider that a number of students need intensive work.

Occupational therapy support problems

School systems in the United States generally have occupational therapists on staff to help students, but far fewer of them than of speech therapists. A 1999 study done for the Ohio legislature found there were 224 occupational therapists in Ohio public schools (Ohio Legislative Office of Education Oversight 1999, Exhibit 2, p.8), an average of fewer than three per county, and those were spread unevenly across the state. I know personally at least three students whose motor deficits appear to me no worse then Andy's who do get occupational therapy at school, at least once a week over a period of years. They are all in school districts in the suburbs of Philadelphia. I have been told repeatedly by the Philadelphia school district that Andy does not meet their criteria for occupational therapy, although they did finally agree to give him five units of occupational therapy. Andy's occupational therapist at Children's Seashore House formerly worked for a school district in Massachusetts, and she was shocked that he did not get more services.

At Andy's multidisciplinary team meeting, his need for occupational therapy came up. The woman running the meeting informed us that occupational therapy was not supposed to be therapeutic; the school district supplied it only if it was needed for an educational purpose. That makes sense in theory. Schools are for education, not medical care, but some districts use that line of reasoning as an excuse for doing nothing. Health insurance companies tend to take the line that such problems are developmental, and therefore should be handled by the school system.

Poorer school districts often give the excuse "He doesn't meet our criteria," but how low are their criteria? Andy's fine motor skills have been the subject of comment by educators since before he started kindergarten, as well as ever since. The special education teacher who pulls him out of his regular class for extra help said in a meeting, "How could he not be eligible?" When I expressed concern to a school district doctor that by third grade his lack of motor skills could inhibit his ability to write complex sentences and paragraphs, she said we could apply for assistance again at that point. It would make more sense to start early. This situation illustrates one more reason to document comments your child's teachers make about his abilities and needs. You can also ask what specific tests were given to your child during a school district occupational therapy evaluation and what his scores were.

Problems with providing social skills training

Although many students could benefit from social skills groups, it is not a traditional support such as speech therapy, occupational therapy, or remedial reading. Schools districts may therefore take the position that such social skills groups are not directly related to education and therefore not part of a free appropriate public education (FAPE). Andy was fortunate enough to be in such a social skills group at school (officially called a social pragmatics group and unofficially called "the lunch bunch"), but he did not have enough sessions with it for various reasons. I know of other such groups in other school districts, usually run by the school guidance counselor. Many students besides those with Asperger's Syndrome could benefit from this sort of club, but there are not enough of them. Perhaps advocates for children with Asperger's will succeed in getting many more established, and they will become a great help to many types of children in American schools.

Problems identifying students with disabilities, and with special education coordinators not knowing how to place them

The IDEA also requires that school districts seek out students with special needs so they can find or create suitable programs for them. Every school district has some provision for this, but their provisions often don't seem to be very effective. Many times it is the parents who bang on the door of the system trying to find help for their child.

Asperger's Syndrome is too complex to depend on a licensed school psychologist making the diagnosis. Their training is not nearly as extensive as a clinical psychologist or psychiatrist. A school district might notice on its own that a child with Asperger's Syndrome was having difficulties and set up an evaluation, but the chances that the evaluation would produce a diagnosis of Asperger's Syndrome are low. Such a diagnosis is best left to the medical community. Even if a child does not have such a complex condition as Asperger's, there is good reason to get an independent psychological evaluation. Because of the financial pressures created by the requirement that it take care of covered conditions, a school district may not be the most impartial evaluator. Once you have a diagnosis from an outside source, a school district cannot ignore it.

Once the evaluation is complete, the school district should see that an appropriate program is developed for the child. Every school district has special education coordinators (they may go by different titles) who are supposed to ensure placement of special needs children in the appropriate program. The onus is not supposed to be on the parent. However, it usually is. Unfortunately many of the special education coordinators are essentially bureaucrats and know little about Asperger's Syndrome. Once we got Andy into a program, we found the school staff helpful, but school district administrative personnel simply did not evince any interest in getting his first placement done: "School placement will be done in August." "I can't handle your son's case; he doesn't have a pupil ID#." "I can't handle your case. It started in another cluster." We found them to be very passive at best. The special education coordinator working on Andy's case never did anything that we did not push her to do, and never seemed to know what his needs were. I never had the impression she knew anything about services for students with Asperger's Syndrome in the district or even had a firm idea of what Asperger's Syndrome is. Months after the file had supposedly been sent to her she told me she did not have any of his paperwork, including evaluations. I had to call around trying to find out what had happened to it, and send again the parts I had.

Nor was our experience unique. According to Echo Fling, one of the founders of Asperger's Syndrome Education Network (ASPEN) in New Jersey, parent of a boy with the syndrome, and author of *Eating An Artichoke: A Parent's Perspective on Asperger's Syndrome*:

> I couldn't simply turn my child over to the authorities and trust that they would make the best decisions for him... Parents were often never told what services were available. It was up to the parent to do the research, scratch for information, and hound the authorities for every single service that the child got. (Fling 2000, p.59)

Problems with promptness

Parents with whom I have come into contact, even in the better funded suburbs, have trouble with promptness. The federal law says every state must set up programs to ensure covered children are identified and served. My state, Pennsylvania, has regulations setting forth timetables for various steps in the IEP process: 45 after request school days for an evaluation or re-evaluation to be done (for preschool children 45 calendar days); Multidisciplinary Team Meeting and Report must be completed within 15 school days of evaluation; IEP must be completed within 30 days of MDT report, and be implemented within 10 days of that. These timetables are part of Pennsylvania's regulations implementing Pennsylvania's version of the IDEA, so other states have different timetables. The 30-day period between a finding that the child is eligible for special education and the first IEP meeting is mandated by federal law (34 CFR 300.343(b)(2)). During our numerous discussions with school officials during the months we tried to work out Andy's public school placement, I saw no evidence of these rules. I was not aware of them until partway through the process. The state's compliance office confirmed the rules and said it could open an investigation if I filed a complaint, but that would take a while.

Problems with regular education teachers not knowing anything about Asperger's

Another problem is that regular education teachers (and often the special education teachers responsible for learning support) rarely understand Asperger's Syndrome. If they are willing to learn, this is easy to ameliorate. Give them printed information on the subject, pick something easy to read, concise, but that separates Asperger's from other disorders they have already heard about. You have probably done the research already, and can pass on something appropriate to them. Tony Attwood's book, *Asperger's Syndrome: A Guide for Parents and Professionals* (1998) contains excellent sections on the cognitive abilities and social skills of individuals with Asperger's Syndrome. Susan Thompson Moore, an elementary school teacher and parent of a child with Asperger's Syndrome, wrote an entire book dedicated to classroom strategies for children with Asperger's Syndrome in the regular classroom, *Asperger's Syndrome and the Elementary School Experience* (2002).

Sue Thompson has written a number of articles on in-school strategies for mainstreamed students with Nonverbal Learning Disability, similar to Asperger's, and these articles are available on the internet (www.ldonline.org

and www.nldontheweb.org). Also, the classroom teacher should talk to a speech therapist or autistic support teacher about the autistic spectrum or attend a conference on Asperger's Syndrome. Push for this teacher training. The IDEA requires "specially designed instruction" in order "to address the unique needs of the child that result from the child's disability." This is difficult to achieve if the teacher has never heard of Asperger's Syndrome until the beginning of the school year, or parent/teacher night. They have got to understand that Asperger's is an autistic spectrum disorder, and therefore it is imperative to teach social skills explicitly to these children. Otherwise, the teacher may be satisfied if the student is functioning academically. Many school report cards have a section on personal/social development. Andy always scores highly on these, usually better than his academic scores. Yet we know his social skills lag far behind his academic skills. The school's scoring system evidently does not pick up the social difficulties of a child with Asperger's. It simply measures compliance with school rules. Even teachers might be lulled by this scoring into believing a child's social skills deficits are not as important as they are.

Problems with rigidity in educational system

School districts also tend to bogged down with rules and regulations, which might be collectively referred to as red tape. Ms. Fling (2000) was at least able to visit classes until she found an appropriate one for her son. He went into a class designed for children with communication impairment, and it was appropriate for him by virtue of its size, structure, and the understanding of the teacher. In some districts it would be very difficult for a parent to visit classes; some schools just won't let you do that. Also, some districts have strict rules about who can be placed where. A student with a diagnosis of Pervasive Developmental Disorder may not be allowed in a class for communication-impaired children on the grounds that the class is for children who have only communication delays and no other symptoms. School districts are supposed to go by a child's needs, not his label, but that is sometimes difficult in a huge bureaucracy. You have to be very careful what label is placed on your child. You may want to investigate the various special education programs first, choose what suits your child best, and then find some professional to give your child the most advantageous label. You can keep a file full of reports and show each entity from which you are trying to get services the reports which are the most useful. You should not have to do this, since the IDEA requires school districts to provide each student with disabilities an appropriate program that suits the child's unique needs, but it may be easier than filing a lawsuit.

Another example of school district rigidity is the case of a Maine family who set up the home program for their autistic son when he was preschool age. When he was old enough to enter kindergarten, they wanted to start him off with half days as recommended by their home program consultant, but they knew the special education coordinator would balk at that request, even though it would cost the school district nothing. That inflexibility may have contributed to their son's failure at school.

At one point I thought Andy might be able to spend some time in a regular education class and some time in the autistic support class there, but was told by the school administration that such an arrangement was impossible. Nonetheless it was exactly the interim arrangement the school administration proposed at the end of our first IEP meeting. We brought a lawyer to the meeting, which probably affected the change of heart, but it was obviously possible. He just switched classes at lunchtime; both classes ate lunch at the same time.

Several years later, Andy's sister started first grade at his school, and was eligible for bussing due to the distance we lived from the school. A bus with special education students already picked him up near our house. I tried to get her placed on the same bus, which had plenty of room, but was initially told the school district just wouldn't do that, just didn't place regular education students on a bus with special education students. This was after more than 25 years of IDEA-related laws, regulations, and court decisions requiring the integration of regular education and special education students to the largest extent possible. Yet the school district was willing to pay extra to bus a regular education student separately from her special education sibling, when their parents wanted them to be together, just because the district was not used to having them on the same bus.

At the time when Andy entered the Philadelphia public school system, the school district was divided into smaller units called clusters. It was difficult to find out what services were in other clusters, the special education coordinator certainly did not seem to know, and if we found out about programs on our own, it was difficult to get him placed in one because it was not in our cluster, even if it was the most appropriate, had room, and our own cluster had nothing appropriate.

Asperger's Syndrome is a newly recognized disorder, at least to schools it is. Although the medical community has been dealing with it since the 1980s, educators are just beginning to realize it exists. Funding is always a problem, as it is with everything in life, but some of the problems in complying with the law are less understandable. They seem to be more a matter of will than of funding, and exist even in the better funded suburbs.

What to do

Wheedle or insist?

What to do about problems in the school district which prevent your child from getting what you believe to be an appropriate education for him or her, depends on what you are looking for. Sometimes it makes sense to wheedle, to butter up the necessary educators, promoting a sense of teamwork, and other times it makes sense to insist on getting what you want, hinting or stating that you will resort to litigation and following through if necessary. I mean that besides your own personal tastes and resources with regard to adversarial relationships and litigation, there are certain results which are more likely to be obtained by the adversarial method and other results which you are more likely to get by wheedling. The "I insist" method – up to and including litigation – seems to work best for when you want a specific service, usually one costing money, rather than compensations, accommodations, modifications, and strategies (CAMS) in a program your child is already in and where you expect him to stay. The specific services insisted on could be intensive speech therapy, occupational therapy, physical therapy, placement in an early intervention program, a one-to-one paraprofessional, special school or program, extended year services, or services for an individual between the ages of 18 and 21. This adversarial approach probably has the fewest negatives when trying to get services from the early intervention system or for someone from age 18 to 21, because only children with disabilities are entitled to these services. Nondisabled children ages 3 to 5 and 18 to 21 are not entitled to public educational services, so it's an all-or-nothing struggle. You do not have to worry about alienating your child's educators because your child won't be seeing those educators at all if you don't insist on it. From looking at law cases involving suits to get more special education services for a child, it appears that a disproportionate number of them involve claims for services from the early intervention system.

The wheedle, or "we're a team," method seems to work best for interventions within the classroom or school. Because so much depends on the quality of individual teachers, assistants, or other professionals, sometimes it doesn't make sense to litigate. As Lorna Wing and Tony Attwood suggest, if the most crucial support for a student with Asperger's Syndrome is the understanding, flexibility, and patience of the teacher, then the most crucial support is something that cannot be written into an IEP or achieved through litigation. How can you achieve through litigation the ability of your child's teacher to push your child just the right amount, and to know when your child needs some private space?

One issue that often comes up in the adversarial processes is the use of a full-time assistant to work with a child in the regular classroom, usually with the parents wanting the assistant, and the school district taking the position either that an aide is not necessary or that the child should be in a special education class anyway. Even if you get what you want on paper, it might not be worth it. Be aware that the quality of one-to-one paraprofessionals varies greatly. Unlike classroom teachers, who usually have a reputation within their school and among parents, parents rarely know anything about paraprofessionals until they start working with their children. Just because a child gets a paraprofessional does not mean that the parapro will be any good or will have any understanding of the autistic spectrum.

Wheedle when asking for extra work from school district employees who are already working with your child. If you want the regular education teacher (or special education teacher who sees your child in the resource room) to know more about Asperger's Syndrome, the autistic spectrum, Developmental Coordination Disorder, or Sensory Integration Disorder, bring them literature, bring them a list of appropriate conferences in your area, hook them up by phone with your child's psychologist. Bring them flowers. Ask them if there are any supplies they need for their classroom and try to get those supplies for them. When suggesting strategies or accommodations, do it in the manner of a colleague or teammate. After all, the IEP team is supposed to be a team including teachers and parents, and the team is supposed to hold together longer than the IEP meeting. Win the principal over as much as you can. Join the Home and School Association or PTA or what the parents volunteer organization is at your school. If possible volunteer in the classroom or elsewhere in the school. Even if you work full time, there may be tasks with which you can help out.

One area where I would advise keeping some pressure on the school district is attention to your child's social skills goals. Too many times, the educational bureaucracy feels successful if a child's standardized test scores are okay. For children with Asperger's Syndrome, it is not uncommon to have decent or high achievement test scores without the ability to express what they have learned, to apply it to practical problems, or the social equipment to find a job after graduating. For a child with Asperger's Syndrome or similar disorders, social skills goals should always be included in an IEP, along with means to measure progress toward them. If a child is making academic progress, especially progress as measured by grades and standardized test scores, but not progress in social skills or peer relations, the school district may be satisfied. The parent should assume a gadfly role in such a case and insist on more social skills training than the child is getting.

But how to insist, and what specifically to insist on? School representatives may look blank when you say you insist on more social skills training, not knowing exactly what you mean. I can think of a number of social skills training strategies, such as more work with a speech therapist, or a social skills club, but how to meet IEP goals is supposed to be left up to the school authorities as professional educators. You can certainly suggest methods. If the school offers no satisfactory method of training your child in social skills, neither your suggestion nor any of its own, you probably should refuse to sign off on the IEP and request due process, detailed in an upcoming section. Or you can complain to the special education supervisor in your district, and threaten to request a due process hearing. In your request for due process, you will probably have to request some specific remedy, a service you want for your child, since the due process hearing officer will not be a expert in this area. Your specific request will put pressure on the school district to come up with a reasonable alternative.

Ways to work the system

Sometimes you can turn disabilities into an advantage in trying to get your child into the best regular education class you can find for him or her. It can be very difficult within public school systems to get any child into the best regular education class you can find for him or her because there are other people vying for it. Often school districts refuse to honor requests for a particular teacher because everybody wants the same teacher, if there are three second grade teachers and one is reputed to be much better than the other. If you can find some reason why the well-thought-of teacher's methods are more suitable for the special needs of your child with a label, you may have an advantage. Do not ever say in your dealings with the school administration that one teacher is just bad; instead give as much detail as you can about why his or her specific methods are not suitable for your child's documented needs. Maybe the desired classroom is quieter and more structured and your child is sensitive to noise and needs structure. A lot of literature supports the need for structure and the sensory sensitivity of children with Asperger's. But what if the unpopular teacher's class is quiet and restrictive and the kids in it do nothing but rote memorization? In that case, possibly your child would actually do better in the unpopular teacher's classroom, but if you are convinced it is not intellectually challenging enough, you can try the argument that your child has memory problems and would do better elsewhere. Analyze any psychological or IQ test reports you have to support this argument. But what if last year you made the reverse argument, then you said the child's memory problems required a lot of memorization work? Probably the school administration won't remember what you said last year, but if they do, you can say your child's needs have changed. Be prepared to point to some passage in some report that can be interpreted as supporting your current argument.

In most school districts, it is very difficult to get a child moved from one elementary school to another unless the child is going into a special education class available only in the non-neighborhood school. In large urban districts, where many of the neighborhood schools are poor, getting children admitted to a better school is the aim of many parents of all sorts of children, as evidenced by use of false addresses and disputes over neighborhood school boundaries. The IDEA's requirement of appropriate supports can be used in this effort by sophisticated parents of children with IEPs. We wanted Andy to go to a particular, well-regarded elementary school, rather than our neighborhood school, which was generally poor, with no one in its graduating class scoring in the top half of the state standardized tests. We argued that the presence of special education teachers and speech therapists with expertise in autism at the school we wanted were an important resource for his classroom teachers. While I am not sure that argument was a key factor in our getting Andy into the school we wanted, it helped. You can try anything from acoustics in the lunchroom to time spent on the bus (a longer time needed to gear up mentally for school or a shorter time necessary because the child can't handle long bus rides, depending on which suits your desired result). Two years after

Andy started at the school we wanted, we used the district's sibling preference criteria to get his younger, non-impaired sibling in there too.

Finding out for yourself what is available

Theoretically you should not have to find out what is available, because the school district is supposed to make sure your child's needs are met regardless of what is available. However, you may want to anyway because otherwise you will have to rely almost completely on the school district's special education coordinator for such information, and in many large districts no one is fully informed on what is available, and even in smaller districts it is not easy to find out what programs or teachers are best.

In order to find out what is available, and what programs or teachers are best, parents simply have to call around to anyone in the school district who knows anything and to other parents in the same situation. Sometimes support groups can be helpful if the people in them are from the same school district. The process of calling around in the school system bureaucracy, trying to find out what is available, seeking permission to observe a class which might be appropriate for your child, can be time consuming, frustrating, and exhausting. You have to budget some time for it. Set aside specific time periods. Approach it as a job – you'll be doing it long term anyway. Be physically organized with your notes and reports, just as you would be for a regular paying job. Keep a folder or several. Finally, commiserate with other parents. Many parents of children without disabilities may have experienced bureaucratic hurdles in the school district.

The summer before Andy started public school, I spoke with the mother of an autistic student of the Philadelphia school district who saw an autistic support class she was pleased with. She had noted serious difficulties in her son at an early age and had obtained considerable assistance from the early intervention unit's programs for three- to five-year-olds in Philadelphia. She told me she had felt very alone as she tried to find appropriate services for her son – "I felt I had no one" – but she did get them and her son progressed greatly. She was visiting autistic support classes at the time of our conversation; her son was soon to start kindergarten. I expressed surprise that she had been able to visit them, but she said she had called a lot of people in the school district and some of them had been amenable.[2] She had not been sure what type of class would be best for her son but she had seen an autistic support class she liked. It had eight kids, a teacher and an assistant, and "there was a lot of learning going on there." She was hoping that her son would be able to spend part of each day in this classroom and part in a regular classroom. I am not sure whether the school district allowed such a schedule, but she did the research on available programs that the school district special education coordinator had not been able to do.

If you want to visit a particular class you feel might be appropriate for your child based on what you have heard about it, and the school in which the class is located refuses to let you observe the class, try wooing the special education coordinator to intervene. Where a school may not routinely allow an unknown parent to visit – and school authorities often reflexively say no to any request which is not routine – the special education coordinator may be able to convince them that a decision on your child's placement is in the final stages and your visit is warranted. Even if you resent having to do the work the special education coordinator is supposed to do, try to make him or her feel like a partner. The special education coordinator is a partner; both of you are bound to know things the other does not.

Ways to confront the system

Sometimes wheedling isn't enough. Sometimes doing things on your own isn't enough. Sometimes your most reasonable arguments are not enough. Perhaps your child needs speech therapy, or occupational therapy, and is getting none. Perhaps he or she requires an aide, needs an extended school year, services from age 18 to 21, or services from the early intervention system, and is not getting them. This is entirely possible despite the laws. In some countries, particularly less developed, impoverished ones, laws setting forth what the educational establishment should do reflect goals rather than reality. Is that what the promises of the IDEA represent?

According to a publication on educating children with autism by the National Research Council: "Legislation can only set the rules; it cannot guar-

---

2   Today school authorities sometimes tell parents that they cannot allow classroom observations because of the Health Insurance Portability and Accountability Act (HIPAA), although it does not specifically prohibit this. You can try offering to volunteer for a class period, or argue about the law.

antee that they will be carried out or followed faithfully. The citizens' recourse, when they think the law is not being faithfully administered, is to turn to the courts for help" (Committee on Educational Interventions for Children with Autism 2001, p.176). In my opinion (I once taught a high school government course), this is a cavalier attitude toward law enforcement. The Executive branch is supposed to enforce the laws. In the case of the IDEA however, the government never allocated the anticipated funding. The US Department of Education was slow to promulgate the necessary regulations, taking two years instead of one to come up with the regulations to implement the 1995 version of the IDEA. The US Department of Education, could, if it wanted to or had the funding to, investigate states' compliance and exact penalties for noncompliance, but it does not.

Yet citizens of the United States have an important tool – litigation. It may appear that the law and the relevant regulations are not in force, but if you hire a lawyer, go to court or even through the administrative grievance process, you can get them enforced to a large degree, at least for your own child, even in a district that is strapped for money. The courts have been friends to children with disabilities. A judge will not take a district's lack of money into account if the minimum requirements of the law are not being met.

Threats of litigation

Many parents do not like the idea of litigation because it is time consuming, emotionally exhausting, expensive, and confrontational. However, often the threat is enough. Consider this story:

> After two months in his first year of school I finally found out, because the teacher told me, that Sammy wasn't getting any speech therapy at all. This is after I was told he needed speech therapy (he is language delayed) and would get it three times a week. I called the special education director and …I told him that Sammy's IEP calls for speech therapy and I expected speech therapy. Then the guy tells me that the speech therapists are overworked; there isn't room for my child – not even one day a week. I said 'OK, I've had it. I'm going to court.' Within an hour – ONE hour – Sammy was granted four sessions of speech therapy a week. That isn't to say that another kid didn't get bumped from the speech therapist's schedule, but is shows you how the system works! (Amatha Smith, cited in Mitchell 1982, p.37)

Sometimes you do not have to be so explicitly confrontational. There are ways to convince a school district that you will insist on getting the services your child requires without saying that you will sue if you do not get what you want. We brought a lawyer to Andy's IEP meeting and, although nominally her purpose there was to facilitate communication, her presence also carried an implicit threat even though she said very little.

Administrative remedies

GRIEVANCE PROCEDURE – DUE PROCESS

If wheedling, threats, and all the persuasion you can muster at the IEP meeting are not effective, and you are convinced your child is not getting the appropriate education which he needs and to which he is entitled by law, the IDEA sets out a system, called due process, for resolving parents' grievances. These due process procedures are administrative remedies. You must go through them before you can file a lawsuit to enforce the law. Every parent of a child who has been referred for evaluation for possible special education is supposed to receive written materials on procedural safeguards. If you did not receive it, ask for a copy. They are usually clearly written and informative. A state office will hold a due process hearing if the parents request it because they disagree with the IEP, or because they disagree with the evaluation or the need for an evaluation. In all states, mediation is an option before a due process hearing. If either the parents or the school district is dissatisfied with the result of the due process hearing, either can bring suit in federal court, but school districts rarely do.

The due process system is set up to be usable by parents. You don't have to have a lawyer, although a lawyer can be very useful and the school district will have one (see Appendix VI). It is easy and free to request due process. The procedural safeguards notice you get from the school district will tell you how to do it. Instead of signing the IEP, sometimes all you have to do is write on it near the parent signature line that you do not agree with it and are requesting due process. Sometimes you have to write a letter saying the same thing; it depends on the state but the basic process is the same. Exactly to whom you address a letter requesting due process varies from state to state but the school must be able to tell you how to do it, and must have a sample request letter on file to show you if you wish to see it. Federal law requires that a decision be rendered within 45 days of the request for due process hearing.

The IDEA requires that states offer mediation, so if you request due process you can try to resolve your differences with the school district without a formal hearing. If you want to try mediation, you and the school district will present your points of view to a mediator hired by the state, who will try to bring you to an agreement. A due process hearing, also called a fair hearing or first level hearing, involves opening statements, presenting evidence, and examining witnesses, with a stenographer keeping a record. Should you appeal the decision in the due process hearing to a court, the stenographic record of the due process hearing will be used in the court case.

Due process is usually used in cases of disagreement over the IEP, but it can also be used in cases of disagreement over the results of an evaluation. Perhaps the evaluation has concluded your child is not eligible for special education, and therefore is not entitled to an IEP, and you feel that he needs and is entitled to special education. Write a letter stating your position and requesting due process.

A disagreement over eligibility for special education could arise concerning a student with Asperger's Syndrome because the seriousness of the syndrome and its effect on the student's education might not be obvious to the school authorities. If the child is very bright, they might not recognize the need for special education. Also, school evaluators are generally not qualified to diagnose Asperger's Syndrome, as such a diagnosis usually requires a psychiatrist or clinical psychologist (school psychologists are generally not clinical psychologists, who have considerably more training). This is an area where an outside evaluation is important. If your child was diagnosed with Asperger's Syndrome years ago and you do not have a report, and are having trouble explaining the diagnosis to the school authorities, contact the diagnostician and ask for a report. If your child never received a formal diagnosis, make sure you get one before proceeding to a due process hearing. At this point, if you know you are going to be using the report to try to get special education services for your son or daughter, you can make sure the report writer knows what you want. You must be able to show that your child's disability, whatever it is, interferes with his education, and to show what he needs to get an education.

The regulations implementing the IDEA, found in the Code of Federal Regulations (CFR), give the following definition of autism:

> Autism means a developmental disability significantly affecting verbal and nonverbal communication and social interaction, generally

evident before age 3, that adversely affects a child's educational performance. Other characteristics often associated with autism are engagement in repetitive activities and stereotyped movements, resistance to environmental change or change in daily routines, and unusual responses to sensory experiences. The term does not apply if a child's educational performance is adversely affected primarily because the child has an emotional disturbance as defined in paragraph (b) (4) of this section. (34 CFR 300.7(c)(1)(i))

The legal definition can apply to a child whose symptoms were not present until after age 3 if the other criteria are met (34 CFR 300.7(c) (1)(ii)).

If your child's conversational skills, nonverbal communication, and social interaction are significantly impaired or delayed, he or she is entitled by federal law to special education.

It is at the due process hearing that the advice people give you on keeping all your child's reports and evaluations (assuming you've followed that advice) comes in handy. You need some clinical evidence to win a due process hearing. In fact, if possible, you should have an expert witness, such as a therapist who has treated your child and knows your child's needs. That expert should also be familiar with the legal standards for special education, that is, what constitutes a disability, an "appropriate" education, and the "least restrictive environment." If, for budget reasons, it comes down to a choice between a lawyer or an expert, you should probably go with the expert. To quote one special education lawyer, "cases can be won without a lawyer, but rarely without some clinical evidence."[3]

COMPLAINTS OVER NONCOMPLIANCE

Due process procedures are set up around disagreements over a child's needs, as stated in either the IEP or evaluation. Sometimes the problem is that the school district never gets to the IEP level, or perhaps not even to the evaluation level, or does not implement the agreed on plan. In this case, your recourse is to complain to the compliance office in your state's education department. The IDEA requires that states have offices of compliance where you can file a complaint if the timetables for evaluation or an IEP meeting are not being met, or if the IEP is not being implemented. An example of the IEP

---

3   Len Rieser, personal communication, 2004

not being implemented would be if the IEP states that your child is entitled to three 30-minute speech therapy sessions a week but he is not getting them. Usually a complaint to the state's compliance office will result in your child's getting an evaluation, IEP meeting, or implementation of the IEP.

Threats might also work here. Sitting in the playground waiting to pick up Andy at school one day, I heard a parent on a cell phone stating that she would file a complaint the day the deadline was up. A special education teacher in Philadelphia told me that she did not get any evaluation in her own child's case until she threatened to file a complaint. Once Andy's IEP meeting had to be delayed so the school could schedule all meetings for the children whose parents had filed or were threatening to file complaints over timeliness. When trying to schedule an occupational therapy evaluation for Andy I was told the district had to schedule a number of children for whom the district was under court order to evaluate. When I spoke to the state's compliance office when Andy's IEP meeting was long overdue and I was having trouble getting it scheduled, a staff person there offered to send me the complaint form saying, "Maybe you can wave it in their faces and that will help."

Delays can work to the advantage of parents trying to get the program they want for their children. If you keep track of all the mandated deadlines and records of your school district's failure to meet those deadlines, they can act as chits in your corner if you proceed to litigation, or even threaten to.

ADMINISTRATIVE REMEDIES FOR SECTION 504 VIOLATIONS

If your child has a Section 504 Plan rather than an IEP, and you have a complaint about it, either that the school district is not following it or you disagree with the district over what the plan should say, and you have not been able to resolve your concern at the school level, you should bring your concern to the attention of the school district's compliance officer for Section 504. If that does not work, or no one in the school district can tell you who that person is, you can bring your complaint to the regional civil rights office of the US Department of Education. They should investigate, and render a decision within 180 days.

Litigation

If you go all the way through due process to the fair hearing (or through Education Department's grievance procedure in case of a Section 504 complaint[4]) and you still don't get what you want and feel that what you want is crucial for your child, you can bring suit in federal court. In many states, you can also bring suit in a state court. A lawyer can advise you on which forum might be better for your case. Which forum moves faster is of course an important consideration, since any significant delay in intervention is meaningful in a child's development.

A lawyer can also advise you on whether it is worthwhile to bring a suit. In deciding whether to litigate, remember that the special education laws do not require the school district to provide your child with the best possible educational program, but with an "appropriate" education. Courts have interpreted an appropriate education to mean one in which the child makes meaningful educational progress. This interpretation is one reason to pay close attention to the goals set out in your child's IEP. From litigation, you may gain a court order for the program you want (equitable relief), but you cannot receive monetary damages for any damage done to your child's potential or emotional distress. You may recover money you spent on educational services for your child if the court rules the school district should have been supplying those services.

Also, the law leaves educational methodology up to the school district, so a dispute over educational methods may be an unwise choice for litigation. In other words, if you think your child should be getting ten hours of speech and/or occupational therapy a week and the school district is willing to provide one hour or less, a court will consider the issue. However, if you think the school district should be supplying your child with sensory integration training and the school district's occupational therapist holds to some other method, a court will probably defer to the school district. Nonetheless, if a school district uses the same methodology for every special education student, you can argue it is not tailored to your child's needs as required by the IDEA. Having worked in the legal world for 15 years, I can tell you that you

---

4   You can bring a lawsuit concerning a Section 504 dispute without waiting for the US Dept of Education to issue a finding, but the Department will close its investigation if you do. In a case of an IDEA dispute, you must go through due process before filing suit.

never know for sure what a court will say. A lawyer in your locality should have some idea.

Although the due process system is set up to be usable by legal laymen, litigation through the courts is not. You will almost certainly need a lawyer with some experience in special education (most lawyers know little about it). A private lawyer will probably charge $100 to $200 an hour, depending in which part of the country you reside. There are some non-profit groups that specialize in disability law, including education, whose lawyers might represent you for a nominal fee, but there are not very many. School districts are required to provide you with a list of free or low cost legal services during due process proceedings, so by the time you proceed to litigation you should already have been given such a list. If not, ask for one.

During due process or litigation, your child's placement remains as it was before your complaint was filed. This provision is helpful to parents and children who are fighting to keep their current placement, but not so helpful to parents who are looking for more services than they are currently getting. If the child was initially getting no special education services, and the disagreement is over how much the child should be getting, the parents and school district may reach an agreement on an interim plan, so that the child may receive some intervention while the process is going on. Alternatively, the parents can pay privately for the services they think their child needs and hope to win reimbursement.

You may have experienced delays within the school district before you got to this point. Sometimes the school district's delays, or other procedural violations, can be a weapon in your arsenal if you do go to court. The IDEA requires that states implement it, and if there is not some degree of promptness in the planning and implementation of each eligible student's special services, the law has not been implemented. There was a legal case in which a school district had not come up with a plan for a student for several months. The court found the school district had violated the IDEA's procedural protections to the extent that the child's right to a free public education had been denied, and it ordered the district to pay the costs incurred by the parents in paying for services for their child (Gerstmyer, 850 F. Supp. 361 (1994)). Of course if the parents had no money to pay for any services, the damage may have been irreparable.

A website (http://home.att.net/~D.FAMILY/Public/sat.html) posted an article warning school districts of increasing litigation aimed at getting them to pay for expensive, intensive applied behavioral analysis at-home programs for autistic children, and pointing out factors common to cases in which parents had prevailed. (This website was aimed at school districts, not at parents, but it was instructive.) The first factor listed was "significant procedural violations by the district." Failure to evaluate, hold IEP meetings, or implement programs on time was the most common type of significant procedural violation. Parents prevailed in many of the cases cited. Apparently the courts held the delays against the school districts, and that helped the parents prevail on other issues as well. Another common theme in the cases was that parents paid for services for an extended period of time; the services were shown to be effective for that particular child, and then the school district was ordered to pick up the cost. The school district had usually done little on its own. These were evidently cases in which the parents had the wherewithal to set up an expensive, difficult-to-arrange program on their own.

Both rich and poor school districts often fail to review a student's records before IEP meetings, even if the student is new to the district. While this is a terrible breech of standards, it can also work to the parents' advantage. If the parents have a clear idea of what the child needs and come in with reports that support their view, and the school district has nothing in its corner with which to respond, the parents may win out.

While litigation is time consuming, emotionally exhausting, expensive, and confrontational, there are ways to minimize those features. Start early and keep up the pressure on the school district. Don't let them have the IEP meeting six months late so that you don't find out until then that they are not going to do anything for your child. The administrative remedies, the due process hearing and attendant mediation are set up so that you don't need a lawyer, but you might want to hire one anyway. This makes it more expensive, but less emotionally exhausting because the lawyer does most of the work for you, and does the confrontation too, and you usually get what you want sooner.

Public v. private school

When is it a good idea to give up on the public schools altogether, and turn to private education? The summer before Andy entered the poorly regarded Philadelphia public school system, I felt desperation and intermittent despair about getting him into an appropriate public school placement. I wished we could find a private school, but it was too late in the process. I felt sure that in a small (10–12 kids) structured class with strong basics and good science and history – much like the school Temple Grandin described in her memoirs (see pp. 90–91) – Andy would flourish. But the private schools near us did not have quite that program. Many emphasized keeping their students stimulated, so they moved from class to class a lot more. At a private school Andy attended for kindergarten and first grade he had two main teachers instead of one, plus others for the less basic subjects. The emphasis on stimulation rather than structure is generally not a plus for students with Asperger's Syndrome. A couple of private schools in Philadelphia suburbs designed for children with learning differences sounded as if they had just the right program, but they cost about $17,000 a year in 2000, and were cool to the idea of having a student with a PDD label. Generally, good private schools are about $10,000 a year.

Catholic schools are much more reasonably priced. A far greater range of people can afford them. They tend to be more structured than most public and nonsectarian private schools, which is usually a plus for students with Asperger's Syndrome. Their class size is usually big though, and it is therefore difficult for the teachers to pay particular attention to children with special needs, and the needs of a child without discipline problems might be overlooked. There are some Catholic schools designed for children with special needs, which are more likely to have a nurturing environment, but they are geared more to remedial academics than to needs of children with Asperger's Syndrome.

Andy's private school was very good about working with us to try to help Andy. The psychologist who worked there two days a week was a clinical psychologist, with far more training then the standard licensed school psychologist at public schools. She observed Andy in the classroom frequently, was the first to suspect Asperger's Syndrome, and was a great resource for the teachers and for us. Because she was on staff there it was easy for her to observe him without Andy or the other students thinking anything of it. In the last couple months of Andy's first grade year there his language arts teacher called us every week to help monitor a incentive program we had set up to get him to write more, pay more attention, and to contribute in class. We gave him points for answering questions and volunteering, and for getting more writing done, and the teacher was happy to provide the necessary monitoring and communication. Often private schools are more flexible than public schools, more willing to meet a student's unique needs without a formal process. Andy's private school had the whole school community involved in one allergic child's anti-peanut plan, making sure nobody brought any peanut product to a school gathering, and that anyone who touched a peanut washed their hands before going near this child. Relations between teachers and parents are often more cordial and less adversarial at private schools than at public schools.

Karen Killilea was admitted to and supported in a private Catholic school kindergarten, when the public schools took the position they had no place for cerebral palsy children (Killilea 1952). Other cerebral palsy children attended private schools when their public schools would not admit them. This was not a matter of those private schools having special equipment or therapists – they didn't. It was a matter of attitude. Sometimes you can find private schools with a more enlightened attitude than your local public school; sometimes not though. Sometimes they are less enlightened, never having to deal with any special needs kids. Some of them put strong emphasis on social graces, and do not admit anyone who does not have them, or throw out students, even kindergartners, who do not meet their social skills criteria. There is often more of a social sameness within private schools that at public schools, which does not bode well for the socially challenged.

The IDEA requires school districts to offer some related special education services, such as occupational therapy, speech therapy, psychological counseling, to a child placed in a private school by his parents, but the school district is required only to spend an amount equivalent to the proportion of federal funds for special education. A school district does not have to spend its own funds on children placed in private schools by their parents. Although these services can be provided at a regular education private school, they are much more integrated with the public school systems. Students at the private Lutheran school where I taught who received services through the school district had to leave our site in a van to get the services as no publicly funded services can be supplied on the site of a religious school. They can be provided on the site of nonsectarian private schools but sometimes they are not. If Andy had received occupational therapy through the school district while at his private school, I would have had to leave work to take him from the private school to a public school for the therapy, and then transport him back; such a giant pain in the butt for a working parent as to be unmanageable for many. When he attended a private school just taking him to an occupational therapy evaluation at the school district (which had to be canceled because the doctor did not show up) took the better part of a work day.

Public schools generally have more special educational supports and more diversity, but it depends where you live. Suburban school districts usually have more money than rural and urban districts, almost always a plus. Large urban districts might have more special education programs than small rural ones. Some districts do more mainstreaming than others. With mainstreaming though, no matter how many supports you have, in a class size of 30, typical of many urban districts – Andy's second and third grade classes had about 30 students each – it is hard for the teacher to give a lot of individual attention to any one student. On the other hand, larger classes often mean more structure. Although regimentation is not much in vogue in educational circles today, it can be comforting to some students with Asperger's Syndrome to be part of a group of children all doing the same task separately and quietly. Where to live is a very personal decision involving many factors, but I have noticed among families with special needs children I know that they generally move to the suburbs if they have more than one child, and pay for private education if they have only one.

There are very few private schools that specialize in educating children with Asperger's Syndrome. There are quite a few more for students with a variety of learning disabilities, or as they put it students who learn differently. These schools almost always have small, structured classes, and specialized instruction for students whose abilities are uneven. They often have speech therapists and occupational therapists around, and activities designed to improve social skills, and they only cost about $18,000 a year!

Generally, the best idea is probably to live in the best school district that you can afford, and then to get the best deal that you can for your child. Wealthier school districts have a lot more resources than poor districts, and you can sue the districts to get them enforced.

Mix of public and private

If you want to keep your child in public school, but feel he is not getting enough support services there, you can try paying for support services yourself. Some school districts may balk at your paying for supports in the classroom, either from a position that the child doesn't need them and would be better off without them, or out of fear that you will subsequently sue for reimbursement. Usually they won't object to parents supplying something like a word processor (some school district supplied keyboards show only a couple lines of text). If a parent wants to hire an assistant for the child, even for only a couple hours a day, schools might object on the grounds that they have no control over that person. You can try to alleviate that concern by going over that person's credentials with the principal, introducing him or her to the principal and classroom teacher in advance, and by reminding them that many times schools have people working who are not their employees, such as paraprofessionals and therapists supplied by Medicaid contractors or mental health agencies, volunteers, and parents.

A school district is required to pay for assistive devices, such as keyboards, for home use if it is necessary for the child's education. Of course, you can buy your own assistive devices for home use. You can teach your child to type over the summer so that he can use a keyboard in school during the academic year. If you feel your child needs an extended school year and the school district won't supply it, you can pay for it privately. If you feel your child would really benefit from a paraprofessional assistant and the school district declines to supply one, you could try hiring a college student with an interest in psychology, or an occupational therapy student if there is an occupational therapy program in your area. The number of hours would depend on the child's needs and your budget. There are parents who spend a lot of time sitting in their child's classroom, functioning as a one-to-one assistant. Also, many parents have obtained some assistance for their children through the early intervention system while arranging for additional support privately. Getting a private evaluation is another example of this mix of private and public. You can pay an occupational therapist or educational psychologist to observe your child in the classroom to help determine what strategies would benefit the child as part of an independent evaluation.

There are several possible reasons for taking on these tasks privately even though the IDEA requires an appropriate education with the necessary supports be provided for free:

1.   You feel they are necessary, but the school district does not, and you do not want to litigate or go through due process.

2.   A due process hearing officer or a court has upheld the school district's refusal to provide these supports but you still feel they are important. This could easily happen considering that a school district is not obligated to provide the best possible education for your child, only an appropriate one, while you may feel your child should have the best possible education.

3.   You feel your child needs these supports while you litigate.

If your reason is the last one, you can use your private payment for these supports to your advantage. If your child makes measurable progress with these supports that he was not making without them, that progress can be evidence in your case, showing that the supports were indeed necessary and appropriate. There are many examples of lawsuits in which the parents prevailed after paying their child's special educational expenses. Also, if a court finds that these supports should have been provided as part of the free, appropriate, public education to which your child is entitled, then the court may order the school district to reimburse you for your costs.

Homeschooling

According to the "least restrictive environment" philosophy of the IDEA, instruction in the home is the least desirable option, the last resort, because the law's intent is that children with disabilities are to be educated with nondisabled children to the largest extent possible. For a child with Asperger's Syndrome, the disadvantage to homeschooling is that the child will not have as many opportunities to observe normal social interchange among his peer group.

However, sometimes children with Asperger's Syndrome need a break from regular school and sometimes, despite the laws, there simply is no appropriate program for them. In the United States, homeschooling is allowed at the parent's wish in every state. Some states regulate homeschooling heavily, while some regulate it so lightly you wonder they lay any claim to having compulsory education at all. Parents of homeschooled children are responsible for teaching their children, unless they hire private tutors, but the parents are not required to have a college education, or even a high school diploma. So, if you feel homeschooling is the best option for your child, the legality of it is the least of your worries.

There are other concerns, such as how to manage financially if you have to quit your job, getting adequate supports, and putting together and teaching an appropriate curriculum, but there is a lot of help out there for the last of these areas. Homeschooling has become much more popular in the last decade than many people ever thought possible, so there are many resources available to support it. All sorts of curriculum packets are marketed to homeschooling parents (many of them developed by fundamentalist Christians). If you have internet access, there are plenty of websites on homeschooling children with special needs. Lise Pyles (2001) describes homeschooling her Asperger's

Syndrome son in her book *Hitchhiking through Asperger Syndrome.* He had been unable to function in his regular school and no one had come up with any strategies there that helped him. She took him out of school and taught him at home, and he learned, whereas at school he had been learning nothing. After a few years, he returned to school, and, although he did not have an easy time, he was not behind academically. He was also ready to learn at school upon his return there. Some students manage in regular school up until high school, but then they no longer can handle it.

Homeschooling does not have to be all or nothing. A child could go to school in the mornings and have a home program in the afternoons. At least theoretically that is possible, but some school districts might put up a lot of resistance to that. The school district would probably agree eventually if you insisted enough. It may be easier to arrange a half-and-half schedule for a high school student, who could attend school for selected classes rather than for a regular day. Theoretically of course, if a child cannot learn in a school setting then the school district should pay for private tutors, but this is unlikely. School districts do pay for home tutors for children who cannot come to school because of illness, but very rarely if ever for children with conditions like Asperger's Syndrome.

A family from Maine published on the internet what they did to set up a home program using the Lovaas method for their son with classic autism. This method involves very intensive one-on-one instruction. They had done this at their own expense (in excess of $16,000 a year including a home program consultant, therapists, and aides plus the time equivalent of a full-time job for the mother) from the time their child was age 3 until he was old enough for kindergarten in the hopes of preparing him to be mainstreamed into a regular kindergarten class. Their school district hired an aide, one with no experience in working with children with autism, to support him in the class. Despite the parents' high hopes and their hard years of intensive work with the boy, the mainstream kindergarten was an obvious disaster for this child after only a few days. The parents withdrew him from school while they scrambled to figure out what program would be best for him, a time period the father referred to as "the dark days." The school district offered to place him in a special education class outside their neighborhood school. Apparently his parents did not consider this offered placement appropriate enough, because they decided to continue their home program, although homeschooling placed a lot of stress on the whole family and was not something they had envisioned or turned to easily for their school-age son. They did not litigate, preferring to use their energy to help their son. They might have lost if they had since the offered self-contained special education class might have been ruled a free, appropriate public education.

I would use homeschooling only as a last resort. It is impossible to second guess any parent's decision, and usually impossible to know if you are doing the right thing, but I wish that Maine family had worked with their school district more, checking out the special education class, maybe pushing for a better one, or insisting on a more experienced paraprofessional (they may actually have done all these things unsuccessfully and not reported it on their website).

Summary

Students with Asperger's Syndrome can usually be mainstreamed, but nevertheless they need considerable special attention. Their social skills must be addressed, as well as their learning styles. Social skills can be addressed in a variety of ways – speech therapy, social skills club, occupational therapy – but they should be included in the IEP. In the classroom itself, structure, small class size, and an understanding teacher are the most important attributes.

Not all students with Asperger's can benefit from a regular classroom, and currently the alternative options are limited. Some special education classes can be suitable for students with Asperger's, but few are designed for them. There are a very few private schools designed for students with Asperger's Syndrome. In my opinion, homeschooling should be a last resort, but many people homeschool now.

The federal IDEA guarantees students with disabilities a free, appropriate education, but, partly for budget reasons and partly for reasons of bureaucratic rigidity, they do not always get it. Students with Asperger's Syndrome are more apt than students with more obvious, better known disabilities to escape the notice and best efforts of the educational establishment. They look so normal. Their differences from the mainstream, their disabilities, are so subtle but so significant. In almost all school districts, inertia is a factor in meeting the needs connected with "new" or unusual disabilities. Therefore their parents must be advocates for their children with Asperger's Syndrome. This advocacy should take the form of working with the teachers as well as insisting on services the child needs. The situation is improving. As Asperger's Syndrome has become better known, more and more has been published about appropriate educational intervention for students with it. There are more social pragmatics or social skills groups in public schools now than there were even a few years ago. Wraparound support was virtually unknown 15 years ago, unless you paid for it yourself. Speech therapists do more work on conversational skills with children who need it (generally, not just in schools). Social skills groups are still hard to find, both in and out of schools, but they do exist. Children with Asperger's Syndrome must get help, but in overburdened public school systems they may well not get it unless their parents push strongly.

PART IV

Daily Life

Progressing in the Maze

11

Coordinating Therapy among Healthcare System, School, and Home

This book is mainly on the struggle to get services, and the difficulties of putting together a coordinated program to meet the special needs of a child with Asperger's Syndrome. However, home life with such a child is part of the program too. All the general books on raising children stress the importance of home life, how home is where children learn to love and be loved, and where they learn responsibility and ethics. The same is true for children with special needs. Children whose social development is delayed must get extra socialization practice at home. Those whose emotional development is delayed must get extra training in loving and being loved, and in demonstrating emotions.

Home is your child's base; it supports the school portion of your child's program and the school and healthcare portions support the home. The weekly hours of occupational therapy, speech therapy, or social skills training don't mean much without school and home. So many times with Asperger's Syndrome, parents must obtain pieces of an intervention program from different sources. Of course, it falls on you, the parent, to coordinate these different pieces. Let us look at coordinating home and school first, and then healthcare, and then examine some home and family issues.

Developing relationships with your child's educators

Good parent–teacher relationships

As you are part of your child's educational team, you want to be on good terms with the rest of the team: the classroom teachers, school administrators, counselor or resource room teacher. It is especially important that you and your child's actual teachers act as a team. If you have any hostile feelings toward the school district, save them for district officials with whom your child has no contact. Badmouthing the teacher never helps your child. It is best not to denigrate any of the educational establishment in front of your child, although if you are having disagreements with the school district and the child is mature enough to understand them, you can certainly explain them.

Good parent–teacher relationships are important for every child, but, as is so often the case with children with special needs, what is important for every child is even more critical for them. You want the teachers on your side since your child needs extra help. If your child is mainstreamed you will be asking a lot of the regular classroom teacher. If you are trying to make a case that the school district should give your child more supports, it bolsters your case to have the teacher on your side.

Teachers are more likely to go the extra mile for your child if you go the extra mile as part of the team. Try to volunteer in the classroom if you possibly can. This is invaluable since it allows you to see your child in the classroom environment, gives you an idea of what the class is like, and allows you to do a favor for the teacher. Even if you work full time, you might be able to come in on an extended lunch break occasionally if your job is not too far from the school. If you cannot spend time in the classroom yourself, perhaps a member of your extended family, the child's grandmother or an aunt or uncle could. If volunteering is not an option, ask the teacher if he or she needs supplies. If she doesn't, you don't have to give anything but at least you asked. If she does, donate a few. Often in the younger grades, teachers want household items like empty paper towel rolls – not a budget-breaker. Giving apples is out of style but there are ways to show the teacher she is appreciated.

Be willing to wait a couple days past the deadlines for IEP conferences if it will help the staff and not harm your child. This is easier if your child is in a somewhat appropriate placement; I wouldn't recommend it if you are waiting for a placement. Talk to the staff so they know you are aware of the deadlines and are exhibiting generosity and flexibility, not ignorance.

In many cases, a child's placement has been determined after some form of adversarial process, either at the IEP level, or through the due process system set out by the IDEA, or even in a court of law. Maybe your child is in one class while you are in the process of suing the school district to get his placement changed. Nonetheless it is entirely possible and desirable to have good relationships with the educators. If you are engaged in litigation with the school district, you want your child's teacher on your side, and frequently the teachers have an adversarial attitude toward the school district. In any case, good parent–teacher relations are crucial for all children, regardless of special needs.

Promoting exchange of information

Getting the special needs of a child with Asperger's Syndrome met requires networking, and teachers are an important resource. School districts, actually the whole education establishment, are such thick, vast bureaucracies that there are often special programs or special specific areas of entitlement, or some sort of funding, that most people working in the district don't know about. Pick the brains of the school staff about special programs. Special programs might range from tutoring, to music lessons, to participation in a study of mainstreamed students with an autistic spectrum disorder, to a wiggle cushion or footrest, or technological support. There are all sorts of reading programs which might serve to get your child into a smaller learning environment for at least some of the time. There may be some unusual after-school programs or extracurricular activities suitable for your child. Part of having a child with Asperger's Syndrome is perpetually casting about for environments where your child can flourish and activities which ground him or her in this world. Any member of the school community may have useful information which you can obtain through informal conversation. Ideally, the teachers, principal, vice-principal, librarian (if there is one), reading specialist (there usually is somebody doubling in that role), school nurse, guidance counselor, physical education teacher, and music or art teacher are all on your team, looking out for your child, along with the speech therapist, occupational therapist, and school psychologist.

Give the staff printed material on Asperger's Syndrome. Encourage them to keep or add to a professional library. If there is no library of professional materials, see if the librarian (or whoever maintains the library if there is no librarian) can keep a shelf for professional materials, including materials on

Asperger's Syndrome; or maybe the resource room or teacher's lounge could keep some available for teachers to peruse. You never know what might help. Maybe as a result of such material another student in the school may be identified as having Asperger's Syndrome, and then you can share concerns and ideas with that student's parents.

From the point of view of advocates for services for children with Asperger's Syndrome, it is crucial to have Pervasive Developmental Disorder listed as a diagnosis on the IEP of any child who has been diagnosed with a form of the disorder. Most IEP forms have space for a primary and secondary diagnosis, but frequently for a child with Asperger's Syndrome the diagnoses given are specific learning disability and/or communication impairment. This is partly because of the definitions given in the special education laws. Asperger's Syndrome, Nonverbal Learning Disorder, and Developmental Coordination Disorder are not specifically covered under the IDEA or mentioned in the implementing regulations. Autism is defined in the regulations as a "developmental disability significantly affecting verbal and nonverbal communication and social interaction…that adversely affects a child's educational performance." Many parents of children with Asperger's Syndrome do not want a diagnosis or label of autism, and many teachers involved in IEPs do not feel these children fit what they think of as autistic. School districts are never going to respond adequately to the needs of students with Asperger's Syndrome unless they are aware of the numbers of students with Asperger's Syndrome they have, but it is difficult for them to be aware of those numbers if is not stamped on the IEPs. If school districts ever get into the business of disseminating information about services for children with autistic spectrum disorders, it will send such information only to parents of children listed as having that diagnosis. Correct listing of diagnoses on IEPs may ultimately help promote communication between the psychiatric community and the educational community.

Behavior at home and school

If a Behavioral Intervention Plan (BIP) is in the works for your child, discuss with the IEP team how it can be reinforced at home as well as at school. Parents and teachers should present a united front in modifying undesirable behaviors. Many behavioral goals must be reinforced at home. Grooming is a case in point, and concentration during homework is related to concentration during class work.

Also think about what the goals in such a plan should be. Think about your child's behavior at home, or what you have observed of it on playgrounds with other children, or with siblings. Think about your goals for your child's behavior. Some children with Asperger's Syndrome behave very differently at home from the way they behave at school. Therefore, in order to contribute intelligently to writing the plan, observe your child at school and think about what behaviors there you would like to see modified.

Even if your child has no formal Behavioral Intervention Plan, discuss with your child's teacher what behaviors you would be like to see modified, and how you can both work on them.

Developing relationships with your child's healthcare professionals

Although there is not as often an adversarial relationship between a child's parents and the child's healthcare providers as there is between a child's parents and the child's educators (hostile feelings in healthcare are generally reserved for the insurance company), it may be harder to get all of your child's healthcare providers to act as a team. The problem is not ill will, but time constraints and lack of physical connection. Many doctors are obliged to see patients at frequent intervals, and so they collaborate with other doctors on the case only when there is an acute need. Your child's healthcare providers are generally not working together in the same building, and they often have no communication with each other unless you arrange it.

What to tell them

Almost any time you visit a new healthcare provider, from dentist to optometrist, you are asked to fill out a health information form asking about your medical history, including any special conditions. Most published advice to parents of children with any sort of "condition" urges them to tell every medical care provider of their child's diagnosis. This advice rests on the belief that healthcare providers will know what special steps to take for your child if they are aware of the diagnosis; possibly, but in practice some healthcare providers may not be familiar with Asperger's Syndrome. You might then have to explain that it is a form of autism or Pervasive Developmental Disorder, and then, if they do in fact remember or pay attention to the health information form, they may baby or talk down to your child more than necessary. You should be prepared to explain your child's form of the diagnosis to providers, with specific attention to its possible effect in that specialist's field.

You might think that the eye doctor whom your child sees once every two years or less does not need to know, but sometimes global coordination problems affect the eye muscles, leading to reading difficulties. I doubt that simply writing Asperger's on the child's form at the eye doctor's office will lead to the doctor checking the tracking muscles, so you may have to be more specific.

Children vary in how they react to dental exams. You probably have some idea of how your child reacts and of whether presenting the dentist with an explanation of your child's Asperger's Syndrome will help. You should probably try to impress on the dentist that your child's reactions to pain might not be typical. Andy's dentist told me that one of his teeth was coming in wrong and that I should bring him in if the tooth hurt him. The dentist did not understand that Andy would not give typical signs of pain, such as complaining that his mouth hurt. More likely he would not complain at all, and we would have to watch closely to see if he was fussy, or if he pulled at his mouth or chewed differently, as you would with an infant. Yet in other ways, such as in explanations of dental matters, it would be better if the dentist treated Andy as an adult.

Pediatricians most of all should know about the diagnosis. Although they may have written referrals to see diagnosing specialists, do not assume that they got the reports written by the specialists for whom they wrote referrals. Ideally, they should have all the reports, in order to help get whatever services are available for the child. Consider giving your child's pediatrician a copy of the Comprehension Evaluation Report done by the school district as preparation for the IEP. But even when a doctor gets the reports, you cannot assume he or she has read them. If you send a doctor reports that other doctors or therapists have written about your child, they may be placed in your child's chart by the medical office staff and only glanced at by the doctor when your child comes in for an appointment, so be sure to mention the reports to the doctor, especially if there is something specific you want him or her to see. Don't ever think pediatricians have told you everything they know about possible services. They may think they have, but there is so much out there and it is so fragmented, and each child with the label is so different, that there may be something the pediatrician can help you with that hasn't occurred to him or her yet. So it is important to keep up the dialogue. At every visit – your other child's sick visit, routine appointments – give the pediatrician a quick update on the status of your child with Asperger's, how he is doing, and what you perceive to be his upcoming needs, in order to stir the pediatrician's brain a bit, and to keep him or her thinking of your child's needs.

Sometimes even service providers who are fully aware of the diagnosis get focused on their specific area and miss the big picture. For example, for a year Andy received occupational therapy at a highly regarded pediatric rehabilitation hospital. Yet for a couple months they had an occupational therapy student working with him in addition to his regular therapist. It was routine for them to use students as part of their role as a teaching hospital, and they were concentrating on his motor skills. But for him that was one more person to concentrate on, which was a distraction. One day Andy was practicing riding a bike in the hallway, as he had been doing for several sessions, and they could not figure out why he was not focusing. It was because it was 5: 00 p.m. and there were hordes of people coming down the hall. We would wait for them to pass but it was one horde after another. How can you expect a child with Asperger's Syndrome to concentrate in that situation?

On another occasion, Andy required alternate recess activities at school. His principal (an educational specialist rather than a medical provider, but the same phenomenon of failing to think through the unique issues associated with Asperger's Syndrome) suggested he report to the language impaired class every day at recess to help out. She did not understand that Andy needed time to unwind during recess, and helping with a strange class was likely to add to his stress.

Coordinating watching for the effects of medication

Asperger's Syndrome is diagnosed by medical professionals, who are the ones who study it, but it is treated mainly through special education. The one part of treatment doctors are significantly involved in is medication. Psychiatrists, and sometimes pediatricians, are the ones who prescribe the medications that can ameliorate some of the symptoms of Asperger's. However, these medical professionals do not see what effect the medication is having. They do not know exactly how its effect meshes with the rest of the treatment program. Parents and teachers have to make those observations. The parent will probably be the link between the doctor and teacher. This is true for any medication, and in fact, for most aspects of the whole treatment program.

Wraparound services

What is wraparound?

Many people have noticed that our patchwork system of social services has many gaps. Families are lucky if their needs fit the existing services. The concept of wraparound was promoted to tailor services to an individual's needs, and has been used in a variety of sectors. One of its most common uses is in the foster care system, as a means of providing services to children in their own homes, to help their whole families stabilize and stay together. Wraparound supports are also used in the arena of mental health services, especially as long-term hospitalization has decreased. It is through the mental health system that individuals with Asperger's Syndrome or similar disorders can access wraparound services if they need them.

So what exactly do wraparound services consist of? In theory, a wraparound coordinator (they can go by different names) meets with the family and comes up with a service plan, much like an Individualized Family Service Plan in the early intervention system, or an IEP except that a wraparound plan goes beyond school. In practice, to many people wraparound support means a paraprofessional coach or aide, sometimes called therapeutic staff support (TSS), to follow the child around for much of his day, with the number of hours depending on needs (or budget). These one-on-one paraprofessionals often shadow a child at school, if that is where the child needs such support most. They are not usually supposed to tutor, if paid for by Medical Assistance or a mental health agency, but to help the child learn to deal with his environment. In the case of autistic children, the TSS can be a social coach.

Some children with classic autism have to be watched all the time, lest they run off, hurt themselves, or hurt others. Of course, this is exhausting for their parents. In these cases, wraparound aides can provide respite care for the parents. Ideally, they are part of the child's whole treatment plan, and strive to ameliorate undesirable behaviors as part of a behavioral intervention plan in place at school and home.

Children at the milder end of the autistic spectrum usually don't need this intensive service, but a trained person acting as a social coach for a few hours a week at school or in an afterschool activity can be very helpful.

HOW TO GET IT

How to get wraparound support varies from state to state, with some states having more available than others. Usually, the place to start is the state's department of mental health (it may have slightly different name, or be a bureau or office rather than a department). To get wraparound support, usually you need an evaluation and a prescription at a minimum, but there is frequently a long wait.

In some states Medical Assistance pays for wraparound aides. All states have a Medicaid program for people under a certain income level, but a number of states extend coverage to people above the income cut-off in certain cases. Some states provide Medical Assistance to children who would otherwise be institutionalized, in order to keep them at home, out of institutions. Pennsylvania provides Medical Assistance to children with disabilities, regardless of income. In Pennsylvania, when Medical Assistance started paying for one-to-one aides, waiting lists mushroomed, and there were stories of severely autistic and other mentally ill children waiting years after getting a prescription, sometimes being hospitalized or attempting suicide during the wait. As a result of these stories, a class action suit was filed, and in December 2000 a court ruled that the state had to provide such services within 60 days of a prescription. There still are not enough wraparound workers to provide such a service to everyone who can convince a doctor they need it. The providers of wraparound services usually insist on doing their own evaluations rather than just reading an outside doctor's prescription. The providers put children on waiting lists for an evaluation, so the children wait for the evaluation rather than waiting for services after getting the prescription.

Even if you get a one-to-one assistant, their quality is very uneven. They may know very little about Asperger's Syndrome. After the court's ruling in Pennsylvania, Lisa M. Lowrie, a children's policy specialist with the Pennsylvania Community Providers Association, told the magazine *Mental Health Weekly*: "We don't have a lot of data to support what the services actually do" (*MHW*, 1/24/00).

If you are referred to an agency that provides such services by the mental health system, you may find it is used to working with a population different from your family. The workers there may not be familiar with Asperger's Syndrome or Nonverbal Learning Disorder. You may also find that your child's pediatrician, and psychologist or psychiatrist, have never heard of this agency.

I was referred to an agency that provided such services by the Medicaid behavioral health HMO (Health Maintenance organisation) for Philadelphia county. I called them and explained my son's diagnosis, and that his doctors and teachers felt he needed a wraparound coach at school. They could not accept an outside doctor's recommendation, but would have to evaluate him themselves. As I was concerned about subjecting him to endless evaluations, I asked to talk to the person who would do the evaluation. This "intake" person was not a doctor, and had never heard of Asperger's. I spoke to the supervisor there, who expressed surprise that I had a job at an office. Apparently most of their clients did not. She said they worked "in the community." When I said I was most interested in help at school, she was not impressed. They were more used to working with people at home, helping the parents learn to work with the children. But I felt I knew more than they did. She said I should go to the school district if I wanted a coach for Andy at school.

It is true, according to the IDEA, that schools are supposed to provide the services a child needs to get an education. If this means a one-on-one coach, then the school district is supposed to provide that. However, school districts are allowed to work with third-party payers, such as Medical Assistance or the mental health system, to provide these services. In Pennsylvania, where disabled children are entitled to Medical Assistance regardless of income, the school districts often rely on the Medical Assistance system for all wrap-around coaches, except those whose job is helping students with severe physical disabilities get from place to place. The special education laws state that if there is a delay in providing services paid for by a third party, the school district is responsible for providing the services in the meantime, but Philadelphia does not seem to have the means to do this. They do not have college-trained aides on staff, and usually blame delays on the third-party payer. There was a lawsuit about that too, and the school district was ordered to provide aides, but their aides are not college trained, and not likely to have any special knowledge of psychological disabilities or how to handle them.

Family therapists, family consultants, home program consultants

In most states, anyone holding themselves out as a family therapist must be licensed as such. As the field becomes more professionalized, more specialized, with its own professional societies, training standards, and licensing requirements, health insurance has become more heavily involved with it. That is, health insurance sometimes covers it, but it also costs more when it doesn't.

Other professionals might give related services, under another name. A psychiatric social worker or occupational therapist who visits the home of an autistic child for the purpose of advising on home life strategies to help the child might be called a family consultant. Such a service might be paid for under some mental health wraparound program, but funding for such a service is not widespread.

A significant number of upper middle class and upper class families have paid for home early intervention programs for their children with classic autism, usually based on the methods of Dr. Ivar Lovaas, or less often on those of Dr. Stanley Greenspan. Both involve long hours of intensive work with the child, the Lovaas method based on the principles of behaviorism (also called Applied Behavioral Analysis, or Discrete Learning Trials) and the other, Greenspan's "Floortime" method, based on using the child's behavior as a basis for socializing with him or her (also called Developmental Individual Relationship model). Parents setting up such a program have often hired a "program consultant," usually a psychologist trained in Applied Behavioral Analysis to teach them how to run the program. John Bald, of Brunswick, Maine, who along with his wife set up such a program for his son in the late 1990s, reported that it cost $8000 to $11,000 a year to pay a consultant to do four personalized training workshops a year, each lasting two to three days, plus telephone consultations.[1] This sort of intense program is rarely set up for a child with Asperger's (either because of the milder symptoms or because of the later age of diagnosis), but someone who advises as a home program consultant might be able to give you some basic advice on things you can do around the house to help with the child, if you pay them.

As mentioned in Part II, an occupational therapist might be someone to turn to for advice on what to do at home to help your child. They could advise on a home sensory integration program, what music to play around the house, and what extracurricular activities would be most beneficial, as well as how to support at home any occupational therapy the child is getting elsewhere.

Treatment of anxiety in children with Asperger's Syndrome
Treatment of anxiety in children with Asperger's Syndrome requires coordination among the medical community, home, and school. In some cases, it seems that the core symptoms of Asperger's Syndrome, that is the absence of

---

1   That was just for the consultant. They paid plenty additionally for other parts of their home ABA program – for students who worked with their son, for supplies.

social and communication skills, and the intense, confining interests in circumscribed areas, grow less pronounced as the child develops, either through intervention or not, but sometimes at the same time secondary symptoms of anxiety and depression increase. As a preschooler, the child may have been happily lost in his or her own world much of the time, but the constant demands of school, along with increased awareness of the world, a growing sense of self and realization of differences and difficulties fitting in, may cause a child with Asperger's Syndrome to suffer from severe anxiety that as parents we hope no children would have to endure.

Sometimes this secondary symptom becomes more disabling than the core features of Asperger's Syndrome. Treatment of anxiety is the province of mental health professionals, but the child's whole environment is involved. Sensory integration therapy may reduce some agitation resulting from oversensitivity to noise or bright lights, but such oversensitivity tends to diminish with age anyway while anxieties connected with peer relations and school work increase. Parents are the part of the home–school–doctor triangle who most closely observe the symptoms.

The good news is that treatment of anxiety is more likely to be covered by private insurance plans than treatment of developmental disorders. Insurance coverage for anxiety treatment may become even more likely in the future if campaigns for parity of funding for treatment of mental health disorders with physical health disorders are effective.

Schools, however, have less expertise in dealing with treatment of anxiety than they do with developmental disorders. In cases where school-related anxiety is severe, the child's school environment may have to be changed to a smaller, more structured, and less rigorous setting, at least for a while. A note from a psychiatrist may help to effect such a change, if strongly worded and well explained. Although anxiety is not covered by the IDEA (unless it qualifies a child as an emotionally disturbed, which you may not want), it is covered by Section 504 of the Rehabilitation Act if it interferes with the student's ability to function. A Section 504 Plan can be written specifically to address a student's anxiety, just as a Section 504 Plan can be written to address the special needs of a student with diabetes (remember that a Section 504 Plan will not put a child in a special class, just make accommodations in the child's existing class).

Even if the child's anxiety results from the school environment and not the home, parents can take steps from home to lessen the child's anxiety at school: maybe walk the child to school, or give him a massage every morning;

or drive the child to school to avoid the bus. Get to the school early to allow time to adjust, or late to avoid the school yard bustle, depending on your child's needs.

Tony Attwood's (1998) book has a section on handling anxiety. He recommends physical exercise, relaxing activities such as listening to soft music, and time set aside for solitude and unwinding.

Loneliness, unhappiness, depression

We all want our children to be happy, to have live happy lives. With Asperger's, we fear they are doomed to be the kid who's left out, who is not invited to birthday parties, last picked for a team (if they even play on any pick-up teams), lonely like Ebenezer Scrooge sitting by himself in Christmas Past, or bullied like the ghost-seeing boy in the movie *The Sixth Sense*. In Japan, there is a social phenomenon called ijime. It occurs relatively suddenly among children, mostly boys, when a child is isolated, and then tormented, not physically, but constantly given to understand that he is the object of dislike by his classmates, for no particular reason. Once it starts to happen to a child, it picks up and doesn't stop. His closest friends will desert him when they see it happening. Adults don't like it, but rarely intervene. Probably all the parents could do in any case is move away, but in Japan this is very difficult because jobs are for life. Children in Japan have committed suicide because of this bullying phenomenon, with some of the victims leaving notes like, "Going to school is worse than hell."

Like ijime, a diagnosis of Asperger's Syndrome seems like a sentence of loneliness and ostracism for a child. With their odd mannerisms, children with Asperger's Syndrome are a natural target. Lise Pyles claimed her child had been bullied on three continents, and that all children with Asperger's had a bull's eye on them when it came to school bullying (Pyles 2001). My mother almost cried when she and my father sent my very socially impaired brother off to overnight camp. I remember my dad saying, "I feel sorry for him too, but he's got to have the experience," and my mother replying, "The experience of being rejected?" Sometimes children with Asperger's Syndrome ignore their peers and are ignored by them until adolescence, when the child with Asperger's tries to make social contacts and is quickly rebuffed. It is probably this situation, and the depression in the children which often results, that leads some experts to say that Asperger's Syndrome is worse than classic autism.

What can you do to prevent or minimize depression in a child or adolescent with Asperger's Syndrome? You can provide a loving home. Let your child know you love him and believe in him, and talk up the things he is good at. Try to get your other children, if any, to do the same thing, to admire their brother for his good qualities.

Be aware that depression tends to be more of a problem in adolescence, and discuss what signs to look for with medical professionals at the beginning of your child's adolescence. Watch for these signs carefully and get professional help fast. Continue to be alert for signs of depression even when your child is a young adult and starts living on his own. Tony Attwood wrote that he knows of several individuals with Asperger's Syndrome who committed suicide. Private health insurance will usually pay for medical treatment of depression.

Home Front Hints

Activities

Many children with Asperger's Syndrome are not very active, or they may be active in a few small selective ways, without much variety. Andy will jump around his room daydreaming for hours, if you call that being active, but he is interested in only a very narrow range of activities. Most children, as they mature, develop interests which involve some sort of activity on their part. When Andy was age five he focused on mazes. He would look at them for hours, tracing possible paths with his fingers. At age nine, his only hobbies seemed to be watching television and daydreaming. He is, or has been, interested in a variety of subjects. "I'm interested in lots of things," he once told me: sure – trains, dinosaurs, Star Wars, history, human biology, and astronomy. For years he was going to become a space scientist. More recently, he is going to become a paleontologist, and dig up dinosaur bones. He likes talking about these subjects, but they do not lend themselves to many conversations with his peers, especially the way he talks about them. These interests in a child, while impressive in some ways, do not lend themselves to the child doing much. Andy has put together a few dinosaur models but does not particularly enjoy that activity, and did it only because we pressed him. He likes to visit museums and has been to the natural history museum in Philadelphia many times. He enjoys watching videos about his favorite subjects. He discusses them to some extent, but he is really just retelling them.

Daydreaming

Many children with Asperger's Syndrome, and other autistic spectrum disorders, tend to daydream a lot, to "zone out" from the rest of the world. Probably this tendency is a result of the amount of effort it requires for them to interact with the world, or of the sensory overload they experience. I have found this tendency to be a difficult problem with my son, who sometimes seems to daydream constantly, because it is intractable. We can keep him from watching too much television, as other parents have limited their Asperger's child's time on the computer or on a gameboy, but limiting daydreaming is more difficult. Some children jump around while daydreaming, or talk out loud, not appropriate in public. Everybody needs some "down time" but autistic individuals need more than most, sometimes far more. As zoning out excessively is no good, especially at school or work, this can be a serious problem, leading to failure in school or a job, or worse, a serious accident while driving a car or riding a bike.

What can you do about it? When the government tries to change people's eating habits, it starts with their current eating habits and tries to modify them in ways that seem possible. If an overwhelming percentage of the population of Georgia eats fried chicken six times a week and has for generations, and has a correspondingly high rate of heart disease, public health officials know they can neither ban fried chicken nor persuade everybody to switch to granola and carrot juice. Instead they promote canola oil, baked chicken, and suggest rice instead of macaroni salad (or at least whole wheat macaroni in the salad). We cannot change our children's personalities, but can try to mold them in appropriate ways, steer them toward wholesome, useful activities that they might like and be able to do. For a child who jumps around while daydreaming, a martial arts class may lead the child to incorporate karate moves into his daydreams, a more normal, useful, and connected to the rest of the world type of daydreaming than aimless movement. If your home has room for a small trampoline, a treadmill, or a stair-stepper, the child can daydream while using this equipment, and will at least be getting some exercise. A child might daydream while jogging, provided the jogging route is safe and he is able to pay some minimal attention to it. Perhaps you can make a deal with your child: he can daydream for an hour but then has to spend 15 minutes writing a story from his daydream. You can try to schedule in daydreaming time (or "zone out," "veg out," or "autistic" time) for your child and persuade him to limit daydreaming to the scheduled time. These children need some time to themselves. It's just a matter of getting them to work it into an acceptable schedule or activity.

Recreational activities

A crucial support for individuals with Asperger's Syndrome in daily life is the development of leisure activities. You cannot be working with them all the time, and they have to learn to do something wholesome or useful independently. Besides the need for children to do something while not being actively supervised or taught by an adult, you have to be concerned about what leisure activities these individuals might like as adults. Daydreaming, staring at fans, stacking blocks in a line repeatedly in the same way, or doing mazes are too limiting to be appropriate activities for all of one's spare time. Many children with Developmental Coordination Disorder watch too much television. It is crucial for parents to find something a bit more active for them to do around the house. However, it is difficult, especially when they are too young to read. Playing with other children is a strain. Crafts and sewing are so difficult that they are not very pleasurable, and cooking is not something you can allow young children to do by themselves. If a child does take to reading, that is a much more acceptable leisure activity than some, but still not very physically active.

Walking, hiking, gardening and baking are possibilities, reasonably consistent with an Asperger's personality, and also checkers and chess (if you can find one person to play against), and computer activities. Checkers and chess are not solitary activities, so they involve input from parents, but if you can get the child started he or she might like to play with a brother or sister. There are chess computer programs for all levels.

Many crafts are recommended as good for fine motor skills, and even Legos for younger children, but they are often too difficult to be pleasurable enough for these children to do them on their own. Legos are fairly easy to work with, and so are K'nex. See what crafts your child might be able to do and enjoy, and to do with little assistance. Playing with clay might be good. There are all kinds of crafts packages for children now; some of them might suit.

You can have the child help you with the housework while young, give him simple tasks and make it as enjoyable as possible, and when older the child might take up cooking. Baking is good, once the child is old enough.

Computer games are an acceptable activity if you try to keep them educational (in a broad sense). Also, some home video games that build up fine motor control are appropriate, but you have to limit the time spent on these. Also, let your child enjoy the things he is good at, and try to build them into some sort of activity. The child could surf the internet concerning his special interest, perhaps even use chatrooms to connect with other fans.

As for physical activities, a child with Asperger's could develop an interest in martial arts, hiking, running, or swimming. There are small, safe trampolines now, low to the ground, without metal springs. You can just tilt them up against a wall when not using them.

Riding a bike is a difficult skill to master for many of these children. Because it is a very common activity among children though, don't give up on it. Take things in small steps. First work on sense of balance, trunk strength, and leg strength, to get ready. Maybe use a stationary bike for leg strength. For balance, try having your child sit on a barrel or giant ball and learn to get himself back on balance with small moves. Then get the right bike. There are a lot of bikes for people with special needs, but they mostly have three wheels. A three-wheeled bike is okay for a start to get the leg strength, but your child might not like to be seen on one. Work with a bike store manager to get the right bike. A regular bike can be modified to make it more stable. There are different schools of thought on training wheels. I'd use them for a particularly uncoordinated kid. Of course, use a helmet. Occupational therapists and physical therapists can help, and sometimes you can even get insurance to pay for it.

When the child is young, these activities require some parental support but not too intensively, and they are activities an older child can do alone or with someone, if they ever have a friend. It is hard to have really varied activities for these children, but make sure to have some more active "screen time" options, such as computer games and surfing the internet, rather than only watching television and looking at books. Any activity they really enjoy will probably have to be limited, as otherwise children with Asperger's tend to engage in it to the exclusion of everything else.

It is difficult to get much help from schools in this area of recreational activities as it is difficult to convince them that the development of leisure skills is necessary for a child's education. However, one of the implementing regulations of the IDEA states that school districts shall take steps to provide extracurricular activities in the manner necessary to afford children with disabilities an equal opportunity for participation, including athletics, recreational activities, and special interest groups of clubs (34 C.F.R. 300.306 (a) and (b)). Section 504 of the Rehabilitation Act also requires that school districts allow children with disabilities to participate in extracurricular activities, but does not require that extracurricular activities be designed especially for them.

Occupational therapists can help in this area, although probably not the ones in school districts. If you have health insurance that covers occupational therapy, the insurance company will probably approve development of leisure activities as a goal.

Television

Television time, like everything else, should be limited. Limited television is okay; at least it keeps these children in some contact with popular culture. With too much television time, they get too sedentary, resulting in low muscle tone. Television is not interactive, but it shows them how people behave to some extent. It demonstrates expressions, gestures, and posture more than reading a book can. In fact, one suggested intervention for children with Non-verbal Learning Disorder is to watch soap operas with the sound off.

Sometimes children with Asperger's prefer educational programs or videotapes (as well as preferring nonfiction books to fiction). Encourage them to watch something that shows children their age interacting normally.

Home-made social skills groups

Various websites discuss how to form your own support group for parents of children with special needs. There is not much information on forming your own social skills group, which might be more useful. Such a group could be something like a brownie group for the socially challenged. Possibly you could get a bunch of parents together and hire an occupational therapist or speech therapist. Finding the right kids, that is the ones with overlapping developmental levels, able to meet at the same time and place is the biggest challenge, just as it is for a therapist trying to start such a group. And where would you meet? People's homes? You could do that. Although private homes do not have as much equipment as an occupational therapy facility, they could easily have enough equipment, plenty of board games, as well as a home atmosphere. Even if you just winged it without a therapist to guide you, you could get ideas from literature, each other, observing therapists in the past or talking with therapists.

Such a club should have a routine – maybe story, crafts, snack, depending on how old the children are – to be followed each time it meets. It could have games requiring verbal interaction or physical cooperation. Also, a social skills group, even if it is not helping your child improve social skills outside the group, may function as a club with safe play for your child. Usually those kids will invite him to birthday parties and come to his. This organized, prear-ranged social life is better than none. Putting two socially inept kids together often doesn't result in warm relationship, but you have to take what you can get.

Anger and disgust with the child

Perhaps you are reading the ideas for activities suggested in this book, or maybe put to you by professional advisors, and thinking, "It's all very well to say 'Have him do this, have him do that' but it's impossible to get my child to do anything." In hearing about other children with disabilities, especially those described as "an inspiring story," you hear of children with cerebral palsy, born without arms, or paralyzed in terrible accidents, who push them-selves to rehabilitate, to learn to ride a bike or mow the lawn without arms, to learn to walk upstairs despite paralyzed legs. You even hear about retarded children who learn as much as they can, or see the movie portrayal of retarded Forrest Gump, who served with distinction in the army and started a success-ful seafood line.

Meanwhile, your child seems to have no interest in learning new activities, activities of which he is clearly physically and intellectually capable. In fact, there seems to be very little wrong with your child, except for poor coordina-tion and a few odd learning characteristics, if he would just do things. But that is part of the problem with autistic spectrum disorders. People with them don't evince much interest in the world, and therefore are less likely to develop hobbies beyond narrow, constricted limits.

Why won't your child just learn to compensate for his or her few obvious problems? According to Lorna Wing, who has studied individuals with autistic spectrum disorders as much as anyone: "Motivation to acquire and use self-care and adaptive skills is conspicuous by its absence in children with autistic spectrum disorders, however high their level of cognitive ability" (Wing 2000, pp.422–423).

Why are these adaptive skills lacking? As so much with this syndrome, researchers have observed this symptom but do not know why it occurs. A. Jean Ayres, the occupational therapist who came up with the idea of Sensory Integration Dysfunction, speculated that the part of the brain that makes us want to do things is not functioning right in autistic individuals. Ayres describes the situations normal people sometimes go through, of not wanting to get up and go, usually if feeling sleepy, of wanting to remain lying down and ignore the world: "This feeling, which the fairly normal person experiences once in a while, is somewhat similar to what the autistic child feels most of the time" (Ayres 1979, pp.127–128).

What can you do to get your child to develop more initiative? Having a child who is physically and cognitively intact, but still apparently unwilling to meet the world is enormously frustrating, but patience is the only viable road. You cannot make a child interested in things, any more than you can make a toddler use the bathroom. Gentle nudges, delivered as part of a larger program, are the only avenue. Only patience and persistence, pushing the child along in small increments, finding activities connected with some interest of the child's, teaching him to play in small steps, getting him to have slightly more normal conversations with practice, will help bring the child out into the larger world. It is very frustrating to search the world over for appropriate activities only to have the child decline to participate in them, but getting angry won't help. The child holds the ultimate weapon – complete withdrawal.

Children with Asperger's Syndrome are usually clued in enough to pick up on what their parents think of them, even if they miss what their classmates think. If you are disgusted with your child, try to remember that Asperger's Syndrome is a very serious, though subtle, disorder. Remember how frustrating it must be to have ability in one area but lack the wherewithal to make use of it. Remember that your child may want to have friends but not know how to make them, may want to show off his knowledge but be unable to communicate it, may want a career as an astronomer or historian, but be unable to get close.

Even remembering all that, it is natural to feel frustrated, angry, or disgusted sometimes. The only advice I can offer is the advice you find elsewhere: talk to your partner, commiserate with other parents. Possibly join a support group. Joining a support group is better than giving way to anger and disgust. And do not minimize the effect that disappointment in offspring can have on a marriage.

Marriage

All children put pressure on a marriage. The parents cannot spend as much time alone together, and there is always the potential for disagreement over childrearing. In an advice column on family life in a general newspaper, the columnist answered someone's question on how they could best help their children by saying "Pay attention to your marriage." This is good advice for all parents.

If children put strain on a marriage, children with special needs add a greater strain, but it is more important than ever that the parents stay together, so work on your marriage even if that appears superficially to be at the expense of the children.

Various websites tell me that families with a "special needs" child face a 50 percent or higher risk of divorce, which is easy to believe considering that is what we hear about all marriages. Hard figures on the subject either do not exist or are nearly impossible to find, but plenty of anecdotal evidence indicates stress on these marriages. But despite the high divorce rate, marriage is more important than ever in cases of children with special needs. A survey done by Bashe and Kirby found that parents of children with Asperger's considered their partner their primary source of support, even if one partner did most of the work related to Asperger's (Bashe and Kirby 2001, p.137). Mitzi Waltz acknowledges the stress a child with special needs can put on a marriage, but reminds readers that even if one parent does most of the extra work involving that special need, the other is still an adult sounding board and a shoulder to cry on (Waltz 1999). Besides the pluses of having another parent around to help, and all the children in the family benefiting from the care of two parents, the parents' marriage is also a model of a relationship for children in the family. For children with Asperger's Syndrome, who in many cases pay little attention to people outside their own families, that relationship is one of the few examples they have of how to treat peers.

Having a child with special needs opens up areas for marital difficulties that would not otherwise exist. The most common problem scenarios include one partner handling all the extra burden of the special needs, disagreement between the parents on how to handle the child's special needs, financial strain, having to change residences, and one partner letting the special needs become consuming.

The unshared burden

In many families, although perhaps less so than ever before, one partner does more than the other in terms of raising children, and the other does more to support the family financially, often working long hours. There is a lot of variation on this theme. I know many marriages in which the partners contributed roughly equal earnings for several years, but when children came along, started school, or started having problems, the mother cut back on work hours and the family became more dependent on the father's income. According to OASIS authors Bashe and Kirby, the mothers of children with Asperger's Syndrome often cut down on their hours or leave their jobs (Bashe and Kirby 2001, p.139). To take a child to weekly or twice-weekly therapy appointments, with the attendant traveling logistics, uses more time than most employers will allow for sick time. Whoever did the most childcare usually starts making the necessary arrangements to meet whatever special needs there are.

In some ways it is good to have one person take the point on the many phone calls, networking, and arrangement making. However, when one partner does most of that sometimes traumatic work, gives up the ability to generate income, or perhaps forgoes dreamt of career opportunities, that partner can feel dumped on, and sometimes is in fact shouldering an unfair share of the burden. Meeting the special needs of a child with Asperger's Syndrome cannot simply be added to the general childcare chores of one partner.

Marriage is sometimes a giant points system, in which every chore is expected to be reimbursed at some future time: I cook, you clean; I do the housework, you pay the bills. Having children only adds to this. I changed the baby in the middle of dinner yesterday; I stayed home with the sick child yesterday; you do it today. I got up in the middle of the night last night. But even if the parent not taking the point on Asperger's Syndrome makes up for it by doing the grocery shopping, the emotional burden would not be shared.

To avoid or minimize this potential marital problem, the other partner can read about Asperger's Syndrome or whatever condition affects the child, take the child to a few of the therapy sessions, and work with the child at home as part of the team. When going to school meetings, not only should both partners go (unless the meeting is very routine), but both should prepare ahead of time, so they are not just passive spectators. In other words, both partners should be part of the team, not just on the sidelines, even if one is taking the point.

Disagreement over handling the child

To some parents it may seem that one partner making all the decisions is a blessing, as it spares disagreements over what to do. Sometimes one parent takes the diagnosis more seriously than the other, not only in reading about it and working on getting an intervention program together, but in how he or she approaches the child. The other parent may think the first one handles the child with kid gloves. In *News From the Border*, Jane McDonnell (1997) shows such a situation in her family. The father took more of a disciplinarian's approach to their autistic child than she did. Mitzi Waltz also describes the possibility of one parent wanting to take a more severe attitude toward the child than the other, running up to add another punishment as the child is being dealt with by the other parent for some infraction (Waltz 1999). To minimize the destructive consequences of this scenario, the parents should be guided by a professional with expertise in Asperger's Syndrome, and work out a general plan for managing the child's behavior. It might help to use something like school forms for behavior improvement plans as a model with specific objectives and strategies, to have a conference between the two parents with such a form in order to see where the areas of disagreement are, and to discuss them away from the child and apart from any immediate crisis.

Financial aspects

There is often some loss of income associated with having a child with Asperger's Syndrome (there is often some loss of income associated with having children at all). Parents may have to curtail their money-earning hours in order to take their child to various service providers. There can also be some heavy expenses. If Asperger's leads the parents to go to a private school rather than a public one, the cost can be $10,000 to $20,000 a year, depending on whether the school is tailored for children with special needs. Many parents pay for speech and occupational therapy beyond what their school district is willing to give them. Special summer camps, or tutoring, can also play a financial role. These expenses, loss of income, or both, can lead to financial strain, and financial strain often leads to marital strain. To minimize this, make a budget, and remember that exceptionally talented children can be very expensive too, what with lessons, and trips to play in tournaments or perform.

Having to change residences

The most likely cause for changing residence would be to locate in a more amenable school district. As soon as our son was diagnosed with special needs, professionals and others advised us to move out of the city to an affluent suburban school district. A news article in the *Seattle Times* stated that families across the country were moving to Seattle for a chance to get a place in one of the special education classes designed for children with Asperger's Syndrome. Of course many families of typical children move to find better school districts; in my home city of Philadelphia it is a leading cause of city population loss. Any decision to change residence should be made with the entire family in mind. In our case it would have cost my husband a job that he loved. Moving should not be done for one member of the family at the expense of the others. You can get your own school district to come up with an acceptable program if you devote enough energy to working with, or struggling with, your district on it.

One partner letting the special needs become all consuming

Sometimes one partner doing all of the work can be more of a problem than the resentment of the unshared burden. Some parents become driven to help their children beat the odds, or to "cure" them. Some mothers talk about their children all the time, becoming obsessed with the need to provide support for them at all costs. They ignore their other responsibilities as wife, mother of other children, homeowner, employee, neighbor, citizen. This is not good. No one child should be the center of family life.

This is yet another reason why both parents should share in managing the special needs of a child with Asperger's Syndrome, even if the total household work is split 50/50. It should be remembered that marriage, not children, is the cornerstone of family life. This is one more reason for remembering that if you do not take care of yourself, you will not be able to take care of others.

Divorce

If divorce, for whatever reasons, does occur, remember the resulting difficulties for all your children may fall hardest on the one with Asperger's Syndrome, who may have unusual difficulty adapting to the abrupt changes. You will need to do everything you can to keep his or her routine the same. To the extent possible, make sure both parents are using the same behavioral modification techniques, and agree on medication, or at least implement it consistently. An abrupt change in school would not be a good idea at any time, but immediately after a parental separation would be particularly bad timing.

If you are eventually remarried, you and your new spouse may model a loving relationship for your children, and the new spouse may be a wonderful stepparent, but family relationships will always be a balancing act for you.

Siblings

Besides the parent's example of a loving relationship, sibling relationships are models of peer relationships, if you have siblings near the same age. Ideally, the siblings play together and the impaired one gets some play practice and friendship practice that way.

In *What About Me? Growing Up With a Developmentally Disabled Sibling*, Bryna Siegal and Stuart C. Silverstein (1994) state that in families where there is a child with a disability, the balance of family life and energy will tilt subtly in favor of the disabled one. This shift can be manifested in many different ways. At worst, the other children might not get enough parental attention or not enough financial support, but more likely the parents' perception of them may be colored by their knowledge of the other child's special needs. The Asperger's child might get a greater share of concern than the siblings in some cases, but in others, especially in undiagnosed cases, the child with Asperger's may be the black sheep. Asperger's is a subtle disorder, with no obvious handicap. Why individuals of normal intelligence, without physical disabilities, should behave as inappropriately as children, even grown-ups, with Asperger's Syndrome are sometimes prone to do, is a mystery to anyone without knowledge of the disorder or exceptional intuition. If the parents protect or give special treatment to the child with Asperger's, without explaining why, the other children may resent it, and turn against their brother or sister.

One variation on the black sheep theme is that the child may be perceived as helpless as a young child and therefore protected and nurtured, but as the child becomes a difficult teenager who appears to have no energy, initiative, or willingness to deal with any of his own problems despite his brains, the kindly attitude drops off and the family turns against him.

In some cases, the child with Asperger's may be babied more than the other children; in some cases the child with Asperger's is pushed more. In high school, I occasionally volunteered to work with handicapped children. These children were severely handicapped, usually paralyzed and retarded. A common theme among their excellent treaters – physical and occupational therapists – was never to do anything for them that they could do themselves. Therefore I rarely did anything for Andy that he could do for himself, at least physical tasks. On the other hand, I have sometimes babied our younger daughter; sometimes I like to baby her, and I figure it is okay to do so since she is developing normally anyway. When she was four and a half, I realized that

Andy had dressed himself better at that age than she did, and I began to resent being a servant to her.

There is no way to avoid any impact on the family. Children always affect a family. Diagnosis is probably the first step to avoiding harmful family attitudes. Diagnosis should probably be shared with all of the family at some point, although young children do not need the name of the disorder. Just let them know their brother or sister has trouble socializing.

Home routine

Mealtimes

In another example of children with special needs having the same needs as other children, only more so, family meals are important for all children to practice manners and intergenerational conversation. Not only is training in these skills extra important to children with Asperger's Syndrome, but family meals give structure to home life.

NEAT EATING

When I was in college, some of my classmates had occasion to visit mental hospitals, and in some cases, to eat with the residents. Even though they were interested in helping these residents, the idea of sharing meals with them filled them with concern, even distaste. One of them asked, "Do they eat, uh, strange?" I also know that at some good programs for retarded children, the staff work hard to instill correct eating habits into their charges. They know many people are put off by sloppy eating habits, especially if their attitude toward the eaters is skeptical to begin with. If I ever had to choose a residential facility for a retarded or autistic child or adult, mealtimes would be one of the first things I would look at.

Eating is a social event, and Asperger's people are already handicapped in the social arena. There is no need to exacerbate the situation by sloppy eating habits. Yet, with poor manual dexterity and obliviousness to social conventions, sloppy eating is a tendency. Therefore, pay close attention to your child's table manners. By table manners, I do not mean saying please and thank you, but physically feeding oneself. If a 7-year-old child has the physical table manners of a 2-year-old, and parental badgering does not seem to be working, consult an occupational therapist for help. This area is very much their purview. Sometimes the mouth muscles as well as the finger muscles are involved if you notice food falling from the child's mouth. They can prescribe oral exercises. Sometimes it is a matter of balancing food on the spoon while it is on the way to the mouth. Sometimes the problem is the ability to get the food onto the spoon without using fingers. As with every type of task, occupational therapists will break the task of eating into discrete parts, and work on the motor skills involved in each one.

Some of the oral exercises occupational therapists suggest include such things as sucking through a straw (we tried practicing with spaghetti with Andy), blowing bubbles, maybe even manipulating bubblegum. For getting food onto the spoon they usually suggest using a knife or spoon as a backstop. The key is to find an activity that your child enjoys which uses the same motor skills as feeding oneself; maybe lifting sand in a sandbox with a small implement, and using that activity as drilling in disguise. One simple formula to help is taking small bites and finishing each one before starting the next.

VERBAL MANNERS

Of course, saying please and thank you and not bolting your food before everyone is seated, which do not require fine motor skills, are such a major part of good table manners that proficiency in them will alleviate the bad impression given by poor feeding skills.

Mealtimes are also a time to practice conversation. As your child probably feels more relaxed at dinnertime in your home than he does at school recess, make sure there are opportunities for conversation at your dinner table. Do not eat with the television on, and have family meals.

Sleeping

Sleeping problems are common with this syndrome. The children need a bedtime routine. Tire the child out. Consult the pediatrician or psychiatrist if the child cannot fall asleep. Dr. Mark Durant (1998) has written a guide for improving the sleep patterns of children with special needs, *Sleep Better! A Guide to Improving Sleep for Children with Special Needs*. Medication may be necessary. Unfortunately, sometimes medication may be contributing to the problem, as antidepressants such as Prozac and its relatives have been associated with some sleep difficulties. A medical doctor will have to advise you on this point.

Hygiene

In writing about adults with Asperger's living alone, Lorna Wing stated that "tactful supervision may be needed to ensure that rooms are kept clean and tidy and clothes are changed regularly" (Wing 1981, p.129). People with an autistic spectrum disorder are not much concerned with personal appearance because they aren't much concerned with social interaction. Of course sloppy, unkempt appearance is one more social handicap.

Margaret Dewey, psychology professor and mother of an adult with Asperger's Syndrome, gives the following advice: keep it simple (Dewey 1991). Have a simple checklist for the mornings. Tape it to the child's mirror. Modify it every once in a while in consultation with the child. My own advice is to keep hair short.

Holidays

Holidays, despite the joy they are meant for, are stressful for many people, with December often a mad scramble and the suicide rates peaking. The sensory stimulation of music and bustling on the streets, people hurrying everywhere, combined with feelings of pressure on the part of adults, and a social whirlwind of parties, festivities, and get-togethers, topped off by travel, may make the holiday season a time to fall apart for those with social and sensory processing impairments. Mothers of typical children have told me "Every year I tell myself that this year I am going to cut back, keep it under control, make it more meaningful" but it is difficult to follow through. If you have a child with an Asperger's-like disorder, congratulations! You now have a real incentive to keep the frenzy out of the holidays and to allow the joy in.

The religious side of the holidays can help with this, if you are raising your children in any religion. Try to see the holidays as part of the liturgical year; that adds a lot of structure. Get an Advent calendar and an Advent wreath. Light the candles each week at home and let the children open the doors on the Advent calendar each day. The daily structure of Ramadan, with the predawn and after dusk meals, and its emphasis on reflection, can be helpful. Schedule daily time for reflection in your household. The eight days of gift giving of Hanukkah can diffuse the intensity that can come with gift giving on a single day. One way to diffuse the possible intensity of Christmas is to stretch out the gift giving over the twelve days of Christmas.

Structure can come from the secular world. Advent calendars are generally not religious at all. Your family can establish a holiday season routine, perhaps having Christmas Eve dinner at home with only nuclear family and Christmas and Christmas Day at grandmother's house every year, or having dinner with certain relatives in a set order during the eight days of Hanukkah. Light the

candles at the same time each day, and make some routine for the gift giving –
opening the presents in order of youngest to oldest or whatever. Develop
certain customs for the holidays that you do annually, such as buying and dec-
orating the tree or house at the same time each year. Most holidays come with
customs; incorporate them into your household. Liturgy, customs, and a
schedule will provide your children with structure for the holidays rather than
frenzy.

Summer camps

For many, summer is a hole in the year. The structure of school is ended; the
child's routine is disrupted. Possibly all the other children in the neighborhood are happily playing outside, while your child is inside in a funk. Then
there is the issue of childcare.

The Philadelphia edition of the magazine *Parents Express* (July 2003) published an article on summer with special needs kids. I looked at it with interest,
hoping for a list of programs, but all it said was to take time this summer to
enjoy your special child: "It's time to reconnect and allow yourself pleasure in
being a parent." That's very nice if possible, but what if the parent's work
schedule forces sticking the child somewhere. Where? There are no IEPs in
summer camps. Will the stress create a backward slide?

There are a few summer overnight camp programs for children with
Asperger's Syndrome and similar disorders. However, they are few, far
between, and quite expensive. Some children may qualify for year-round
instruction from the school district. However, in most school districts
remedial summer programs focus on academics only. There are a few
examples of school districts paying for recreational programs during the
summer if the parents could prove that the child would otherwise regress over
the summer to the point where ability to make progress during the school year
would be impaired, but these few examples occurred after litigation, and such
litigation is cutting edge with inconsistent results.[1]

---

1   In *Dracut Public Schools* (35 I.D.E.L.R. 57), a Massachusetts school district was
       ordered to pay for a student to attend a recreational day camp during the
       summer, as cited by Bazelon Center for Mental Health Law in "Teaming Up:
       Using the IDEA and Medicaid to Secure Comprehensive Mental Health
       Services for Children and Youth," p.10.

Most summer day camps are too sportsy to be a good match for children with Asperger's Syndrome or other disorders involving coordination dysfunction. Day camps in urban settings may feature field trips to cultural institutions, which such children may find more appealing. Pick one with as much structure as possible. There may be camps which cater to your child's special interest, but they are usually expensive and brief, and then you have to switch to another program which your child may have to enter in mid-session. Such camps might still be an excellent idea if you can arrange the rest of the summer. The best plan might be to find a structured day camp that your child likes, and then send him to it year after year.

Services for mildly autistic adults

I have often thought, while watching severely disabled children, that their childhoods are not so sad or abnormal. They live with their families and go to school, and are usually in more or less appropriate programs. It is when they become adults that their disabilities really prevent them from leading any kind of a life. Severely retarded children in appropriate programs seem happy enough, but I wonder whether adults living in an institution are happy. So much depends on their program, upon which they are completely dependent.

However, for retarded adults there does seem to be something of a continuum of alternative placements. Some, who need a great deal of care and supervision, are placed in hospitals, group homes, or homes with custodians. Others, who are semi-independent, sometimes live in private apartments with someone to check on them. One apartment complex I knew of had one three-bedroom apartment for three mildly retarded adults, who had a social worker spend several hours a day there. At night they were on their own. In several adjacent apartments were higher functioning adults, who had some degree of mental retardation, to whom the social worker was available, but they were more independent, had their own individual kitchens. Something like that is needed for autistic adults, but right now such services are usually available to autistic people only if they are also retarded, and even for mildly retarded adults there are not enough of these semi-dependent placements.

Autistic adults are only now getting any attention at all. A few small advocacy groups made up of parents have started agitating for some attention to the need in this area. A recently founded advocacy group in Connecticut called Friends of Autistic People says on its website: "Autistic children have recently been noticed and through legislation many services have become available to them. Autistic adults, however, are completely forgotten." An organization of parents in Illinois called the Foundation for Autism Services Today and Tomorrow is trying to raise money to establish a farm community for autistic adults. These groups are mainly concerned with adults with classic autism, who may be inappropriately placed in institutions for people with severe mental disabilities other than autism, or living in their aging parents' homes with no community services.

There has been growth in interest in services for high-functioning autistic individuals. Small advocacy groups are springing up in various states. The state of Connecticut recently decided to fund a study on providing services like those for retarded citizens to young autistic adults who are not retarded. There is a group in Pennsylvania, called Autism Living and Working (ALAW), which is involved in setting up housing for higher functioning adults with autistic spectrum disorders, with parents joining together to buy houses for them and working with government agencies to provide services to the residents of those houses.

But more needs to be done. Mildly autistic adults, including those with Asperger's Syndrome, are often unemployed or underemployed, and socially isolated. I am acquainted with several adults who strike me as probably having Asperger's, and they have a very difficult time fitting in anywhere. Various websites posted by adults who identify themselves as having Asperger's Syndrome tell of unhappy, wasted lives. Some of them live on disability, some do not qualify for disability as seeming too high functioning, and very few seem really happy.

I do not know of any significant services specifically tailored to this population. I know at one point Miami-Dade's Recreational Department offered a recreation program for mildly autistic adults which met about an hour a week for several weeks. A self-help group comprised of adults with Asperger's Syndrome in New Jersey has occasional picnics and social events. I am sure there are a few other programs scattered about the country, but they barely touch the surface of the need. There are some programs for people with disabilities that adults with Asperger's Syndrome can sometimes take advantage of, but these programs are not tailored to their needs.

The Comprehensive Employment and Training Act (CETA) was formerly a source of temporary jobs and training for adults with disabilities. Its services, at least the training aspect, have been partially replaced by state vocational rehabilitation programs. Check with your state's vocational rehabilitation program to see if your child is eligible for job training or counseling. Be careful of diagnosis at this point though. States differ, but Pervasive Developmental Disorder, or Developmental Coordination Disorder, both in the DSM, are more likely to get help than Nonverbal Learning Disorder or Sensory Integration Disorder, which are not in the DSM.

The Social Security Administration may also be a source of assistance, but it has its own definitions of disability. The Social Security Administration administers two payment programs for adults with disabilities, Social Security disability benefits and Supplemental Security Income (SSI). Social Security disability benefits are available to individuals who have worked and paid into the Social Security system but who are now too disabled to work. Supplemental Security Income benefits are paid to individuals who are poor and disabled. These individuals do not necessarily have to have ever been employed and paid into the system, as this program is funded by general tax revenues rather than by Social Security contributions. There is an income ceiling for this benefit, but an adult with no income meets it unless he or she has significant assets. The financial requirements are complicated and take into account living with parents, but there is a sliding scale, and most people qualify who are unemployed as a result of disability. A medical review board decides whether an applicant meets the requisite definition of disability. Although disability benefits can be a lifeline, parents do not look forward to having their children with Asperger's Syndrome spend their adult lives on disability, which is a horrible waste of these intelligent people.

Increasing interest and information

One of the biggest problems in the US social service system is lack of information. There is a lot of information around, but with 50 different states with their own laws, regulations, and funding, and the lack of coordination between the healthcare system and the educational system, it is difficult to sift through all the bits of information and difficult to have a comprehensive notion of how to proceed. Networking is helpful, but not easy because Asperger's is so rare. Networking may work best with other parents in social skills groups. Of course, if the group is school based, which is in some ways ideal, networking is much harder than if you are taking the child to the social skills group and hanging around the waiting room with other parents. Providers sometimes have brochures available, which give phone numbers. The local or state chapter of the American Society for Autism (ASA) has some useful information, and it now has chapters in all 50 states.

There is a burgeoning amount published about Asperger's Syndrome, website after website, news article after news article, book after book. Diagnoses are escalating too, especially mild ones. Mostly this attention is good. Schools and employers are bound to get more familiar with the syndrome.

Advocacy

When I think about advocacy for children and adults with autistic spectrum disorders, the model I look to is the work done by the ARC. Advocates for citizens with mental retardation have been enormously successful in getting services for retarded children and adults. The ARC was founded in 1950 as the National Association for Retarded Citizens in response to the exclusion of retarded children from schools, lack of community services, long waiting lists for residential facilities, and parental dissatisfaction with conditions in state institutions. Long-term placement in state hospitals was commonplace then, and those hospitals usually let their residents languish with few programs and no education. Eventually scandals erupted over poor treatment.

At the same time as hospitalization was considered the way to handle retarded people, schools restricted the enrollment of retarded children. Schools instituted IQ cut-off limits and tests for kindergartners such as tying shoes, much like literacy tests for voting in Southern states. In the 1950s and 1960s, some parents of retarded children started organizing to run educational programs on their own, in their homes, in rented space, in church basements. In the 1960s, some parents tried to enroll their children in school, but were turned away. In 1971, inspired by the civil rights movement, the Pennsylvania ARC brought a lawsuit against the Commonwealth of Pennsylvania in federal court, complaining of the exclusion of retarded children from public schools. In a seminal decision, the court prohibited Pennsylvania from applying its statute excluding children with mental retardation from public education, and ordered the Commonwealth to provide all retarded children from ages 6 to 21 with a free public education appropriate to each one's learning capacity.[2] This court decision, along with other triggers, led Congress to study the situation regarding handicapped children in US schools. The Rehabilitation Act, with its Section 504 prohibiting discrimination in public schools, followed shortly after in 1973. The Education for All

---

2   This decision can be found at 334 F. Supp. 1257.

Handicapped Children Act, the IDEA predecessor, with its emphasis on integration, followed soon after in 1975.

But advocates for children with mental retardation did not stop there. Various ARCs across the country started afterschool and summer programs, or pushed others to start them, and campaigned for programs for retarded adults. In Philadelphia, a lawsuit filed by advocates of retarded adults led to a 1977 court decision which closed a notorious hospital and provided generous funding for community services for the discharged residents.

In the last 30 years, thanks to these advocates, there has been a revolution in care for citizens with mental retardation, even in the long-term hospitals. Not only that, but it is largely due to their efforts that we owe the IDEA. Maybe most important of all, these advocates, together with the effects of the measures they brought to pass, have caused a revolution in the way most citizens think about people with disabilities. They are no longer simply to be cared for, but to be educated and integrated into society at large to the greatest extent possible.

Asperger's Syndrome has been getting a lot of attention in the mainstream press, but advocates for those whom it affects are just beginning to get organized, and at this point mainly just share information – certainly valuable work. More needs to be done in terms of making services available. With just a little more education, people may start recognizing the odd individuals they thought of as weirdos as having a specific, manageable disability along with a lot of talents. With more social programs for these individuals, our children, their lives could be a lot less lonely. With more teachers educated about their profile of needs and strengths, their education could be much more productive. With more job counselors trained to work with them, their employment possibilities could go way up. There is no reason at all for them not to lead happy lives, using their abilities as productive members of society.

Conclusion

Diagnosis is not fixed, but may vary depending on who gives you the diagnosis, how you describe the symptoms or how thoroughly the diagnostician conducts the evaluation. Although Asperger's Syndrome and the other conditions described in Part I are lifelong, their symptoms, or presentation, do sometimes change as the individuals develop. But while diagnosis can be fluid, the system for delivering services uses fixed definitions, so labels are important to obtaining services.

All the treatments, interventions, and supports for Asperger's Syndrome, with the exception of medication, fall under the category of special education, broadly defined. People with Asperger's need help learning to converse, to socialize, to be flexible, and, in most cases, to use their hands effectively. This specialized training is the province of both the world of healthcare and the world of education. Unfortunately, these worlds do not work together very closely. The diagnosticians, who know the most about these conditions, usually have no involvement in their treatment. Speech, occupational, and physical therapists from outside the school system work in something of a vacuum when it comes to treating developmental disorders, and are often able to work only on discrete skills. The system of healthcare delivery is a huge patchwork of private and public funding at all levels, and not everyone can get the necessary supports for Asperger's Syndrome from it. Because of the IDEA, and because there is universal public education, children with Asperger's Syndrome are entitled to assistance from the school system, but schools are just beginning to develop an understanding of Asperger's Syndrome.

Public policy makers need to do more to integrate services; school districts and health insurance should not be at odds. If a special need is described as educational the school district is supposed to take care of it; if it is described as medical then health insurance is supposed to take care of it. With Asperger's Syndrome and other handicaps, the medical and educational aspects are not easily separated.

Asperger's Syndrome is getting more attention. More doctors are aware of the range of autistic spectrum disorders, and there are more social skills training groups than ever before. More services may soon be tailored to it. That would certainly be a wonderful thing, but it would also be helpful if there were better coordination of services. Perhaps in the future it will be routine for psychiatrists to be on school district staffs. Perhaps some social workers will specialize in autistic disorders, and be in a position to advise parents on how to get services from different segments of the social service system, and which services and which providers might be best for their child. (I am not sure who would pay these social workers, who are now usually employed by one entity within the social service system.) Individuals with Asperger's Syndrome are all so different that until then, and to some extent always, their parents, and later they themselves, are going to have to be the "program managers," stitching together what services are available in consultation with whatever experts they can find.

Diagnostic Criteria for Disorders Related to Asperger's Syndrome

DSM-IV definitions for related disorders

Reprinted by permission of the American Psychiatric Association. What follows are the American Psychiatric Association's criteria for several disorders similar to Asperger's Syndrome. You may find your child is close to fitting one of these sets of diagnostic criteria.

Diagnostic Criteria for 299.00 Autistic Disorder:

A.   A total of six (or more) items from (1), (2), and (3), with at least two from (1), and one each from (2) and (3):

(1) qualitative impairment in social interaction, as manifested by at least two of the following:

    (a) marked impairment in the use of multiple nonverbal behaviors such as eye-to-eye gaze, facial expression, body postures, and gestures to regulate social interaction

    (b) failure to develop peer relationships appropriate to developmental level

    (c) a lack of spontaneous seeking to share enjoyment, interests, or achievements with other people (e.g., by a lack of showing, bringing, or pointing out objects of interest)

    (d) lack of emotional reciprocity

(2) qualitative impairments in communication as manifested by at least one of the following:

    (a) delay in, or total lack of, the development of spoken language (not accompanied by an attempt to compensate through alternative modes of communication such as gesture or mime)

    (b) in individuals with adequate speech, marked impairment in the ability to initiate or sustain a conversation with others

        (c) stereotyped and repetitive use of language or idiosyncratic language

        (d) lack of varied, spontaneous make-believe play or social imitative play appropriate to developmental level

  (3) restricted repetitive and stereotyped patterns of behavior, interests, and activities, as manifested by at least one of the following:

        (a) encompassing preoccupation with one or more stereotyped and restricted patterns of interest that is abnormal either in focus or intensity or focus

        (b) apparently inflexible adherence to specific, nonfunctional routines or rituals

        (c) stereotyped and repetitive motor mannerisms (e.g., hand or finger flapping or twisting, or complex whole-body movements)

        (d) persistent preoccupation with parts of objects

B. Delays or abnormal functioning in at least one of the following areas, with onset prior to age 3 years: (1) social interaction, (2) language as used in social communication, or (3) symbolic or imaginative play.

C. The disturbance is not better accounted for by Rett's Disorder or Childhood Disintegrative Disorder.

Diagnostic criteria for 315.4 Developmental Coordination Disorder

A. Performance in daily activities that require motor coordination is substantially below that expected given the person's chronological age and measured intelligence. This may be manifested by marked delays in achieving motor milestones (e.g., walking, crawling, sitting,), dropping things, "clumsiness," poor performance in sports, or poor handwriting.

B. The disturbance in Criterion A significantly interferes with academic achievement or activities of daily living.

C. The disturbance is not due to a general medical condition (e.g., cerebral palsy, hemiplegia, or muscular dystrophy), and does not meet criteria for a Pervasive Developmental Disorder.

D. If Mental Retardation is present, the motor difficulties are in excess of those usually associated with it.

Diagnostic criteria for 313.23 Selective Mutism

A. Consistent failure to speak in specific social situations (in which there is an expectation for speaking, e.g., at school) despite speaking in other situations.

B. The disturbance interferes with educational of occupational achievement or with social communication.

C. The duration of the disturbance is at least one month (not limited to the first month of school).

D. The failure to speak is not due to a lack of knowledge of, or comfort with, the spoken language required in the social situation.

E. The disturbance is not better accounted for by a Communication Disorder (e.g., Stuttering) and does not occur exclusively during the course of a Pervasive Developmental Disorder, Schizophrenia, or other Psychotic Disorder.

Appendix II

Sample Individualized Education Programs (IEPs), Notices of Recommended Assignments (NORAs), Behavioral Intervention Plans (BIPs), and Functional Behavioral Assessments (FBAs)

As every child with Asperger's Syndrome is different, there is no one plan to suit them all. What follows are merely sample IEPs for two hypothetical children with different presentations of Asperger's Syndrome. They are not intended as recommendations, but they may suggest some ideas. Both children are fictional eight-year-old boys.

There is also no one IEP form; different districts use different forms. All IEP forms, though must have the elements required by the IDEA, a description of the student's current educational performance, a description of the student's disability and how it affect his or her education, measurable annual goals for the student, a description of how the school system plans to meet the student's needs, what special educational services the student is supposed to receive, including related services such as occupational therapy, if any (per CFR section 300.347). An IEP also must include a statement of how progress toward the annual goals will be measured, how the child's parents will be informed of the child's progress, and any special information about the child's participation in state-wide assessments (standardized tests). Many school districts' forms have a checklist format in some sections, as well as large sections which may be marked "Not Applicable" for some students, making those IEP forms look more "form-like" than these samples. Also included here, right before each IEP, is a Notice of Recommended Educational Placement (NOREP), which describes what level of support the child should receive – regular or special school, regular or special education class. This Notice is used in Pennsylvania; other states may call it something else or give the placement information in different format.

Also included are Behavioral Intervention Plans (BIPs, sometimes called Behavior Support Plans). These plans are often associated with children whose behavior is disruptive to others, but that is not the case with these two fictional students. Rather, their withdrawn behavior interferes with their own education. Sometimes educators are reluctant to give such students BIPs, but they can be helpful in identifying or clarifying measurable goals for behavior and encouraging consistency in responding to a student's behavior among school staff. They can be prejudicial, causing some people who are aware of them to think the student is disruptive, but they are confidential, so not many people do know about them. As both of these Individualized Education Programs include speech and occupational therapy, the speech therapist and occupational therapist should have been present at the IEP meeting or meetings at which the programs were set up. The BIP is followed by a Functional Behavioral Assessment (FBA).

NORA, IEP, BIP, and FBA for a mainstreamed child with Asperger's Syndrome

---

Notice of Recommended Placement (NORA)

1. **Action proposed:** Joseph will receive itinerant level of learning support service with speech therapy consultation.

2. **Why action is proposed:** Joseph's condition directly affects his academic progress.

3. **Description of other options considered:** Giving Joseph a 504 service plan rather than a special education designation.

4. **Reasons why above options rejected:** Joseph's academic progress requires more consistent monitoring in order to proceed at an adequate pace.

5. **Evaluation procedures, tests, records or reports used as a basis for the proposed action:** teacher evaluation, standardized tests, classwork, report cards, social interactions.

6. **Other factors relevant to proposed action:** Socialization and communication skills are in need of monitoring and remediation as well as academic skills.

The recommended educational placement for this child is as follows:

Type of support: Autistic support.

Level of support: Itinerant/resource room.

Individualized Education Program (IEP)

I. **Present Levels of Educational Performance**
   A. **Student's progress in past year:** Joseph is currently performing at grade level in both reading and math. Classwork and standardized tests (Babcock

Reading Inventory) verify this. He has above average mastery of science and social studies content areas. His social skills have continued to show delay.

B. **Student's current strengths:** Joseph grasps and retains information easily.

C. **Student's current needs:** Joseph needs intensive training in social and communication skills. He needs extra help in writing, both in physical handwriting and composition skills.

D. **How student's disability affects his/her progress in the regular education curriculum:** Joseph is unable to contribute to group work or class discussion, even when he knows the subject matter well. He is unable to express what he has learned in a written format. He is often unable to complete assignments due to his difficulty with handwriting and difficulty concentrating in the sensory atmosphere of a normal classroom.

II. **Goals and Objectives**

A. **Communicating/Speaking:** Joseph has difficulty initiating verbal communication. Joseph will improve his ability to initiate verbal communication in the school setting. Short-term objectives are that he will raise his hand at least five times a day for ten consecutive school days, and he will initiate asking a question or making a statement during class once a day for ten consecutive days. Once these are met Joseph will meet new objectives as follows: Joseph will greet at least two classmates at the beginning of the school day for ten consecutive school days, and Joseph will speak to at least two classmates during recess for ten consecutive school days.
Method of evaluation: Teacher observation.

B. **Communication/Writing:** Joseph's ability to compose a written composition is below the expected level for his grade. Joseph will be able to compose a paragraph in a given amount of time. Short-term objectives are Joseph will be able to start writing within two minutes of being given the topic. Joseph will compose a topic sentence within four minutes of being given the topic.

III. **Participation in Statewide Assessments**

Joseph will participate in statewide assessments, but will be allowed extra time in which to complete test sections.

IV. **Related Services**[1]

Speech therapy: One 40-minute session a week to work on strategies to improve conversational skills.

---

1   Since speech therapy and occupational therapy are part of Joseph's Individualized Education Program, the speech therapist and occupational therapist should attend the IEP meeting.

Occupational therapy: One 40-minute session a week, to work on handwriting and typing, and on strategies to handle sensory overload.

V. **Supports Needed for School Personnel**
Classroom teacher to receive specific professional development, either to attend conference on strategies for effective inclusion of students with Asperger's Syndrome, or if conference not available to receive printed information on the same subject and time to study same.

Behavioral Intervention Plan (BIP)

Measurable Annual Goals

1. Joseph will complete class assignments in the given amount of time.

    Short-term objectives: Joseph will start assignments in class immediately after directions are given. Joseph will stay on task until assignment is done. Joseph will have his materials lined up immediately before directions are given.

    Strategies to help meet objectives: Joseph will be asked to repeat the directions orally. Teacher will announce time remaining for completion of assignment. Joseph will have an hour glass on his desk to provide visual cues for passage of time. Joseph will have to complete class work not done in allotted time at home.

2. Joseph will contribute to the group when working on a group project, both offering appropriate information to peers and following appropriate group etiquette in conversational turn taking.

    Short-term objectives: Joseph will offer at least two pieces of information or advice to peers when working in a group for a 15-minute interval. Joseph will not talk for more than one minute at a time within the group.

    Strategies to help meet objectives: In advance of group project, Joseph will be given an outline of specific information that he needs to find to contribute to the group. This information should be a critical piece of the project, yet one that will not be difficult for Joseph to complete. Joseph will also be given a limit on the number of times he may speak in the group, depending on the length and complexity of the group project.

Reporting of Progress toward Goals and Objectives: Each piece of written work sent home will indicate Joseph's starting time in relation to being given the assignment and indicate how sustained his attention to the project was. After group activities, Joseph's outline will be sent home with an indication of whether he contributed to group.

Functional Behavioral Assessment (FBA)

1. **Behavior of concern:** Joseph engages in many self-stimulation behaviors at very close intervals during the course of the school day, including finger snapping, facial movements, pulling on clothes, touching parts of body (including privates), coughs and clears throat. He also daydreams a lot.

2. **Antecedents to the behavior of concern:** It is difficult to identify any single trigger, but it is believed that related to Joseph's diagnosed condition of Asperger's Syndrome, the school day in a regular education setting is intense for him and causes him anxiety.

3. **At what times does the behavior occur more or less?** These behaviors occur less when Joseph is in a one-to-one situation. They occur most frequently during recess.

4. **Could the behavior be related to educational or skills deficits?** Joseph has significant deficits in social skills. Therefore, any situation requiring peer interaction is difficult, and it is in these situations Joseph is most likely to exhibit these inappropriate behaviors.

5. **Reinforcers that maintain the behaviors of concern:** Sensory stimulation appears to satisfy Joseph momentarily, but he does not seem to use it as a strategy to gain any material reward or benefit. These behaviors do allow Joseph to avoid interaction with others.

6. **A. Describe any educational or skill deficits the student may have which may be promoting this undesirable behavior:** Joseph lacks the social skills to interact with other children and chooses to be by himself at most times. He appears to escape into a dream world. He usually does not ask for assistance.

   B. What supports in the student's IEP address the related deficits? Speech therapy, class participation strategies. Joseph will be provided with a "wiggle cushion" to help focus his sensory processing. When Joseph's "stimming" behavior becomes intense, Joseph will be allowed some solitary time, but will have to complete all work that he missed.

NORA, IEP, BIP, and FBA for a child in a self-contained classroom

Notice of Recommended Placement (NORA)

1. **Action Proposed:** Daniel will be placed in the self-contained autistic support class nearest to his neighborhood school.

2. **Why action is proposed:** Daniel's previous year in regular education classroom with resource room support was not successful in that he did not meet IEP or BIP goals. He withdrew from all social and academic activities and seemed to retreat completely into himself.

3. **Description of other options considered:** Placement in language-impaired class; remaining in regular education class with additional support.

4. **Reasons why above options rejected:** Language-impaired class required an hour's bus ride. Remaining in regular education classroom with additional support would require frequent switching between resource room and regular education classroom, and transitions seem to strain Daniel; also, his social skills require more intensive intervention than can be given in resource room.

5. **Evaluation procedures, tests, records or reports used as a basis for the proposed action:** Teacher observation, classwork, report cards, observation of social interaction by speech therapist.

6. **Other factors relevant to proposed action:** Daniel appears to be very anxious in large group settings, according to teacher observation of extreme physical tension, including rigid body, extreme fidgeting, holding hands over ears, and avoidance of looking at others.

The recommended educational placement for this child is as follows:

Type of support: Autistic support.

Level of support: Self-contained special education classroom most of day. Daniel will be included in regular education class for science.

Individualized Education Program (IEP)

I. **Present Levels of Educational Performance**

    A. **Student's progress in past:** Daniel is currently performing two years below grade level in both reading and math. Classwork and standardized tests verify this. He has above average mastery of content areas of science and social studies, according to class tests.

    B. **Student's current strengths:** Grasps and retains factual information.

    C. **Student's current needs:** Intensive training in social and communication skills, and occupational therapy for fine motor skills, as well as remedial education in reading and math.

    D. **How student's disability affects his/her progress in the regular education curriculum:** Seems too withdrawn in past year in regular education class to benefit from general curriculum, but may be able to access general curriculum in a smaller, more structured classroom.

II. **Goals and Objectives**

    A. **Communicating/Speaking:** Daniel will respond when spoken to. Daniel will ask for help when he needs it. Daniel will exchange greetings with his classmates and with adults. Short-term objectives that he will look at teacher and answer her questions when she sits near him and talks to him one on one. Objectives for later in year are that he will first answer questions when called on in class, then raise his hand to answer questions during class, and later initiate greetings to classmates and teachers.
    Method of evaluation: Teacher observation.

    B. **Communication/Writing:** Daniel will be able to write two consecutive paragraphs expressing what he learned in class or on an experience or emotion he had. Short-term objectives are that Daniel will be able to make an outline for the paragraphs, and later will be able to write five sentences, then two paragraphs, and by end of year will be able to review and self-correct his spelling and punctuation.

    C. **Reading:** Daniel will be able to read at no more than one year below grade level, will be able to read short chapter books fluently. Short-term objectives are that Daniel will be able to decode four syllable words, then will be able to answer yes-or-no questions on a short passage he has read, then identify the main idea in a paragraph, and then will be able to retell the meaning of the paragraph in his own words (one on one with a teacher known to him). By the end of the year he will be able to explain what happened in a chapter of a story.

    D. **Math:** Daniel will be able to do math at no more than one year below his grade level. He will be able to perform simple addition, subtraction, multiplication, and division operations in his head, and will be able to do more complex ones on paper. Short-term objective is to improve his time for adding and subtracting in his head. By the end of the year, he will have the multiplication tables up through times ten memorized.

III. Participation in Statewide Assessments

Daniel will participate in statewide assessments with the following accommodations: extra time, directions repeated, test administered to him in isolation with one proctor.

IV. Related services

Occupational therapy: 1x/week, to work on handwriting and fine motor skills.

Psychological counseling: 1x/week, to work on reducing level of anxiety.

Speech therapy: 2x/week, to work on listening skills, including looking at others, and on maintaining dialogue.

Behavioral Intervention Plan (BIP)

Measurable Annual Goals: Daniel will look at people when they speak to him 90 percent of the time. Daniel will answer questions when asked 95 percent of the time. Daniel will initiate at least ten conversations a week by the end of the school year.

Short-term objectives: By December, Daniel will look toward people when they speak to him 50 percent of the time. Daniel will answer people when they speak to him, in at least a monosyllable, 60 percent of the time. Daniel will initiate four conversations a week.

By March, Daniel will look toward people when they speak to him 75 percent of the time. Daniel will answer people when they speak to him, in at least a monosyllable, 75 percent of the time. Daniel will initiate four conversations a week.

Strategies to help meet objectives: When Daniel's teacher tries to initiate conversation with Daniel, she (or he) will keep speaking to Daniel until he responds and looks toward her (or him).

Five chips will be placed on Daniel's desk every day, and one will be taken away each time he speaks or holds up his hand. A reward program, to be administered by parents, will be attached to use of chips.

Reporting of Progress toward Goals and Objectives: A chart of chip use will be sent home daily.

Functional Behavioral Assessment (FBA)

1. **Behavior of concern:** Not talking at all, not looking at people who are talking to him, putting head on desk.

2. **Antecedents to the behavior of concern:** During last school year, Daniel was silent essentially at all times during school day, although the previous year he talked in one-on-one situations.

3. **At what times does the behavior occur more or less?** He keeps his head on desk when classroom is noisy, and during group work, and at lunch. Stayed in corner during recess (spent second half of year in nurse's office for recess, looked at picture books there).

4. **Could the behavior be related to educational or skills deficits?** It is thought to be related to social and communications skills deficits, and possibly Sensory Integration Dysfunction, associated with Daniel's diagnosis of Pervasive Developmental Disorder, Asperger's Syndrome. Daniel can talk. He talked in previous school year. Parents report that he talks at home. He does talk to speech therapist and school nurse when alone with them and after much coaxing. Speech therapy evaluation done by school district speech pathologist two years ago found articulation skills within normal range. Independent evaluation obtained by parents at local pediatric hospital found deficits in pragmatic language skills.

5. **Reinforcers that maintain the behaviors of concern:** Not being bothered; being ignored by others.

6. **A. Describe any educational or skill deficits the student may have which may be promoting this undesirable behavior:** May be unable to process the numerous stimuli of a large, bustling classroom. May be unable to concentrate on more than one person, speaking calmly, at a time.

   B. What supports in the student's IEP address the related deficits? Smaller, very structured class, located in quiet part of school building. Speech therapy. Psychological counseling.

Appendix III

Sample Blank Section 504 Service Plan

What follows is a blank Section 504 Service Plan. These plans are known by different names in different states, sometimes taking their names from the section number of the state's implementing regulation. All these service agreements must comply with Section 504 of the Rehabilitation Act, the federal law designed to eliminate barriers to the education of people with disabilities. This particular form is used in Pennsylvania, where it is often called a Chapter 15 Service Agreement, after the PA Code chapter implementing the federal law. Services which can be obtained through these plans include speech therapy, occupational therapy, accommodations such as extra time on class assignments or standardized tests, extra time getting from class to class, or permission to enter the building early, among others. You can see eligibility for these plans outlined in federal regulations in Appendix V. The services which can be obtained through such a plan can also be obtained through an IEP, and IEPs have more detailed goals and objectives.

Sample Service Agreement

Attachment to Basic Education Circular
SUBJECT: Implementation of Chapter 15
22 Pa. Code Chapter 15

Student Name: _____
Date Services Begin: _____
Date Services End: _____
Initial Agreement: _____
Modified Agreement: _____

I am writing as a follow-up on our recent evaluation concerning your child and to summarize our recommendations and agreements for aids, services or accommodations. The aids, services or accommodations are as follows:

_____
_____
_____
_____

The following procedures need to be followed in the event of a medical emergency:

_____
_____

The attached letter outlines your rights to resolve any disputes that you may have concerning the recommended aids, services or accommodations. If you have any questions concerning your rights or the aids, services or accommodations recommended, please feel free to contact me.

_____   _____
School District Administrator   Date

DIRECTIONS: Please check one of the options and sign this form.

☐ I agree and give permission to proceed as recommended.
☐ I do not agree and do not give permission to proceed as recommended.
☐ I would like to schedule an informal conference to discuss my concerns.

My reason for disapproval is: _____
_____

_____   _____
Parent(s) Signature   Date

Appendix IV

Key Sections of IDEA Regulations

Congress enacts laws such as the IDEA, but the US Department of Education issues regulations implementing the law. These regulations can all be found in Title 34 of the Code of Federal Regulations (the CFR). The entire Code is available online on government websites, including www.gpoaccess.gov. You can also find it online by doing a search for "Code of Federal Regulations" or "IDEA regulations." I have rearranged the order of these selected regulations to keep topics together. Only a small fraction of the implementing regulations are reprinted here, and in most cases, only portions of a given numbered section.

Remember, your state has its own laws and regulations, but your state's rules and practices must be consistent with these federal regulations.

In these regulations, FAPE stands for Free Appropriate Public Education, SEA stands for State Education Authority (that is, State Department of Education), and LEA stands for Local Education Authority (that is, the school district).

Definitions

Sec. 300.7 Child with a disability.

(a) (1) As used in this part, the term child with a disability means a child evaluated ... as having mental retardation, a hearing impairment including deafness, a speech or language impairment, a visual impairment including blindness, serious emotional disturbance (hereafter referred to as emotional disturbance), an orthopedic impairment, autism, traumatic brain injury, any other health impairment, a specific learning disability, deaf-blindness, or multiple disabilities, and who, by reason thereof, needs special education and related services.

    ...

(b)   The term child with a disability for children aged 3 through 9 may...include a child –

(1) Who is experiencing developmental delays...in one or more of the following areas: physical development, cognitive development, communication development, social or emotional development, or adaptive development; and

(2) Who, by reason thereof, needs special education and related services.

191

(c) (1) (i) Autism means a developmental disability significantly affecting verbal and nonverbal communication and social interaction, generally evident before age 3, that adversely affects a child's educational performance. Other characteristics often associated with autism are engagement in repetitive activities and stereotyped movements, resistance to environmental change or change in daily routines, and unusual responses to sensory experiences. The term does not apply if a child's educational performance is adversely affected primarily because the child has an emotional disturbance, as defined in paragraph (b)(4) of this section.

(ii) A child who manifests the characteristics of "autism" after age 3 could be diagnosed as having "autism" if the criteria in paragraph (c)(1)(i) of this section are satisfied.

...

(c) (4) Emotional disturbance is defined as follows: ...a condition exhibiting one or more of the following characteristics over a long period of time and to a marked degree that adversely affects a child's educational performance:

(A) An inability to learn that cannot be explained by intellectual, sensory, or health factors.

(B) An inability to build or maintain satisfactory interpersonal relationships with peers and teachers.

(C) Inappropriate types of behavior or feelings under normal circumstances.

(D) A general pervasive mood of unhappiness or depression.

(E) A tendency to develop physical symptoms or fears associated with personal or school problems.

...

(c) (10) Specific learning disability is defined as follows: ...a disorder in one or more of the basic psychological processes involved in understanding or in using language, spoken or written, that may manifest itself in an imperfect ability to listen, think, speak, read, write, spell, or to do mathematical calculations, including conditions such as perceptual disabilities, brain injury, minimal brain dysfunction, dyslexia, and developmental aphasia.

(c) (11) Speech or language impairment means a communication disorder, such as stuttering, impaired articulation, a language impairment, or a voice impairment, that adversely affects a child's educational performance.

...

Sec. 300.24 Related services.

(a)   ... Related services means transportation and such developmental, corrective, and other supportive services as are required to assist a child with a disability to benefit from special education, and includes speech-language pathology and audiology services, psychological services, physical and occupational therapy, recreation, including therapeutic recreation, early identification and assessment of disabilities in children, counseling services, including rehabilitation counseling, orientation and mobility services, and medical services for diagnostic or evaluation purposes. The term also includes school health services, social work services in schools, and parent counseling and training.

...

(b) (7) Parent counseling and training means –

(i) Assisting parents in understanding the special needs of their child;

(ii) Providing parents with information about child development; and

(iii) Helping parents to acquire the necessary skills that will allow them to support the implementation of their child's IEP or IFSP.

...

(b)(10) Recreation includes –

(i) Assessment of leisure function;

(ii) Therapeutic recreation services;

(iii) Recreation programs in schools and community agencies; and

(iv) Leisure education.

Sec. 300.26 Special education.

(a) (1) Special education means specially designed instruction, at no cost to the parents, to meet the unique needs of a child with a disability, including –

(i) Instruction conducted in the classroom, in the home, in hospitals and institutions, and in other settings; and

(ii) Instruction in physical education.

...

(2) (ii) Travel training; and

(iii) Vocational education.

...

(3) Specially-designed instruction means adapting ... the content, methodology, or delivery of instruction –

(i) To address the unique needs of the child that result from the child's disability; and

(ii) To ensure access of the child to the general curriculum, so that he or she can meet the educational standards within the jurisdiction of the public agency that apply to all children.

(4) Travel training means providing instruction, as appropriate, to children with significant cognitive disabilities, and any other children with disabilities who require this instruction, to enable them to –

(i) Develop an awareness of the environment in which they live; and

(ii) Learn the skills necessary to move effectively and safely from place to place within that environment (e.g., in school, in the home, at work, and in the community).

...

Evaluation

This evaluation is to determine whether a child has a disability under the IDEA and is entitled to special education and related services.

Sec. 300.532 Evaluation procedures.

Each public agency shall ensure...that the following requirements are met:

...

(b)   A variety of assessment tools and strategies are used to gather relevant functional and developmental information about the child, including information provided by the parent..., that may assist in determining –

(1) Whether the child is a child with a disability under Sec. 300.7; and

(2) The content of the child's IEP.

...

(d)   Tests and other evaluation materials include those tailored to assess specific areas of educational need and not merely those that are designed to provide a single general intelligence quotient.

(e)   Tests are selected and administered so as best to ensure that if a test is administered to a child with impaired sensory, manual, or speaking skills, the test results accurately reflect the child's aptitude or achievement level or whatever other factors the test purports to measure, rather than reflecting the child's impaired sensory, manual, or speaking skills (unless those skills are the factors that the test purports to measure).

(f)   No single procedure is used as the sole criterion for determining whether a child is a child with a disability and for determining an appropriate educational program for the child.

(g)   The child is assessed in all areas related to the suspected disability, including, if appropriate, health, vision, hearing, social and emotional status, general intelligence, academic performance, communicative status, and motor abilities.

(h)   In evaluating each child with a disability under Secs. 300.531–300.536, the evaluation is sufficiently comprehensive to identify all of the child's special education and related services needs, whether or not commonly linked to the disability category in which the child has been classified.

...

Sec. 300.533 Determination of needed evaluation data.

(a) ... As part of an initial evaluation (if appropriate) and as part of any reevaluation, a group...shall –

(1) Review existing evaluation data on the child, including –

(i) Evaluations and information provided by the parents of the child;

(ii) Current classroom-based assessments and observations; and

(iii) Observations by teachers and related services providers; and

(2) On the basis of that review, and input from the child's parents, identify what additional data, if any, are needed to determine –

(i) Whether the child has a particular category of disability, as described in Sec. 300.7, or, in case of a reevaluation of a child, whether the child continues to have such a disability;

(ii) The present levels of performance and educational needs of the child;

(iii) Whether the child needs special education and related services, or in the case of a reevaluation of a child, whether the child continues to need special education and related services; and

(iv) Whether any additions or modifications to the special education and related services are needed to enable the child to meet the measurable annual goals set out in the IEP of the child and to participate, as appropriate, in the general curriculum.

...

Sec. 300.542 Observation.

(a) At least one team member other than the child's regular teacher shall observe the child's academic performance in the regular classroom setting.

...

Sec. 300.534 Determination of eligibility.

...

(a) (2) The public agency must provide a copy of the evaluation report and the documentation of determination of eligibility to the parent.

...

(c) (1) A public agency must evaluate a child with a disability in accordance with Secs. 300.532 and 300.533 before determining that the child is no longer a child with a disability.

...

Sec. 300.543 Written report.

...

(b)   Each team member shall certify in writing whether the report reflects his or her conclusion. If it does not reflect his or her conclusion, the team member must submit a separate statement presenting his or her conclusions.

Sec. 300.535 Procedures for determining eligibility and placement.

...

(b)   If a determination is made that a child has a disability and needs special education and related services, an IEP must be developed for the child in accordance with Secs. 300.340-300.350.

Sec. 300.536 Reevaluation.
Each public agency shall ensure –

...

(b)   That a reevaluation of each child ... is conducted if conditions warrant a reevaluation, or if the child's parent or teacher requests a reevaluation, but at least once every three years.

Sec. 300.502 Independent educational evaluation.

...

(a) (3) (i)   Independent educational evaluation means an evaluation conducted by a qualified examiner who is not employed by the public agency responsible for the education of the child in question.

...

(b) (1) A parent has the right to an independent educational evaluation at public expense if the parent disagrees with an evaluation obtained by the public agency.

(2) If a parent requests an independent educational evaluation at public expense, the public agency must, without unnecessary delay, either –

(i) Initiate a hearing under Sec. 300.507 to show that its evaluation is appropriate; or

(ii) Ensure that an independent educational evaluation is provided at public expense...

(3) If the public agency initiates a hearing and the final decision is that the agency's evaluation is appropriate, the parent still has the right to an independent educational evaluation, but not at public expense.

...

(c)   Parent-initiated evaluations. If the parent obtains an independent educational evaluation at private expense, the results of the evaluation –

(1) Must be considered by the public agency, if it meets agency criteria, in any decision made with respect to the provision of FAPE to the child; and

(2) May be presented as evidence at a hearing under this subpart regarding that child.

...

Sec. 300.501 Opportunity to examine records; parent participation in meetings.

(a)   General. The parents of a child with a disability must be afforded ... an opportunity to –

(1) Inspect and review all education records with respect to –

(i)   The identification, evaluation, and educational placement of the child; and

(ii) The provision of FAPE to the child; and

(2) Participate in meetings with respect to –

(i)   The identification, evaluation, and educational placement of the child; and

(ii) The provision of FAPE to the child.

...

(c) (3) If neither parent can participate in a meeting in which a decision is to be made relating to the educational placement of their child, the public agency shall use other methods to ensure their participation, including individual or conference telephone calls, or video conferencing.

...

Individualized Education Program (IEP)

Sec. 300.346 Development, review, and revision of IEP.

(a) (1) In developing each child's IEP, the IEP team shall consider –

(i)   The strengths of the child and the concerns of the parents for enhancing the education of their child;

(ii) The results of the initial or most recent evaluation of the child; and

(iii) As appropriate, the results of the child's performance on any general State or district-wide assessment programs.

(2) ... The IEP team also shall –

(i) In the case of a child whose behavior impedes his or her learning or that of others, consider, if appropriate, strategies, including positive behavioral interventions, strategies, and supports to address that behavior;

…

(v) Consider whether the child requires assistive technology devices and services.

…

(c) Statement in IEP. If, in considering the special factors described in paragraphs (a)(1) and (2) of this section, the IEP team determines that a child needs a particular device or service (including an intervention, accommodation, or other program modification) in order for the child to receive FAPE, the IEP team must include a statement to that effect in the child's IEP.

…

(d) Requirement with respect to regular education teacher. The regular education teacher of a child with a disability, as a member of the IEP team, must, to the extent appropriate, participate in the development, review, and revision of the child's IEP.

…

Sec. 300.347 Content of IEP.

(a) General. The IEP for each child with a disability must include –

(1) A statement of the child's present levels of educational performance, including –

(i) How the child's disability affects the child's involvement and progress in the general curriculum (i.e., the same curriculum as for nondisabled children); or…

(2) A statement of measurable annual goals, including benchmarks or short-term objectives, related to –

(i) Meeting the child's needs that result from the child's disability to enable the child to be involved in and progress in the general curriculum (i.e., the same curriculum as for nondisabled children), or for preschool children, as appropriate, to participate in appropriate activities; and

(ii) Meeting each of the child's other educational needs that result from the child's disability;

(3) A statement of the special education and related services and supplementary aids and services to be provided to the child, or on behalf of the child, and a statement of the program modifications or supports for school personnel that will be provided for the child –

(i) To advance appropriately toward attaining the annual goals;

(ii) To be involved and progress in the general curriculum ... and to participate in extracurricular and other nonacademic activities; and

...

(4) An explanation of the extent, if any, to which the child will not participate with nondisabled children in the regular class and in the activities described in paragraph (a)(3) of this section;

(5) (i) A statement of any individual modifications in the administration of State or district-wide assessments of student achievement that are needed in order for the child to participate in the assessment; and

(ii) If the IEP team determines that the child will not participate in a particular State or district-wide assessment of student achievement (or part of an assessment), a statement of –
(A) Why that assessment is not appropriate for the child; and
(B) How the child will be assessed;

(6) The projected date for the beginning of the services and modifications described in paragraph (a)(3) of this section, and the anticipated frequency, location, and duration of those services and modifications; and

(7) A statement of –

(i) How the child's progress toward the annual goals described in paragraph (a)(2) of this section will be measured; and

(ii) How the child's parents will be regularly informed (through such means as periodic report cards), at least as often as parents are informed of their nondisabled children's progress, of –
(A) Their child's progress toward the annual goals; and
(B) The extent to which that progress is sufficient to enable the child to achieve the goals by the end of the year.

(b) Transition services. The IEP must include –

(1) For each student with a disability beginning at age 14 (or younger, if determined appropriate by the IEP team), and updated annually, a statement of the transition service needs of the student under the applicable components of the student's IEP that focuses on the student's courses of study (such as participation in advanced-placement courses or a vocational education program); and

(2) For each student beginning at age 16 (or younger, if determined appropriate by the IEP team), a statement of needed transition services for the student, including, if appropriate, a statement of the interagency responsibilities or any needed linkages.

...

Sec. 300.308 Assistive technology.

(a)   Each public agency shall ensure that assistive technology devices or assistive technology services, or both ... are made available to a child with a disability if required as a part of the child's –

(1) Special education ...;

(2) Related services ...; or

(3) Supplementary aids and services ....

(b)   On a case-by-case basis, the use of school-purchased assistive technology devices in a child's home or in other settings is required if the child's IEP team determines that the child needs access to those devices in order to receive FAPE.

Sec. 300.309 Extended school year services.

...

(a) (2) Extended school year services must be provided only if a child's IEP team determines, on an individual basis ... that the services are necessary for the provision of FAPE to the child.

(3) In implementing the requirements of this section, a public agency may not –

(i) Limit extended school year services to particular categories of disability; or

(ii) Unilaterally limit the type, amount, or duration of those services.

(b)   ...The term extended school year services means special education and related services that –

(1) Are provided to a child with a disability –

(i) Beyond the normal school year of the public agency;

...

Sec. 300.306 Nonacademic services.

(a)   Each public agency shall take steps to provide nonacademic and extracurricular services and activities in the manner necessary to afford children with disabilities an equal opportunity for participation in those services and activities.

(b)   Nonacademic and extracurricular services and activities may include counseling services, athletics, transportation, health services, recreational activities, special interest groups or clubs sponsored by the public agency, referrals to agencies that provide assistance to individuals with disabilities, and employment of students, including both employment by the public agency and assistance in making outside employment available.

Least restrictive environment

Sec. 300.550 General LRE requirements.

...

(b)   Each public agency shall ensure –

   (1) That to the maximum extent appropriate, children with disabilities, including children in public or private institutions or other care facilities, are educated with children who are nondisabled; and

   (2) That special classes, separate schooling or other removal of children with disabilities from the regular educational environment occurs only if the nature or severity of the disability is such that education in regular classes with the use of supplementary aids and services cannot be achieved satisfactorily.

Sec. 300.551 Continuum of alternative placements.

(a)   Each public agency shall ensure that a continuum of alternative placements is available to meet the needs of children with disabilities for special education and related services.

(b) (1) The continuum must...include the alternative placements listed...(instruction in regular classes, special classes, special schools, home instruction, and instruction in hospitals and institutions); and

   (2) Make provision for supplementary services (such as resource room or itinerant instruction) to be provided in conjunction with regular class placement.

Private school placements by parents

Sec. 300.403 Placement of children by parents if FAPE is at issue.

(a)   General. This part does not require an LEA to pay for the cost of education, including special education and related services, of a child with a disability at a private school or facility if that agency made FAPE available to the child and the parents elected to place the child in a private school or facility. ...

...

(c)   Reimbursement for private school placement. If the parents of a child with a disability, who previously received special education and related services under the authority of a public agency, enroll the child in a private preschool, elementary, or secondary school without the consent of or referral by the public agency, a court or a hearing officer may require the agency to reimburse the parents for the cost of that enrollment if the court or hearing officer finds that the agency had not made FAPE available to the child in a timely manner prior to that enrollment and that the private placement is appropriate. ...

(d)   Limitation on reimbursement. The cost of reimbursement described in paragraph (c) of this section may be reduced or denied –

(1) If –

    (i) At the most recent IEP meeting that the parents attended prior to removal of the child from the public school, the parents did not inform the IEP team that they were rejecting the placement proposed by the public agency to provide FAPE to their child, including stating their concerns and their intent to enroll their child in a private school at public expense; or

    (ii) At least ten (10) business days (including any holidays that occur on a business day) prior to the removal of the child from the public school, the parents did not give written notice to the public agency of the information described in paragraph (d)(1)(i) of this section;

(2) If, prior to the parents' removal of the child from the public school, the public agency informed the parents, through the notice requirements described in Sec. 300.503(a)(1), of its intent to evaluate the child (including a statement of the purpose of the evaluation that was appropriate and reasonable), but the parents did not make the child available for the evaluation; or

(3) Upon a judicial finding of unreasonableness with respect to actions taken by the parents.

    …

Dispute resolution

Sec. 300.503 Prior notice by the public agency; content of notice.

(a)   Notice.

(1) Written notice…must be given to the parents of a child with a disability a reasonable time before the public agency –

    (i) Proposes to initiate or change the identification, evaluation, or educational placement of the child or the provision of FAPE to the child; or

    (ii) Refuses to initiate or change the identification, evaluation, or educational placement of the child or the provision of FAPE to the child.

    …

(b)   … The notice required under paragraph (a) of this section must include – …

(2) An explanation of why the agency proposes or refuses to take the action;

(3) A description of any other options that the agency considered and the reasons why those options were rejected;

(4) A description of each evaluation procedure, test, record, or report the agency used as a basis for the proposed or refused action;

    …

Sec. 300.504 Procedural safeguards notice.

(a)   General. A copy of the procedural safeguards available to the arents of a child
       with a disability must be given to the parents, at a minimum –

   (1) Upon initial referral for evaluation;

   (2) Upon each notification of an IEP meeting;

   (3) Upon reevaluation of the child; and

   (4) Upon receipt of a request for due process under Sec. 300.507.

       ...

Sec. 300.506 Mediation.

(a)   ... Each public agency shall ensure that procedures are established and imple-
       mented to allow parties ... to resolve the disputes through a mediation process
       that, ... must be available whenever a hearing is requested under Secs. 300.507...

(b)   ... The procedures must meet the following requirements:

   (1) The procedures must ensure that the mediation process –

      (i) Is voluntary on the part of the parties;

      (ii) Is not used to deny or delay a parent's right to a due process...; and

      (iii) Is conducted by a qualified and impartial mediator who is trained in effective
           mediation techniques.

      ...

   (3) The State shall bear the cost of the mediation process...

   (4) Each session in the mediation process must be scheduled in a timely manner and
       must be held in a location that is convenient to the parties to the dispute.

      ...

   (6) Discussions that occur during the mediation process must be confidential and
       may not be used as evidence in any subsequent due process hearings or civil pro-
       ceeding. ...

      ...

Sec. 300.507 Impartial due process hearing; parent notice.

(a) (1) A parent or a public agency may initiate a hearing on any of the matters ...
        relating to the identification, evaluation or educational placement of a child with
        a disability, or the provision of FAPE to the child).

   (2) When a hearing is initiated under paragraph (a)(1) of this section, the public
       agency shall inform the parents of the availability of mediation described in Sec.
       300.506.

   (3) The public agency shall inform the parent of any free or low-cost legal and other
       relevant services available in the area if –

(i) The parent requests the information; or

(ii) The parent or the agency initiates a hearing under this section.

...

(c)   Parent notice to the public agency.

(1) General. The public agency must have procedures that require the parent of a child with a disability or the attorney representing the child, to provide notice (which must remain confidential) to the public agency in a request for a hearing under paragraph (a)(1) of this section.

(2) Content of parent notice. The notice required in paragraph (c)(1) of this section must include –

(i) The name of the child;

(ii) The address of the residence of the child;

(iii) The name of the school the child is attending;

(iv) A description of the nature of the problem of the child relating to the proposed or refused initiation or change, including facts relating to the problem; and

(v) A proposed resolution of the problem to the extent known and available to the parents at the time.

(3) Model form to assist parents. Each SEA shall develop a model form to assist parents in filing a request for due process ...

(4) Right to due process hearing. A public agency may not deny or delay a parent's right to a due process hearing for failure to provide the notice required in paragraphs (c)(1) and (2) of this section.

Sec. 300.509 Hearing rights.

(a)   ... Any party to a hearing conducted pursuant to Secs. 300.507... or an appeal conducted pursuant to Sec. 300.510, has the right to –

(1) Be accompanied and advised by counsel and by individuals with special knowledge or training with respect to the problems of children with disabilities;

(2) Present evidence and confront, cross-examine, and compel the attendance of witnesses;

(3) Prohibit the introduction of any evidence at the hearing that has not been disclosed to that party at least 5 business days before the hearing;

(4) Obtain a written, or, at the option of the parents, electronic, verbatim record of the hearing ... .

(b) (1) At least 5 business days prior to a hearing conducted pursuant to Sec. 300.507(a), each party shall disclose to all other parties all evaluations completed by that date and recommendations based on the offering party's evaluations that the party intends to use at the hearing.

(2) A hearing officer may bar any party that fails to comply with paragraph (b)(1) of this section from introducing the relevant evaluation or recommendation at the hearing without the consent of the other party.

(c) (1) Parents involved in hearings must be given the right to –

    (i) Have the child who is the subject of the hearing present; and

    (ii) Open the hearing to the public.

(2) The record of the hearing and the findings of fact and decisions described in paragraphs (a)(4) and (a)(5) of this section must be provided at no cost to parents.

(d)   ... The public agency, after deleting any personally identifiable information, shall ... make those findings and decisions available to the public.

Sec. 300.510 Finality of decision; appeal; impartial review.

...

(1) General. If the hearing required by Sec. 300.507 is conducted by a public agency other than the SEA, any party aggrieved by the findings and decision in the hearing may appeal to the SEA.

(2) ... If there is an appeal, the SEA shall conduct an impartial review of the hearing.

...

(d)   Finality of review decision. The decision made by the reviewing official is final unless a party brings a civil action under Sec. 300.512.

Sec. 300.511 Timelines and convenience of hearings and reviews.

(a)   The public agency shall ensure that not later than 45 days after the receipt of a request for a hearing –

(1) A final decision is reached in the hearing; and

(2) A copy of the decision is mailed to each of the parties.

(b)   The SEA shall ensure that not later than 30 days after the receipt of a request for a review –

(1) A final decision is reached in the review; and

(2) A copy of the decision is mailed to each of the parties.

(c)   A hearing or reviewing officer may grant specific extensions of time beyond the periods set out in paragraphs (a) and (b) of this section at the request of either party.

(d)   Each hearing and each review involving oral arguments must be conducted at a time and place that is reasonably convenient to the parents and child involved.

Sec. 300.512 Civil action.

(a)   ... Any party aggrieved by the findings and decision made under Secs. 300.507...who does not have the right to an appeal under Sec. 300.510(b), and any party aggrieved by the findings and decision under Sec. 300.510(b), has the right to bring a civil action with respect to the complaint presented pursuant to Sec. 300.507. The action may be brought in any State court of competent jurisdiction or in a district court of the United States without regard to the amount in controversy.

(b)   Additional requirements. In any action brought under paragraph (a) of this section, the court –

(1) Shall receive the records of the administrative proceedings;

(2) Shall hear additional evidence at the request of a party; and

(3) Basing its decision on the preponderance of the evidence, shall grant the relief that the court determines to be appropriate.

...

Sec. 300.513 Attorneys' fees.

(a)   ... The court...may award reasonable attorneys' fees as part of the costs to the parents of a child with a disability who is the prevailing party.

...

Sec. 300.514 Child's status during proceedings.

(a)   Except as provided in Sec. 300.526 [involving disciplinary procedures], during the pendency of any administrative or judicial proceeding regarding a complaint under Sec. 300.507, unless the State or local agency and the parents of the child agree otherwise, the child involved in the complaint must remain in his or her current educational placement.

(b)   If the complaint involves an application for initial admission to public school, the child, with the consent of the parents, must be placed in the public school until the completion of all the proceedings.

(c)   If the decision of a hearing officer in a due process hearing conducted by the SEA or a State review official in an administrative appeal agrees with the child's parents that a change of placement is appropriate, that placement must be treated as an agreement between the State or local agency and the parents for purposes of paragraph (a) of this section.

Appendix V

Key Sections of Section 504 Regulations

As discussed in Part III of this book, Section 504 of the Rehabilitation Act prohibited discrimination in an attempt to help people with disabilities obtain access to existing services, and applies to most entities receiving federal funding. The word "recipient" as used in these regulations refers to such entities, including public and private schools, colleges, and local government programs. Like the IDEA regulations, the regulations excerpted here are found in Title 34 of the Code of Federal Regulations, as well as online (see www.gpoaccess.gov, or do a search for "Section 504 regulations"). Unlike the IDEA regulations, they apply directly to covered entities and are not filtered through state laws and regulations.

Definition of disability
Sec. 104.3 (j)

Handicapped persons means any person who (i) has a physical or mental impairment which substantially limits one or more major life activities, (ii) has a record of such an impairment, or (iii) is regarded as having such an impairment.

(i) … Mental impairment means…any mental or psychological disorder, such as mental retardation, organic brain syndrome, emotional or mental illness, and specific learning disabilities.

(ii) Major life activities means functions such as caring for one's self, performing manual tasks,…learning, and working.

(iii) Has a record of such an impairment means has a history of, or has been misclassified as having, a mental or physical impairment that substantially limits one or more major life activities.

(iv) Is regarded as having an impairment means
   (A) has a physical or mental impairment that does not substantially limit major life activities but that is treated by a recipient as constituting such a limitation;

(B) has a physical or mental impairment that substantially limits major life activities only as a result of the attitudes of others toward such impairment;

(C) has none of the impairments defined in...this section but is treated by a recipient as having such an impairment.

Discrimination prohibited (Thrust of Act)

Sec. 104.4

No qualified handicapped person shall, on the basis of handicap, be excluded from participation in, be denied the benefits of, or otherwise be subjected to discrimination under any program or activity which receives Federal financial assistance.

...

Sec. 104.3 (k)

Program or activity means all of the operations of –

(1) (i) A department, agency, special purpose district, or other instrumentality of a State or of a local government; or

(ii) The entity of such State or local government that distributes such assistance and each such department or agency (and each other State or local government entity) to which the assistance is extended, in the case of assistance to a State or local government;

(2) (i) A college, university, or other postsecondary institution, or a public system of higher education; or

(ii) A local educational agency..., system of vocational education, or other school system;

(3) (i) An entire corporation, partnership, or other private organization,...Which is principally engaged in the business of providing education, health care, housing, social services, or parks and recreation; ...

...

Regarding public school systems

Sec. 104.33 Free appropriate public education.

(a)   General. A recipient that operates a public elementary or secondary education program or activity shall provide a free appropriate public education to each qualified handicapped person who is in the recipient's jurisdiction, regardless of the nature or severity of the person's handicap.

(b)   Appropriate education.

(1) For the purpose of this subpart, the provision of an appropriate education is the provision of regular or special education and related aids and services that (i) are

designed to meet individual educational needs of handicapped persons as adequately as the needs of nonhandicapped persons are met. ...

(2) Implementation of an Individualized Education Program developed in accordance with the [IDEA] is one means of meeting the standard established in paragraph (b)(1)(i) of this section.

...

(**Author's Note:** Sections 104.34 and 104.35 require the education of handicapped students with other students to the extent possible and set out evaluation procedures for identifying students who need extra help in order to obtain the education to which they are entitled. These sections are similar to analogous sections in the IDEA implementing regulations, but are not as detailed.)

Sec. 104.37 Nonacademic services.

(a)   General.

(1) A recipient to which this subpart applies shall provide non-academic and extracurricular services and activities in such manner as is necessary to afford handicapped students an equal opportunity for participation in such services and activities.

(2) Nonacademic and extracurricular services and activities may include...physical recreational athletics,...recreational activities, special interest groups or clubs sponsored by the recipients,...

...

(c) Physical education and athletics.... A recipient that offers physical education courses or that operates or sponsors interscholastic, club, or intramural athletics shall provide to qualified handicapped students an equal opportunity for participation.

...

Regarding private schools

Sec. 104.39

(a)   A recipient that provides private elementary or secondary education may not, on the basis of handicap, exclude a qualified handicapped person if the person can, with minor adjustments, be provided an appropriate education...within that recipient's program or activity.

(b)   A recipient to which this section applies may not charge more for the provision of an appropriate education to handicapped persons than to nonhandicapped persons except to the extent that any additional charge is justified by a substantial increase in cost to the recipient.

...

Postsecondary education: subpart E

Sec. 104

Subpart E applies to postsecondary education programs or activities, including postsecondary vocational education programs or activities, that receive Federal financial assistance and to recipients that operate, or that receive Federal financial assistance for the operation of, such programs or activities.

Sec. 104.42 Admissions and recruitment.

. . .

(b)   Admissions. In administering its admission policies, a recipient...

    (2) May not make use of any test or criterion for admission that has a disproportionate, adverse effect on handicapped persons or any class of handicapped persons unless

        (i) the test or criterion, as used by the recipient, has been validated as a predictor of success in the education program or activity in question and

        (ii) alternate tests or criteria that have a less disproportionate, adverse effect are not...available.

    (3) Shall assure itself that (i) admissions tests are selected and administered so as best to ensure that, when a test is administered to an applicant who has a handicap that impairs sensory, manual, or speaking skills, the test results accurately reflect the applicant's aptitude or achievement level or whatever other factor the test purports to measure, rather than reflecting the applicant's impaired sensory, manual, or speaking skills (except where those skills are the factors that the test purports to measure); (ii) admissions tests that are designed for persons with impaired sensory, manual, or speaking skills are offered as often and in as timely a manner as are other admissions tests. ...

    . . .

Sec. 104.43 Treatment of students; general.

(a)   No qualified handicapped student shall, on the basis of handicap, be excluded from participation in, be denied the benefits of, or otherwise be subjected to discrimination under any academic, research, occupational training, housing, health insurance, counseling, financial aid, physical education, athletics, recreation, transportation, other extracurricular, or other postsecondary education aid, benefits, or services to which this subpart applies.

    . . .

(d)   A recipient to which this subpart applies shall operate its program or activity in the most integrated setting appropriate.

Sec. 104.44 *Academic adjustments.*

(a)   *Academic requirements.* A recipient to which this subpart applies shall make such modifications to its academic requirements as are necessary to ensure that such requirements do not discriminate or have the effect of discriminating, on the basis of handicap, against a qualified handicapped applicant or student. Academic requirements that the recipient can demonstrate are essential to the instruction being pursued by such student or to any directly related licensing requirement will not be regarded as discriminatory within the meaning of this section. Modifications may include changes in the length of time permitted for the completion of degree requirements, substitution of specific courses required for the completion of degree requirements, and adaptation of the manner in which specific courses are conducted.

(b)   *Other rules.* A recipient to which this subpart applies may not impose upon handicapped students other rules, such as the prohibition of tape recorders in classrooms,...that have the effect of limiting the participation of handicapped students in the recipient's education program or activity.

(c)   *Course examinations.* In its course examinations or other procedures for evaluating students' academic achievement, a recipient...shall provide such methods for evaluating the achievement of students who have a handicap that impairs sensory, manual, or speaking skills as will best ensure that the results of the evaluation represents the student's achievement in the course, rather than reflecting the student's impaired sensory, manual, or speaking skills (except where such skills are the factors that the test purports to measure).

(d)   *Auxiliary aids.*

  (1) A recipient...shall take such steps as are necessary to ensure that no handicapped student is denied the benefits of, excluded from participation in, or otherwise subjected to discrimination because of the absence of educational auxiliary aids for students with impaired sensory, manual, or speaking skills.

  .... Recipients need not provide attendants, individually prescribed devices, readers for personal use or study, or other devices or services of a personal nature.

Appendix VI

When and How to Hire a Lawyer

The most common area for hiring a lawyer to get help for a child with Asperger's Syndrome is special education. This is probably because of the crucial importance of a child's school situation, because school authorities, while well meaning, usually lack of understanding of Asperger's Syndrome, and because the law provides for payment of counsel fees in cases where parents prevail. Other areas where lawyers might be of assistance are in Medical Assistance, Supplemental Security Insurance (SSI), or lack of reasonable accommodations for adults with Asperger's Syndrome.

As mentioned before, both the IDEA and Section 504 of the Rehabilitation Act set out grievance procedures which are designed to avoid lawsuits and to minimize the need for a lawyer. Nonetheless, you can have a lawyer represent you at any step in the process. Legal representation may even be helpful at the IEP meeting, depending on the circumstances. Generally I would not recommend it, as it may over-formalize the proceedings and make what should be a team effort into an adversarial process, but if you have a clear sense of your child's needs and feel certain the school district will not meet them without coercion, the presence of a lawyer at the IEP meeting may help you get what you want faster and earlier in the process, avoiding the need for litigation. At due process hearings, school districts typically have lawyers representing them. A due process hearing does involve opening statements and presenting evidence, and examining witnesses, activities which lawyers are trained in but most people are not. Also, should you appeal the decision in the due process hearing to a court, the record of the due process hearing will be used in the court case. Although new evidence can be introduced, the hearing record will control much of the case. If you do go to court, a lawyer is almost always necessary. The legal system is not designed for unrepresented litigants (and as the child is the actual litigant in these cases rather than the parent, some courts have held that the parent cannot represent the child, only a lawyer can).

Most lawyers do not know much about special education law. The lawyer who drew up your will or helped you in the purchase of your house probably cannot help you here, but may be able to give you the name of someone who can. Advocacy groups in your area might have the names of some local special education lawyers. If you are connected with any kind of support group for parents of children with special needs, someone there probably knows someone involved in special education law. Also, school districts are required to maintain a list of free or low-cost attorneys for parents to consult (per CFR Section 300.507(a)(3)).

There are a few occasions where it is helpful simply to have a lawyer present, without the lawyer actually doing much of anything, even if the lawyer does not know much about special education law. Perhaps you already know what you want to say at an IEP meeting or a due process mediation session, and want a lawyer by your side so that the school district takes you seriously. In such a case, a neighbor who works as a real estate lawyer who is willing to give you some free time might be very helpful, but he or she will not be managing the case for you.

Because legal fees vary so much and are constantly changing, it is impossible to give a likely hourly rate, but the hourly rate for special education matters tends to be much lower than the hourly legal fees for commercial litigation, and higher than the hourly rates for a private occupational therapist (not much higher). The total cost of a lawyer also depends on how much time the lawyer spends on your case, which depends partly on how much litigating you are willing to do. The *New Yorker* magazine recently profiled a couple who spent $30,000 in legal fees suing their school district in Westchester County, MD, and their suit was not successful. My husband and I spent about $400 paying a lawyer to represent us at one meeting, without filing any complaint, and felt we were fairly successful. Besides the amount of litigation, the total cost is affected by how efficiently the lawyer works. Remember, the lawyer is an expert in special education law, not in teaching techniques or learning difficulties or Asperger's Syndrome. You are not going to a lawyer for advice on your child's program, just for advice and assistance in getting what educational services you have already determined that your child needs, in consultation with whatever expert advice you have already obtained on this subject. Keep in mind that lawyers bill in small time increments, usually in tenths of an hour, so every telephone call gets billed. If you talk with your lawyer about your case or your child for 20 minutes, expect to be billed for a third of an hour. If your lawyer is chatty, try to keep him or her on the subject as much as possible. Either one of you might be tempted to discuss a story you read or heard about Asperger's Syndrome the other day, but expect to be billed for it if you do discuss it.

While private lawyers who specialize in special education law are not as common as personal injury lawyers or real estate lawyers, they are more common than lawyers who specialized in obtaining Medical Assistance or SSI, especially Medical Assistance. Because of the low income required to be eligible for these services, and because the law does not provide for payment of prevailing parents' legal fees in these areas as it does in special education matters, representing clients here is not sufficiently lucrative to make it a big area of practice. Nonetheless, there is a professional organization for advocates of social security claimants, the National Organization of Social Security Claimants Representatives.[1] Although Medical Assistance is not part of the Social Security system (and SSI technically isn't either), this organization may be able to give you the names of

---

1   Its telephone number, at the time this went to press, was 800-431-2804, and the address was 6 Prospect Street, NJ.

some lawyers in your area who know something about resolving disputes over Medicaid eligibility and benefits.

Disputes or claims over lack of accommodations for people with Asperger's Syndrome can be handled by lawyers specializing in disability issues or in civil rights. There are advocacy groups for people with disabilities all over the country now, many of which have some knowledge of disability lawyers in their locality. These advocacy groups are often a source of information and referral for many types of disputes involving people with disabilities. For better or worse, disability law is becoming a bigger area of legal practice than it ever has been.

State Government Numbers
for Information on Medical Assistance

Many states have health care coverage programs for children with disabilities that go beyond the eligibility limits of traditional Medical Assistance. These programs vary greatly from state to state. These numbers were taken from state and federal government websites. Most numbers were verified by the author, but many of the toll-free numbers can be reached only from within their own state.

Alabama

Alabama Medicaid Information Agency Automated Helpline
1-800-362-1504

SCHIP (ALLKIDS)
1-888-373-KIDS (5437)

Alaska

KidCare Hotline (Child Health Insurance Program, CHIP)
1-888-318-8890
(907-269-6529 for Anchorage residents)

Medicaid Hotline, covers provided services, eligibility questions
1-800-271-7470
(907-562-3671 for Anchorage residents)

Division of Medicaid
1-907-465-3355

American Samoa
684-633-4590/4036

Arizona

CHIP (called CHP+ for Child Health Plan Plus)
1-800-359-1991

Denver Metro Area
303-866-3513

Enrollment
1-800-334-5283

MCH/Family Health
1-800-688-7777

Operator (in-state)
1-800-654-8713

Operator (out-of-state but not nationwide)
1-800-523-0231

Verifications
1-800-962-6690

Connecticut (in-state)
Alternate Care
1-800-445-5394

Connecticut Partnership Long Term Care
1-800-547-3443

Customer Information Center
1-800-385-4052

Disability Determination
1-800-842-8320

Pre-admission Screening and Resident Review (PASARR)
1-800-445-5394

Public Information (Dept. of Social Services)
1-800-842-1508

Delaware
Delaware Health Children Program
1-800-996-9969

Delaware Hotline
1-800-464-4357

Dept. of Health and Social Services
1-800-372-2022

Health Benefits Manager for Managed Care Enrollment
1-800-996-9969

District of Columbia
Eligibility
1-202-724-5506

Healthy DC Kids
1-800-666-2229

Managed Care Hotline (English and Spanish)
1-202-639-4030

Florida
Agency for Health Care Administration Consumer Hotline
1-888-419-3456

Florida Health Kids and KidCare
1-888-352-5437
(1-888-FLAKIDS)

SCHIP (KidCare)
1-888-540-5437
(1-888-540-KIDS)

Georgia
Division of Medical Assistance
1-800-211-0950

SCHIP (PeachCare for Kids)
1-877-427-3224

Guam
Dept. of Public Health and Social Services
671-735-7102

Hawaii (restricted to islands listed)
Hawaii (East)
1-808-933-0339

Hawaii (West)
1-808-327-4970

Kauai
1-808-241-3575

Lanai
1-808-565-7102

Maui
1-808-243-5780

Maui, Molokai
1-800-894-5755

Molokai
1-808-553-1758

Oahu (applicants)
1-808-587-3521

Oahu (recipients)
1-808-587-3540

Idaho

Idaho CareLine and Children's Health Insurance Program
1-800-926-2588

Illinois

Department of Human Services (DHS) Customer Inquiry (in-state only)
1-800-252-8635

Dept. of Human Services Customer Inquiry (out-of-state)
1-800-843-6154

KidCare Hotline
1-866-468-7543

KidCare Health Benefits Hotline (in-state only)
1-877-204-1012

Indiana

Customer Assistance
1-800-577-1278

Disability, Aging and Rehabilitation Services
1-800-545-7763

Disability Determination Bureau
1-800-622-4968

Hoosier Healthwise Helpline - Medicaid and CHIP
1-800-889-9949

Indiana Family Help Line (free provider locator/referral services)
1-800-433-0746

Medicaid Recipient Hotline
1-800-457-4584

Iowa

Iowa Children's Health Insurance Program (CHIP)
1-800-257-8563

Medicaid Recipient Hotline
1-800-338-8366

Kansas

Health Wave
1-800-792-4884

Recipient's Assistance Unit
1-800-766-9012

Kentucky Member Services

Children's Health Insurance Program (CHIP) (in-state only)
1-877-524-4718

Medicaid Member Services
1-800-635-2570

Louisiana

Bureau of Health Services Financing (handles Medicaid matters)
225-342-5774

Medicaid Hotline (also handles CHIP questions)
1-888-342-6207

Maine

The Bureau of Medical Services administers Medicaid but does not determine medical eligibility. To apply for Medical Assistance, contact local or regional office of the State Department of Human Services, as follows:

Augusta Regional Office
207-624-8200, 1-800-452-1926

Bangor Office
207-561-4100, 1-800-432-7825

Biddeford Office
207-286-2400, 1-800-322-1919

Calais Office
1-800-622-1400

Caribou District Office
207-493-4000, 1-800-432-7366

Ellsworth Office
207-667-1600, 1-800-432-7823

Farmington Office
207-778-8211, 1-800-442-6382

Houlton Office
207-532-5000, 1-800-432-7338

Kent Office
207-834-7700, 1-800-432-7340

Lewiston Office
207-795-4300, 1-800-482-7517

Machias Office
207-255-2000, 1-800-432-7846

Portland Office
207-822-2000

Rockland Office
1-800-432-7802

Sanford Office
207-490-5400, 1-800-482-0790

Skowhegan Office
1-800-452-4602

South Paris Regional Office
1-888-593-9775

Maryland
Dept. of Human Resources Customer Service, includes Medicaid information
1-800-332-6347

Medicaid beneficiary services hotline
1-800-492-5231

Massachusetts
Mass Health Customer Service (for inquiries on entire program)
1-800-841-2900

Mass Health Enrollment Centers
1-888-665-9993

Michigan
Beneficiary Helpline
1-800-642-3195

Beneficiary Managed Care Enrollment
1-888-367-6557

Children's Health Insurance Program (CHIP)
1-888-988-6300

Children's Special Health Care Services Family Phone Line and Family Support Line
1-800-359-3722

Michigan Children with Special Health Care Services Health Plan Helpline
1-877-274-2737

Minnesota

Minnesota Care Help Desk (CHIP)
1-800-657-3672

Recipient Help Desk
1-800-657-3739

Mississippi

Division of Medicaid
1-800-421-2408

General Information ACS Provider and Beneficiary Services
1-800-884-3222

SCHIP (MS Health Care Benefits Program)
1-800-421-2408

Missouri

Eligibility
1-800-392-1261

MC+ for Kids (CHIP) Eligibility
1-888-275-5908

Medicaid Managed Care Enrollment (MC+) Helpline
1-800-348-6627

Recipient Services
1-800-392-2161

Montana

Citizens Advocate Office
1-800-332-2272

SCHIP
1-877-543-7669

Nebraska

Behavioral Health Services
1-402-479-5117

Children's Improvement Program (CHIP)
1-877-632-5437

Dept. of Health and Human Services
1-402-471-8845

Developmental Disabilities
1-402-479-5102

Disabled Persons and Family Support/Medically Handicapped Children's Program
1-800-358-8802

Disability Services
1-402-471-9345

Nebraska Health Connection/Access Medicaid (Lincoln)
1-402-471-7715

Nebraska Health Connection/Access Medicaid (Omaha)
1-402-595-1000

Systems Advocate (for individuals with concerns about or problems with the Dept. of Human Services)
1-800-254-4202

Nevada
Dept. of Human Resources, includes Medicaid
1-800-992-0900

State Child Health Insurance Program (SCHIP)
1-877-543-7669 or 800-360-6044

New Hampshire
Dept. of Health and Human Services
1-800-852-3345

New Hampshire Health Kids Program (CHIP)
1-877-464-2447

New Jersey
Medical Assistance Hotline (General Medicaid)
1-800-356-1561

New Mexico
Human Services Dept.
1-800-432-6217

Medicaid Client Server
1-888-997-2583

Medicaid Managed Care Information Line
1-888-532-8093

New York
Child Health Plus Hotline (CHIP)
1-800-698-4543

Office and Temporary and Disability Service
1-800-342-3009

Office of Managed Care Certification
1-800-206-8125

North Carolina
CARE-LINE, referral line
1-800-662-7030

Mental Health Case Manager (Value Options) 24-hour call center
1-800-753-3224

North Dakota
Medical Services Division of Dept. of Human Services
1-800-755-2604

Ohio
Dept. of Human Services, Medicaid Consumer Hotline
1-800-324-8680

Oklahoma
Children's Health Insurance Program (CHIP)
1-800-987-7767

Medicaid Claims (Client Line)
1-800-522-0310

Specialized Behavioral Health Needs (Client Line)
1-800-652-2010

To Enroll in Medicaid Department of Human Services (Care Inquiries Line)
1-888-521-2778

Oregon
Client Advisory Services
1-800-273-0557

Oregon Health Plan Application Center
1-800-359-9517

Oregon Medical Assistance Programs (OMAP) Information
1-800-527-5772

Pennsylvania
Dept. of Health, Kids Helpline
1-800-986-5437

Dept. of Public Welfare (handles Medical Assistance)
1-800-692-7462

Medicaid/Children's Health Insurance Program (CHIP) questions
1-800-842-2020

Puerto Rico
General Medicaid
1-787-250-7429

Rhode Island
Dept. of Human Services Information Line
1-401-462-5300

Dept. of Human Services Rite Care Information Line
1-401-462-1300

South Carolina
South Carolina Medical Programs (including CHIP)
1-888-549-0820

South Dakota
CHIP Eligibility
1-800-305-3064

Medicaid/Medicaid Expansion for CHIP
1-800-452-7691, 1-605-773-6383

Medicaid questions
605-773-4678

Tennessee
TENNCare Information Line (Medicaid and SCHIP)
1-800-669-1851

Texas
Dept. of Human Services Consumer Assistance Hotline
1-800-448-3927

Dept. of Human Services, includes eligibility questions
1-888-834-7406

Utah
Children's Health Insurance Program (CHIP) Helpline
1-877-543-7669

Health Medicaid Information Line ·
1-800-662-9651

Virginia
Family Access to Medical Insurance Security Plan
1-800-873-2647

Vermont
Healthcare Ombudsman
1-800-917-7787

Medicaid Eligibility (Vermont Health Access Member Services)
1-800-250-8427

Virgin Islands
General Medicaid Number
1-340-774-4624

Washington
Children's Health Insurance Program (CHIP, Kids Helpline)
1-877-543-7669

Eligibility Questions
1-800-865-7801

West Virginia
Children's Health Insurance Program (CHIP)
1-888-983-2645

Dept. of Health and Human Services/Client Services
1-800-642-8589

Providers' Medicaid hotline
1-800-688-5810

Wisconsin
Managed Care Enrollment Specialists
1-800-291-2002

Medicaid Recipient Hotline
1-800-888-7989

Medicaid Recipients Services and BadgerCare Hotline
1-800-362-3002

Program for Children with Special Health Care Needs
1-800-642-7837

Wyoming
Client Link to Department of Health
1-800-251-1269

Dept. of Family Services Eligibility Information
1-888-996-8678

Medicaid Hotline, Questions on Policy and Benefits
1-800-252-8263

References

Abbott, M., Franciscus, M.L. and Weeks, Z.R. (2001) *Opportunities in Occupational Therapy Careers.* Chicago: VGM Career Books.

American Board of Medical Specialities (ABMS) (2003) *The Official ABMS Directory of Board Certified Medical Specialists,* 35th edn. St. Louis, MO: Saunders.

American Occupational Therapy Association (AOTA) (1985) *AOTA Manpower Report.* Bethesda, MD: American Occupational Therapy Association.

American Physical Therapy Association (APTA) (2001) *Physical Therapist Employment Survey Fall 2001 – Executive Summary.* Alexandra, VA: American Physical Therapy Association.

American Psychiatric Association (2000) *Diagnostic and Statistical Manual of Mental Disorders,* 4th edn. Washington, DC: American Psychiatric Association.

Asperger, H. (1950) as cited by M.A. Felder (2000) in "Foreword" to *Asperger Syndrome.* A. Klin, F.R. Volkmar, S.A. Sparrow (eds), New York, The Guildford Press, pp.xii–xiii.

Attwood, T. (1998) *Asperger's Syndrome: A Guide for Parents and Professionals.* London: Jessica Kingsley Publishers.

Attwood, T. (2000) "Should Children With An Autistic Spectrum Disorder Be Exempted from Doing Homework?" *The Morning News 12,* 2.

Ayres, A.J. (1979) *Sensory Integration and the Child.* Los Angeles: Western Psychological Services.

Bashe, P.R. and Kirby, B. (2001) *OASIS Guide to Asperger Syndrome.* New York: Crown.

Bauer, S. (1996) "Asperger Syndrome." Published on OASIS website, copyright Stephen Bauer. www.udel.edu/bkirby/asperger/aspergerpapers/html

BBC News (2002) "Autism misdiagnosis 'ruined a life.'" *BBC News,* 27 June. http://news.bbc.co.uk/1/hi/health/787526.stm

California Department of Developmental Services (1999) *Changes in the Population of Persons with Autism and Pervasive Developmental Disorders in California's Developmental Services System: 1987 through 1998: A Report to the Legislature.* Sacramento, CA: Department of Developmental Services.

Centers for Disease Control and Prevention, National Vaccine Program Office (NVPO), *Vaccine Fact Sheets.* Washington, DC: US Dept of Health and Human Services.

Committee on Children with Disabilities (1985) "School-aged children with motor disabilities." *Pediatrics 76,* 4, 648.

Committee on Children with Disabilities (1996) "The role of the pediatrician in prescribing therapy services for children with motor disabilities." *Pediatrics 98,* 2, 308.

Committee on Children with Disabilities (1998) "Auditory Integration Training and Facilitated Communication for Autism." *Pediatrics 102,* 2, 431–433.

Committee on Educational Interventions for Children with Autism, National Research Council (2001) *Educating Children with Autism.* Washington, DC: The National Academies Press.

Dewey, M. (1991) "Living with Asperger's Syndrome." In U. Frith (ed) *Autism and Asperger's Syndrome.* New York: Cambridge University Press.

Durrant, V.M. (1998) *Sleep Better! A Guide to Improving Sleep for Children with Special Needs.*
    Baltimore, MD: Paul H. Brookes Publishing Co.

Fling, E.R. (2000) *Eating An Artichoke: A Mother's Perspective on Asperger's Syndrome.* London:
    Jessica Kingsley Publishers.

Fombonne, E. (2003) "The prevalence of autism." *Journal of the American Medical Association 289,*
    87–89.

Frankel, F. (1996) *Good Friends Are Hard To Find.* Los Angeles: Prospective Publishing.

Frith, U. (1989) *Autism: Explaining the Enigma.* Oxford: Blackwell Publishers.

Gerstmyer v. Howard County Public Schools, 850 F. Supp. 361 (D.Md. 1994)

Gillberg, C. and Gillberg, I.C. (1989) "Asperger's Syndrome – Some epidemiological
    considerations: A research note." *Child Psychology and Psychiatry 30,* 631–638.

Grandin, T. (1992) "An inside view of autism." In E. Schopler and G.B. Mesibov (eds)
    High-Functioning Individuals With Autism. New York: Plenum.

Grandin, T. (1996) *Thinking in Pictures and Other Reports from my Life with Autism.* New York:
    Vintage Books.

Grandin, T. (2000) "Foreword" in M.D. Powers (ed) *Children With Autism,* 2nd ed. Bethesda,
    MA: Woodbine.

Greenfeld, J. (1972) *A Child Called Noah: A Family Journey.* New York: Henry Holt.

Hyatt-Foley, D. and M.G. (2000) "First advocate." In A. Klin, F.R. Volkmar and S.S. Sparrow
    (eds) *The Asperger Syndrome.* New York: Guilford Press.

Holliday Willey, L. (1996) *Pretending to be Normal: Living with Asperger's Syndrome.* London: Jessica
    Kingsley Publishers.

Holliday Willey, L. (2001) *A Bit about Liane and her Life with Asperger's Syndrome.*
    http://www.aspie.com/Bio.html

Howlin, P. and Asgharian, A. (1999) "The diagnosis of autism and Asperger Syndrome:
    findings from a survey of 770 families." *Developmental Medicine and Child Neurology 41,* 12,
    834–839.

Kanner, L. (1943) "Autistic Disturbances of Affective Contact." *Nervous Child 2,* 217–250.

Killilea, M. (1952) *Karen.* Englewood, NJ: Prentice Hall.

Klin, A. and Volkmar, F.R. *Asperger's Syndrome and Pursuing Eligibility for Services: The Case of the
    'Perfect Misplacement.'* Asperger Syndrome Education Network (ASPEN).

Klin, A., Volkmar, F.R. and Sparrow, S.S. (eds) (2000) *The Asperger Syndrome.* New York:
    Guilford Press.

Kranowitz, C.S. (1998) *The Out-of-Sync Child.* New York: Berkley.

The Lancet (2000) "Lifeline." *The Lancet 356,* 9223, 1 July, p.84.

McDonnell, J.T. (1993) *News from the Border: A Mother's Memoir of Her Autistic Son.* New York:
    Ticknor and Fields.

Mental Health Weekly (2000) "Legal dispute puts rehab services for children in spotlight."
    Mental Health Weekly 10, 29, 24 July.

Mitchell, J.S. (1982) *Taking On The World: Empowering Strategies for Parents of Children with
    Disabilities.* New York: Harcourt Brace Jovanovich.

Moore, S. T. (2002) *Asperger Syndrome and the Elementary School Experience: Practical Solutions for
    Academic and Social Difficulties.* Shawnee Mission, KS: Autism Asperger Publishing Co.

New York Times (2004) "Autism cases up: cause is unclear." *New York Times,* 26 January.

Ohio Legislative Office of Education Oversight (1999) *Availability of Therapists to Work in Ohio
    Schools.* Columbus, OH: Ohio Legislative Office.

Parker, P. (2000) "A chance like no other for autistic children." *Seattle Times*, 8 August.

Portwood, M. (1999) *Developmental Dyspraxia*, 2nd edn. Philadelphia: David Fulton.

Pyles, L. (2001) *Hitchhiking through Asperger Syndrome*. London: Jessica Kingsley Publishers.

Rieser, L. (2004) *personal communication* Education Law Center, Philadelphia, January.

Rogers, E. (2000) "Mother Claims Drugs Ruined Daughter's Life." *Hillingdon and Uxbridge Times*, 1 June.

Sacks, O. (1985) *The Man Who Mistook his Wife for a Hat and Other Clinical tales*. New York: Simon and Schuster Books.

Schafer, D. (2003) "Special Kids. Special Needs." *Parents Express*, July 2003.

Schaeffer, J.L. and Ross R.G. (2002) "Childhood-onset schizophrenia: premorbid and prodromal diagnostic and treatment histories." *Journal of the American Academy of Child and Adolescent Psychiatry 41*, 5, 538–545.

Seattle Post-Intelligencer (2002) *Special Reports*. Downloaded 2 February http://seattlepi.nwsource.com/autism

Siegal, B. and Silverstein, S.C. (1994) *What About Me? Growing Up With a Developmentally Disabled Sibling*, Cambridge, MA: Da Capo Press.

Stancliff, B.L. (1997) "Smart, honest, trusting, loving – what's the problem?" Article posted to an NLD website. Accessed OT Practice, August. www.nldline.com

Stehli, A. (1990) *The Sound of a Miracle: A Child's Triumph Over Autism*. Wetport, CT: Georgiana Organization.

Szatmari, P. (2000) "Perspectives on the classification of AS." In A. Klin, F.R. Volkmar and S.A. Sparrow (eds) *Asperger Syndrome*. New York: Guilford Press.

US Dept of Labor, Bureau of Labor Statistics (2000) *Occupational Outlook Handbook, 2000–2001 Edition*. Washington, DC: US Dept of Labor.

Vandegrift, B. (2001) *A Tiger by the Tail*. iUniverse. http://memebers.aol.com/bertvan

Waltz, M. (1999) *Autistic Spectrum Disorders: Understanding the Diagnosis and Getting Help*. Sebastopol, CA: O'Reilly and Associates.

Watling, R., Deitz, J., Kanny, E.M. and McLaughlin, J.F. (1999) "Current practice of occupational therapy for children with autism." *American Journal of Occupational Therapy 53*, 5, 498–505.

Weisberg, D. (2000) 'Fallout from the autism explosion.' *Pittsburgh Post-Gazette*, 19 December.

Westat (2002) *Study of Personnel Needs in Special Education*. Washington, DC: Office of Special Education, US Department of Education.

WHO (1993) *ICD-10 Classification of Mental and Behavioral Disorders: Diagnostic Criteria for Research*. Geneva: World Health Organization.

Williamson, G.G. and Anzalone, M.E. (2001) *Sensory Integration and Self-Regulation in Infants and Toddlers*. Washington, DC: ZERO TO THREE: National Center for Infants, Toddlers and Families.

Wing, L. (1981) "Asperger's Syndrome: a clinical account." *Psychological Medicine 11*, 115–129.

Wing, L. (1996) "Autistic spectrum disorders." *British Medical Journal 312*, 327–328.

Wing, L. (2000) "Past and future of research on Asperger Syndrome." In A. Klin, F.R. Volkmar and S.A. Sparrow (eds) *Asperger Syndrome*. New York: Guilford Press.

Wing, L. and Gould, J. (1979), "Severe impairments of social interaction and associated abnormalities in children: epidemiology and classification." *Journal of Autism and Developmental Disorders 9*, 1.

Subject Index

Author Index

Abbott, M. 68
Anzalone, M E. 72
Asperger, H. 27, 29, 89–90, 98
Attwood, T. 19, 29, 33, 59, 79, 90, 95, 98,
    114, 118, 153, 154
Ayres, A.J. 40, 76, 160–1

Bald, J. 151
Bashe, P.R. 162, 163
Bauer, S. 33
Berard, G. 79–80
Bligh, S. 64

Dewey, M. 75, 169
Durant, M. 168

Fling, E. 32, 49, 51, 105, 113, 115
Foley, M.G. 105
Fombonne, E. 54
Franciscus, M.L. 68
Frankel, F. 52–3
Frith, U. 40

Garcia-Winner, M. 105
Gillberg, C. 31
Gillberg, I.C. 31
Grandin, T. 41, 79, 90–1, 131
Greenfeld, J. 26, 27, 44–5, 50
Greenspan, S. 151

Hall, H. 66
Hyatt-Foley, D. 105

Jenzen, D. 79

Kanner, L. 27, 29
Killilea, K. 99, 132
Kirby, B. 162, 163

Klin, A. 105
Kranowitz, C. 40

Lovaas, I. 151
Lowrie, L.M. 149

McDonnell, J. 164
Mitchell, J.S. 124
Moore, S. Thompson 90, 91, 95, 114

Portwood, M. 39, 72
Pyles, L. 135–6, 153

Roman, M. 34
Ross, R.G. 50
Rourke, B. 34

Sacks, O. 81
Schaeffer, J.L. 50
Siegal, B. 166
Silverstein, S. C. 166
Smith, A. 124
Stancliff, B.L. 34
Stehli, A. 80
Szatmari, P. 20

Tomatis, A. 80

Volkmar, F.R. 105

Waltz, M. 162, 164
Weeks, Z.R. 68
Holliday Willey, L. 32–3, 48, 74, 75
Williamson, G.G. 72
Wing, L. 29, 41–2, 54, 90, 92, 98, 118, 160,
    168–9